Divine Hiddenness
and Human Reason

A volume in the series

Cornell Studies in the Philosophy of Religion

EDITED BY WILLIAM P. ALSTON

A list of titles in this series is available at www.cornellpress.cornell.edu.

J. L. Schellenberg

Divine Hiddenness and Human Reason

Cornell University Press, Ithaca and London

First published 1993 by Cornell University Press
First printing, Cornell Paperbacks, 2006

Library of Congress Cataloging-in-Publication Data

Schellenberg, J. L., 1959–
    Divine hiddenness and human reason / J. L. Schellenberg.
       p.   cm. — (Cornell studies in the philosophy of religion)
    Includes index.
    ISBN-13: 978-0-8014-7346-3 (pbk. : alk. paper)
    ISBN-10: 0-8014-7346-2 (pbk. : alk. paper)
       1. Theism.   2. Hidden God.   3. God—Knowableness.   4. Knowledge,
Theory of (Religion)   I. Title.   II. Series.
BL200.S34   1993
212'.6—dc20   92-32633

Paperback printing   10 9 8 7 6 5 4 3 2 1

Contents

Preface to the
Paperback Edition

The problem for theism that has come to be associated with the term "Divine hiddenness" was very largely hidden from view during many centuries of philosophical rumination about the existence of God. Hints of it can be found in Hume and Nietzsche and a few other writers, but only in the last decade or so have the shape and seriousness of the problem truly come to light. For this, I suppose the present book, the first full-dress presentation of a hiddenness argument for atheism, can take some credit. (I was originally opposed to such labels for the argument—see pp. 5–6—but I have succumbed in the face of popular usage.) This book has provoked many reactions (see, for example, Daniel Howard-Snyder and Paul Moser, eds., *Divine Hiddenness: New Essays* [Cambridge: Cambridge University Press, 2002]), and a much fuller discussion of hiddenness issues is now well underway. I hope that the book's reissue in paperback will only add fuel to the fire, enticing many more inquirers to engage its themes.

In this new Preface I offer readers some clarifications and intensifications of thoughts expressed herein (in making my selections I have been guided by misunderstandings and oversights to which some of the first readers of the book fell prey). In conjunction, these additions provide a sort of frame for the book's discussion that might usefully be consulted both before and after reading it.

(1) A basic point to remember is that the central notion of "reasonable nonbelief" *emerges* from reflection on Divine love. I do not

start with reasonable nonbelief as philosophers might ordinarily think of it, arguing that such exists but would not exist if there were a God. Rather, I begin with reflection on Divine love and allow the problematic phenomenon to receive its shape therefrom, as I work out what hiddenness-related facts would be absent from the world if such love were present in it. (The emphasis on *inculpable* nonbelief, for example, is a direct result of this process, and "reasonable" is just a prettier word for "inculpable.") Failure to see this point can result in the misunderstanding that I am committed to the reasonableness of nonbelief as defined by certain antecedently accepted criteria of epistemology, or, even worse, that my focus is reasonable *doubt* (the familiar reflective nonbelief of the agnostic) instead of inculpable nonbelief however instantiated. (Doubt of a certain kind *is* the topic of Chapter 3, but it is discussed only as a prominent *example* of reasonable or inculpable nonbelief.)

(2) A related point is that it is not the trauma of a certain kind of anguished doubt or unrequited seeking for God that leads to my argument—indeed, this phenomenon has no role in my argument at all. (Supposing otherwise is one way of confounding the hiddenness argument with the argument from evil.) My deepest claim is rather about the connection between love and openness to relationship—a personal and positively meaningful and explicit relationship of the sort that logically presupposes each party's belief in the other's existence. Though I do not go this far in the book, I would now be inclined to view this connection as a conceptual one: when we use the word "loving" *discriminatingly*—not just as a synonym for "good"—and also *admiringly* of persons, in a manner that can provide a model for talk about God, it is part of the very meaning of what we say that the loving one is available for an explicit and positively meaningful relationship of just this sort with the one she loves, insofar as the latter is capable of it. In any case, as I understand it, the Divine Parent's motivation to make Divine-human relationship possible includes much more than do the motives to which we appeal when we argue, if we do, that God would prevent trauma or anguish.

(3) Another related point is this: the most provocative premise of my argument—that if there is a loving God, reasonable nonbelief does not occur—must always be viewed as grounded in the deeper claim just mentioned, which (when filled out) tells us that *if there is a perfectly*

loving God, anyone capable of explicit and positively meaningful relationship with God who is not resisting relationship with God is in a position to participate in such relationship. Indeed, the latter claim, the central result of my examination of the notion of Divine love, is the most important feature of my reasoning. That it is not part of the formal structure of the argument presented at the beginning of Chapter 4—though notice that the provocative premise is there said to be *based on* earlier reflections about love—has led some to overlook this claim and its fundamental role and to fall into the misunderstanding that there is nothing behind the provocative premise except, perhaps, a weakness for entertaining signs and wonders. But as the present point shows, what my arguer claims has nothing to do with some independent craving for the evidence of signs and wonders. Rather, it is anchored in and governed by reflection on the love of God—the results of which, as it happens, are at odds with talk of stunning signs and wonders and lead much more naturally to an emphasis on evidence deriving from religious experience, with a texture and forcefulness modulated according to our moral and other needs.

(4) A further misunderstanding that readers should beware of involves conflating what my argument claims—that if God exists, reasonable nonbelief does not occur—with "If God exists, reasonable nonbelievers receive evidence sufficient for belief." What the former claim says is that if God exists, there is *never* a time when someone inculpably fails to believe (belief is made available as soon as there is a capacity for relationship with God). In other words, if there is a God, *there are no reasonable nonbelievers about who may be treated in the imagined fashion.* So it is no use showing that God would not interrupt the lives of reasonable nonbelievers with evidence; what we need is a way of understanding how God could have permitted them to become reasonable nonbelievers in the first place.

(5) Such points as I have made about relationship with God ought to be assessed in light of another: that given the infinite richness and depth of any God there may be, relationship with God would be capable of an indefinite degree of development, with always more to discover and overcome for one who participated in it. Critics often argue as though there are goods God would desire for us that must somehow be fitted in *prior* to such relationship, but if we look at things from only a slightly nonconventional slant, we will see how such

goods must in a multitude of forms arise as the relationship progresses. What cause could there be, then, for anyone ever to be prevented from so much as *beginning* the relationship?

(6) This brings me to a point that is not so much about particular misunderstandings or oversights as about a general condition that may make us susceptible to them. Most of us are not accustomed to thinking of God nonconventionally due to the influence of our environment and of the religious teaching to which we have been exposed. We may, for example, have learned to tolerate solitary males and distant fathers and—still picturing God with a bit of both in mind—find the notion of Divine hiddenness unproblematic, even romantic. Moreover, we certainly have been influenced by centuries of theologizing that, committed from the start to the existence of God, must find some way of establishing a "fit" between God and the way things go. (So the evidence is weak? It must somehow be God's plan.) Philosophy is different. Philosophers must think for themselves about what a truly *ultimate* reality that was fully *personal* and *perfectly loving* would be like. And I am suggesting that when we do, a somewhat different picture of God from the one we are used to will emerge.

(7) Finally (and here we have what is in the first instance a misunderstanding or oversight of my own), let me say that if I had it to do all over again I would use gender-sensitive language not only in speaking of humans but also in reference to God. The fact that I have found it possible to do so in writing *after* 1993 puts the lie to the claim—still heard from time to time—that when discoursing about the Divine, personal pronouns suggesting masculinity or femininity cannot gracefully be avoided. I challenge those philosophers still offering that excuse to give it up and to use language about God, in this way as in others, with due care.

I remain grateful to everyone who helped me with the original edition of this book. I particularly want to acknowledge John Ackerman, director of Cornell University Press, whose advice and support both then and now are much appreciated.

My deepest thanks go to Regina Coupar, for teaching me ever more about the art of life and being my partner and inspiration in all things.

J. L. S.

August 2006

Divine Hiddenness
and Human Reason

Introduction

Many religious writers, sensitive to the difficulties in which our evidence for God is involved, have held that God would wish (or at any rate, permit) the fact of his existence to be obscure. God, so it is said, is a *hidden* God. But upon reflection, it may well appear otherwise. Why, we may ask, would God be hidden from us? Surely a morally perfect being—good, just, loving—would show himself more clearly. Hence the weakness of our evidence for God is not a sign that God is hidden; it is a revelation that God does not exist.[1]

1. Several contemporary writers have touched on this problem. See Terence Penelhum, *God and Skepticism* (Dordrecht: Reidel, 1983), pp. 156–158, esp. p. 158; John Hick, *Faith and Knowledge*, 2d ed. (London: Macmillan, 1988), p. 121; Ronald Hepburn, "From World to God," in Basil Mitchell, ed., *Philosophy of Religion* (Oxford: Oxford University Press, 1971), p. 178; Frank B. Dilley, "Fool-Proof Proofs of God?" *International Journal for Philosophy of Religion*, 8 (1977), 19–27, 35; Anthony O'Hear, *Experience, Explanation, and Faith* (London: Routledge and Kegan Paul, 1984), pp. 238–239; George Schlesinger, "The Availability of Evidence in Support of Religious Belief," *Faith and Philosophy*, 1 (1984), 422–427; William Alston, "Religious Diversity and Perceptual Knowledge of God," *Faith and Philosophy*, 5 (1988), 445; C. Robert Mesle, "Does God Hide From Us? John Hick and Process Theology on Faith, Freedom, and Theodicy," *International Journal for Philosophy of Religion*, 24 (1988), 97; Thomas V. Morris, "The Hidden God," *Philosophical Topics*, 16 (1988), 5–7, 11; Mark R. Talbot, "Is It Natural to Believe in God?" *Faith and Philosophy*, 6 (1989), 160–161; and Robert McKim, "The Hiddenness of God," *Religious Studies*, 26 (1990), 141–143. But few of these writers have

In this book I argue that there is support for such claims as these. The weakness of evidence for theism, I maintain, is itself evidence against it. Paving the way for my argument will be a discussion of certain important questions raised by its central claim: What *reasons* are there to suppose that God would be more clearly revealed? (It is not obvious a priori that he would, so reasons need to be provided.) If reasons there be, what is suggested by them as to the *degree* of clarity, and of accessibility, we might expect to find? Should we look for proof—perhaps an overwhelming manifestation—or would something less than this serve God's purposes? And would the evidence be made available to all, or only to those who satisfy certain conditions beforehand? More generally, what explications of "weak" and "strong" ought we to give here? It seems clear enough that these questions need answering if our problem is to be properly developed, but they have not been addressed in previous discussions, even by those (few) who have seen that there may be an argument for atheism lurking here. Our discussion will seek to remedy this neglect—to state with some precision why we might expect stronger evidence for theism to be available if God exists, and what sort of evidence God might be expected to provide.

The argument that will emerge from this discussion is, in broad outline, as follows. A perfectly loving God would desire a reciprocal personal relationship always to obtain between himself and every human being capable of it. But a logically necessary condition of such Divine-human reciprocity is human belief in Divine existence. Hence a perfectly loving God would have reason to ensure that everyone capable of such belief (or at any rate, everyone capable who was not disposed to resist it) was in possession of evidence sufficient to bring it about that such belief was formed. But the evidence actually available is not of this sort (the claim that it is "weak" is to be read simply as the claim that it is not "strong" in this sense). The most obvious indication that it is not is that inculpable—or as I prefer to term it, *reasonable*—nonbelief actually

---

offered suggestions as to how the weakness of theistic evidence might yield an argument for atheism; and the remarks of those who have are sketchy.

occurs.[2] Hence we can argue from the weakness of theistic evidence (where this is understood as indicated), or more specifically, from the reasonableness of nonbelief, to the nonexistence of a perfectly loving God. But God, if he exists, is perfectly loving. Hence we can argue from the reasonableness of nonbelief to the nonexistence of God.

In Part 1 of the book (Chapters 1–4), I fill out the argument here briefly sketched, and detail the considerable initial support that it can claim. I show, first, that there are indeed grounds to suppose that a perfectly loving God would put his existence beyond reasonable nonbelief. I argue, further, that although it is possible for God to prevent it, reasonable nonbelief occurs. In Part 2 (Chapters 5–7), I examine various possible rebuttals, explicit or implicit in the literature—arguments of Pascal, Joseph Butler, Kierkegaard, John Hick, and others which might be thought to defeat the prima facie case of Part 1 by showing that there are reasons for God to remain hidden from us that override or at least offset the reasons for revelation (where "hiddenness" and "revelation" are understood in terms of the permission and of the prevention of reasonable nonbelief, respectively). Not all of these arguments have been given a clear shape in the past or are applicable as they stand, and so my procedure is to clarify them and adapt them for my purposes as I go along. That they are in many cases less than fully developed is at least in part due to the fact that the problem to which they must be seen as responses—the problem of weak theistic evidence—has not heretofore been carefully articulated. My claim in Part 2 is that no available argument is an adequate defense against the version of the problem that I present. The final claim of the book is accordingly that for anyone who accepts my judgments (along with certain assumptions, to be indicated later in the Introduction), the argument from the reasonableness of nonbelief goes through, providing good grounds for atheism.[3]

2. Nonbelief is reasonable, I will stipulate, if and only if it is not the result of culpable actions or omissions on the part of the subject.
3. It may seem to some, upon reading my argument, that it might just as well have been developed in terms of Divine *justice*—that an emphasis on the implications of love is not essential to my case. For, it may be argued, a perfectly just God would distribute good evidence of his existence *evenly*, and so ensure that the op-

I have suggested (and the title of this book also suggests) that the question here raised for discussion is connected to the idea of the hiddenness of God. But the notion of God's hiddenness is ambiguous, and so this way of referring to our topic can be misleading. It can mislead, first of all, by suggesting that *all* the ways in which God may be said to be hidden pose problems for theology. It can also mislead in a very different way, by suggesting that the absence of persuasive and readily available theistic evidence is *not a problem*—that since theology has always insisted on God's hiddenness, the question I am raising can be dismissed a priori, as displaying theological naïveté. In order to avoid being misled in these ways, we must make some distinctions. The notion of God's hiddenness can be interpreted in at least three ways: as referring to the obscuring of God's existence, the incomprehensibility of God's nature, or our inability to detect the exact pattern of God's activity in the world. To the question I am raising, only "hiddenness" in the first sense is relevant. All I seek to show is that we might expect God's *existence* to be more obvious. I am happy to allow that the same claim made in respect of the depths of God's nature or the exact pattern of his activity would have much less to recommend it.

Can it now be argued, however, that theologians have always insisted on God's hiddenness in *all three* senses? I think not. Although some writers, such as Karl Barth, seem to refer to God as hidden not only in the second and third of the above senses, but also in the first, it is important to note that this is largely a post-Enlightenment phenomenon.[4] The majority of patristic, medieval,

---

portunity to acquire belief and the benefits of belief was missed by no one (see Schlesinger, "Availability of Evidence," 424–425). But if only God's justice need be saved, the theist may always point to the possibility that everything will even out in the end—that those who fail to benefit from belief in this life will be compensated hereafter. Or else she may claim that it is not unjust to give a gift to someone while not giving it to others, unless everyone can be shown to be *entitled* to it. Such easy "outs" are, however, not possible where Divine love is concerned. If God is loving as well as just, he is motivated to pursue personal relationship with each of us in this life as well as in the hereafter. In the interests of a stronger argument, therefore, I have decided to fill out the reasoning suggested by the question "Why, if there is a God, is his existence not more obvious?" in terms of love rather than in terms of justice.

4. For Barth's view, see his *Church Dogmatics*, vol. 2, pt. 1 (Edinburgh: T&T

and reformation theologians affirmed that God's existence could be "clearly seen, being understood through the things that have been made" (Rom. 1:20), while maintaining that "such knowledge or demonstration could not comprehend God as he was in himself."[5] Even Martin Luther, who championed the idea of a hidden God, wrote by way of comment on Romans 1:20 that "there must be that which is more sublime than anything else, which is higher than all and helps all."[6] According to Jaroslav Pelikan, Luther ascribed to natural reason "the recognition, even apart from Scriptures, that God was almighty and his foreknowledge was infallible."[7] We may therefore conclude that the traditional emphasis of theology on the hiddenness of God does not imply that the evidence for God's existence must be weak, and hence does not sanction a dismissal of our inquiry, as it might otherwise be thought to do.

There is, however, a third way in which the description of our problem in terms of the hiddenness of God can be misleading. "God is hidden" (in the sense of "hidden" that concerns us) is perhaps most naturally construed as equivalent to

> (1) God exists and has intentionally withheld (or permitted to be obscured) strong evidence of his existence.

But (1) entails that God exists, and so it would be contradictory, on this understanding of "God is hidden," to speak of an argument *from* the hiddenness of God *against* God's existence. Of course, those who think of the hiddenness of God as an epistemic problem of the sort here discussed may well be understanding it solely in terms of the absence of strong evidence for God's existence. But it is not clear to me that this is so; and it is even less clear that this would be an acceptable understanding. It seems much more natural

---

Clark, 1957), p. 187. He writes: "That God is, lies as little in the field of our spiritual oversight and control as what He is. We lack the capacity both to establish His existence and to define His being."

5. Jaroslav Pelikan, *The Christian Tradition*, vol. 3 (Chicago: University of Chicago Press, 1978), p. 289.

6. Martin Luther, quoted in Jaroslav Pelikan, *The Christian Tradition*, vol. 4 (Chicago: University of Chicago Press, 1984), pp. 165–166.

7. Ibid., p. 166.

to interpret talk of God's hiddenness as implying a commitment to God's existence, and to understand the *problem* of God's hiddenness as a nonepistemic problem—a theological, or perhaps pastoral, problem of the sort that only believers may admit.[8] This, at any rate, is the understanding I will assume. Accordingly, our problem is not to be understood as the problem of God's hiddenness, nor my argument as an argument *from* God's hiddenness. This, however, is not to deny that the claim that God is hidden, and suggested reasons for such hiddenness, are relevant to our problem, or that my argument has no implications for how the idea of Divine hiddenness should be assessed. Quite the contrary. Such claims and such reasons may, as we have seen, function in a *solution* to the problem, and if no purported solution succeeds, the claim that God is hidden (as well as the claim that God exists) must be relinquished. Human reason may, as the title of this book suggests, have something to say about the idea of Divine hiddenness, and what it has to say may be of great significance for the philosophy of religion.

It is interesting to note at this juncture that the problem posed for theology by the argument I develop may also be construed as a special instance of the problem of evil. But it is important to be clear about what is meant by this. Philosophers who discuss the problem of evil usually restrict their attention to the question whether certain events, actions, and states of affairs that we would all naturally view as negative or destructive and so as evil (e.g., wrong actions, physical pain, mental anguish) provide the basis for a strong argument against the existence of an omnipotent, omniscient, and morally perfect God (a *logical* argument showing the existence of such evils to be incompatible with the existence of God, or an *empirical* argument showing that their existence renders his unlikely). The phenomena commonly discussed are, furthermore, ones whose elimination would be a great good even if atheism were true—facts which, as we might say, the world would be much better without whether God exists or not. But as an article by Terence Penelhum suggests, to pose a problem of evil, an event,

8. Of course, the theological problem is closely connected to ours inasmuch as any solution to the former might well provide the theist with a response to the latter. But insofar as the theological problem presupposes God's existence, the two are not to be identified.

action, or state of affairs need not be of this sort.⁹ It need only be such that the affirmation of its existence comes into conflict with what theists are committed to saying about the nature of God—in particular, about the moral nature of God: it poses a problem of evil if it seems that a morally perfect God who was also omnipotent and omniscient could not allow it, or if it seems improbable that he would. Hence the state of affairs discussed in this book—the reasonableness of nonbelief—though it is not a state of affairs that we would all naturally view as negative or destructive and so as evil, and though it is not a state of affairs the world would be much better without even if God does not exist, may still legitimately be viewed as posing a problem of evil *if* the affirmation of its existence comes into conflict with what theists are committed to saying about God's moral nature. And that it does so is my claim. Hence I seem to be in a position to claim that the problem of reasonable nonbelief is a problem of evil. However, the "evil" to which it refers is, as we have seen, not of the ordinary sort (for it does not consist in pain or suffering or any other commonly recognized evil, nor would its removal be a great good unless personal relationship with God is possible); and so, to mark this difference, it may be appropriate to refer to it as a *special instance* of the problem of evil.

It remains only to point out the *sort* of conflict I have in mind here: Do I consider the problem of reasonable nonbelief to be a special instance of the logical, or of the empirical, problem of evil? If the former, then the claim I advance is tantamount to the claim that

(2) If God exists and is perfectly loving, reasonable nonbelief does not occur

is *necessarily* true, or equivalently, that

(3) God exists and is perfectly loving

is *logically incompatible* with

(4) Reasonable nonbelief occurs.

9. Terence Penelhum, "Divine Goodness and the Problem of Evil," *Religious Studies*, 2 (1967), 95–107.

And in reply to such a claim, it would surely be tempting to argue, in the spirit of Alvin Plantinga's famous response to the logical problem of evil, that the compatibility of (3) with (4) can quite easily be demonstrated.[10] It might be argued, for example, that there is a possible world in which humans are constructed in such a way that strong evidence for God's existence causes them to conform automatically to what they perceive as God's will. If such a world were actual, even a perfectly loving God concerned to facilitate reciprocal personal relationship would surely allow reasonable nonbelief to occur, for his doing so would be a necessary condition of human moral freedom. Thus, it might be concluded, the claim that God exists and is perfectly loving can easily be shown to be compatible with the claim that reasonable nonbelief occurs: there is a possible world (one in which humans are as described) in which both claims are true.

Now it seems to me that the compatibility of (3) with (4) is not so easily demonstrable as our imaginary critic imagines. For the critic must show not only that there is a possible world in which humans are so constituted, but also that there is a possible world in which a loving God has *made* them so; and the latter possibility has not been demonstrated. To demonstrate it, the critic would have to show either (i) that there is a possible world containing God in which humans are as described and in which God would not have any inclination to seek personal relationship, or (more hopefully) (ii) that there are possible goods which require for their existence that humans be so constituted, and which outweigh or offset the goods that would be sacrificed by a loving God in so making them. But while it seems to me, for this reason, that it would be rash to suppose that the claim that (2) is necessarily true can *easily* be shown false, I will not seek to defend it. It will be more convenient for our purposes to concentrate on the question whether (2) is true. If we do, a Plantinga-style response will be not just difficult but irrelevant. And in any case, it will at some points in the argument be necessary to appeal to features of the actual world which we cannot assume are replicated in every possible world containing

10. See Alvin Plantinga, *The Nature of Necessity* (Oxford: Clarendon Press, 1974), chap. 9.

human beings. Accordingly, the problem of reasonable nonbelief, as I develop it, must be viewed as a special instance of the *empirical* problem of evil: the claim at issue, properly understood, is that because of what we have reason to believe about the connection between Divine love and the prevention of reasonable nonbelief, and because states of affairs for the sake of which even a loving God might permit reasonable nonbelief to occur apparently do not actually obtain, there is good reason to suppose that (2) is true, and so (given the occurrence of reasonable nonbelief) good reason to suppose that a loving God does not exist.[11]

In a philosophical work of this sort, one must always decide what to assume and what to defend or oppose. It will be useful at this point to indicate several important assumptions I will be making—claims for which no explicit argumentation is provided in later parts of the book.

(1) The first of these is that belief is involuntary in the sense that we cannot believe a proposition at a moment's notice. If we could decide to "believe" where formerly we had not, and our decisions were immediately efficacious, we would know that our "beliefs" were the result of our decisions and not determined by how things are. But in that case we would not have any reason to suppose that

---

11. It may be worthwhile to point out here that there is a way of construing my claim as a *necessary* truth that is equally immune to a Plantinga-style response. This can be seen as follows. The claim that some state of affairs obtains and the claim that it obtains in the actual world (α) are truth-functionally equivalent. (I assume here that "the actual world" and "α" designate rigidly.) Hence we may with perfect propriety rephrase (2) as follows:

> (2') α includes the state of affairs consisting in God's being perfectly loving only if reasonable nonbelief does not occur.

But as Plantinga's own work shows, "α-claims" like (2') are noncontingent—either necessarily true or necessarily false. For if α includes some state of affairs S, it *necessarily* includes it. And if α does not include S, it *necessarily* excludes it. (See Plantinga, *Nature of Necessity*, pp. 45–46, 55.) Hence if (2') is true, it is necessarily true, which was what we wished to show. So anyone who wishes to do so may interpret the claim for which I will be seeking to make a prima facie case as a claim with respect to what is necessarily true: no susceptibility to Plantinga-style maneuvers need thereby be incurred. But for myself, I will continue to view it simply as the claim that if God is perfectly loving, reasonable nonbelief does not occur—a claim which purports to be no more than true.

what we "believed" was true and so would not really believe.[12]
That belief is involuntary has been convincingly argued by a number of writers, and the force of their arguments would be conceded
by perhaps the majority of contemporary philosophers.[13]

(2) A second assumption is that humans have libertarian free
will. As Richard Swinburne has concisely put it, a being has free
will in this sense if "he acts intentionally and . . . how he acts is not
fully determined by prior states of the world; his choices are to
some extent up to him."[14] The claim that human beings have libertarian free will is of course highly controversial, but I will assume
it because it is accepted by most of the contemporary philosophers
and theologians to whom this work is addressed and often presupposed in their arguments.

(3) I will further assume that it is constitutive of the idea of God
that God, if he exists, is *unsurpassably great*. As such, God is to be
described (minimally) as ultimate (i.e., the source or ground of all
existence other than his own, to whom nothing stands as a ground
of existence), personal (that is to say, one of whom agential, intellectual, and affective qualities may appropriately be predicated),
and (in some sense) all-powerful, all-knowing, perfectly good, and
perfectly loving. I will not, with one exception, offer a defense of
any of the several parts of this description, for it would, I think, be
accepted by the majority of contemporary theologians and philosophers of religion. The exception concerns the claim that God is to
be understood as perfectly loving—a claim central to my argument. It might be thought that this is a claim only Christians have
any reason to accept. But I would deny this. Without offering any-

12. I have taken this argument from Richard Swinburne, *Responsibility and
Atonement* (Oxford: Clarendon Press, 1989), pp. 165–166. See also Bernard Wil-
liams, *Problems of the Self* (Cambridge: Cambridge University Press, 1973), pp.
147–149. There will be more on the nature of belief in Chapter 1, second section.

13. While it is impossible, as I am suggesting here, to will belief directly, it may
be possible to will it *indirectly*, and so belief may be said to be indirectly voluntary.
But this is a very different notion. Getting oneself to believe, for example, that
there is a God when the evidence does not seem initially to support that belief
requires deliberate self-deception, and such self-deception—since it involves viewing the evidence selectively *and* forgetting that one has done so—requires a considerable period of time.

14. Richard Swinburne, *The Existence of God* (Oxford: Clarendon Press, 1979),
p. 153.

thing like a complete explication of "Divine love," I think we can say that what usually goes by that name—at a minimum, self-giving, unconditionally accepting, relationship-seeking love—is such that any being who lacked it would be a being whose greatness *could* be surpassed, and therefore not God. Love of the sort in question is clearly one of the highest manifestations of personal being; so if God is conceived as embodying the perfections of personal life, he must be conceived as perfectly loving.

Now it may be said that this picture of God as perfectly loving is a picture of God peculiarly suited to my purposes and so one I will naturally be inclined to defend. But it should be noted that very many who are not antecedently committed to the conclusion of my argument would nonetheless accept this premise without hesitation. As H. H. Price puts it, "What could conceivably be better than universal and unconditional love?"[15] In the unconditional love of a Mother Teresa, for example, we see reflected a quality of being that most of us would intuitively say must belong to God, if God exists. For it is something to which we are inclined to ascribe very great value indeed. When we reflect on the nature of such love, all the power and knowledge in the world fade by comparison. Hence it would seem (and I will assume) that *all* who espouse a form of theism are rationally committed to the truth of the claim that God, if he exists, is perfectly loving.

(4) A fourth assumption is that the claim that God exists is *coherent*. I do not wish to suggest that there are no problems of coherence which theists must resolve, but these problems will not concern us here. That some description of God falling within the parameters laid down above is coherent is in any case assumed by most contemporary philosophers of religion to be in principle demonstrable.[16] The questions that concern philosophers of religion writing today are more commonly questions of truth than questions of coherence.

(5) I will further assume that the relevant evidence (exclusive of

15. H. H. Price, "Faith and Belief," in John Hick, ed., *Faith and the Philosophers* (London: Macmillan, 1964), p. 5.
16. See, for example, Richard Swinburne, *The Coherence of Theism* (Oxford: Clarendon Press, 1977), and J. L. Mackie, *The Miracle of Theism* (Oxford: Clarendon Press, 1982), pp. 1–3.

evidence adduced in this book) does not clearly favor either the conclusion that there is a God or its denial. This assumption seems warranted in light of recent discussions in the philosophy of religion, which often end in deadlock, and is accepted by many, both inside and outside the academic study of religion.[17] In the Conclusion, however, I will consider the implications of our discussion for those who would view belief in the existence of God as having considerably more in the way of evidential support than I here allow.

(6) Finally, I will assume that it is coherent to suppose that human beings survive their deaths. This assumption, like the assumption of libertarian free will and of the coherence of theism, is made in full recognition of its controversial status, for the sake of *argument*: it too is accepted and commonly presupposed by those to whom this book is addressed.

My description in this Introduction of the argument to follow may seem to suggest that it is my wish to defend atheism—to show that God does not exist. But this is not an accurate representation of my intent; and I would like to emphasize that it is not. The intended contribution of this book is more correctly characterized as a demonstration that there *is* an argument here—an argument of considerable force, which deserves much more attention than it has heretofore received. It is true, as noted earlier, that I will conclude by declaring all the available counterarguments to be bankrupt, and by suggesting that anyone who accepts my conclusion (as well as the fifth assumption above) has good grounds for a denial of theism. But I by no means wish to rule out the possibility that better arguments than the ones here discussed may one day be devised. It is indeed my hope that those who read this book may be motivated to seek to provide such arguments. Thus although I do believe that, where there is a prima facie case, the failure of all the arguments one can think of to rebut that case provides good grounds for believing its conclusion, and that no *available* counter-

---

17. The deadlock is exemplified by, for example, the opposed arguments of Swinburne's *Existence of God*, and Mackie's *Miracle of Theism*.

argument defeats the case that I present, my claim should be construed by theists not as a cry of triumph but rather as a challenge, an invitation, to find for the problem herein discussed the solution I myself have been unable to uncover.

Part 1

Framing the Argument

[1]
Some Epistemic Implications
of Divine Love

We saw in the Introduction that the concept of God is the concept of a being who is, among other things, perfectly loving. But what is it for God to be loving? More specifically, what is it for God to love *us*—to love human beings? One term that may seem important here is "benevolence": if God is loving, he desires our well-being. And indeed, it can hardly be denied that a reference to benevolence must find its way into any adequate explication of Divine love, for the sort of love that can be viewed as a perfection of personal being is clearly other-regarding. The one who claims that benevolence is a feature of Divine love can also point out that this is entailed by the understanding of God's love as agape, a self-giving love.[1] As Robert Adams writes, "There cannot be Agape at all without benevolence."[2] But there is more to love than a general reference to benevolence can capture. What more there is cannot be fully detailed here, but most important for our purposes is the (often neglected) connection between Divine love and the seeking of *personal relationship*. In the present chapter, I seek to clarify this

1. The classic treatment of the concept of "agape" is to be found in Anders Nygren, *Agape and Eros*, Philip S. Watson, trans. (Philadelphia: Westminster Press, 1953). But as later discussion will suggest, Nygren's distinction between the two forms of love mentioned in his title may be too sharply drawn.
2. Robert Adams, *The Virtue of Faith* (New York: Oxford University Press, 1987), p. 190.

connection and to develop certain of its implications.[3] In particular, I argue that if a perfectly loving God exists, all human beings capable of personal relationship with himself are, at all times at which they are so capable, in a position to believe that he exists.

A Neglected Feature of Divine Love

"God seeks to be personally related to us." In claiming that this proposition is essential to any adequate explication of "God loves human beings," I am claiming that God, if loving, seeks *explicit, reciprocal* relationship with us, involving not only such things as Divine guidance, support, and forgiveness, but also human trust, obedience, and worship. So understood, this proposition seems obviously required. For only the best human love could serve as an analogy of Divine love, and human love at its best clearly involves reciprocity and mutuality. If I love you and so seek your well-being, I wish to make available to you all the resources at my disposal for the overcoming of difficulties in your life. But then I must also make it possible for you to draw on me *personally*—to let you benefit from my listening to your problems, from my encouragement, from my spending time together with you, and so on. In other words, I wish to make available to you the resources of an intimate personal relationship with me. This, indeed, is part of what is involved in self-giving. As W. H. Vanstone puts it, "the authenticity of love must imply a totality of giving—that which we call the giving of self or self-giving. The self is the totality of what a man has and is: and it is no less than this that is offered or made available in love."[4] Therefore, if I am to act toward you with perfect benevolence, I must, it seems, seek personal relations with you.

This emphasis seems especially appropriate in the Divine case: personal relationship with *God* would *immeasurably* enhance our well-being, and so God as perfectly benevolent must seek it for us.

---

3. In line with earlier discussion in the Introduction, claims with respect to this connection are defended as true, not as necessarily true. Needless to say, if they are necessarily true as well, the argument will be none the worse for it.

4. W. H. Vanstone, *Love's Endeavour, Love's Expense* (London: Darton, Longman and Todd, 1977), p. 45.

Before endorsing this claim, however, we must examine it a little more closely. What are the benefits such a relationship would make available? We may begin by noting the ethical benefits. It seems clear that explicit relationship with a perfectly loving God would have a certain moral influence and make available certain resources for dealing with the moral weakness endemic to humanity; and few would deny that, were we to become ethically stronger in this way, our well-being would be enhanced. But that is not all. If God exists and is perfectly loving, and if the life of God is unsurpassably good, as by definition it must be, and if, in addition, God has created us and wills *our* good, then the love of which we are in some measure capable must be seen as a significant clue to the nature of our deepest well-being. Growth in self-giving love must, in other words, lead to a deeper realization of well-being, and so God as perfectly benevolent will naturally seek to facilitate it. In helping us replace self-centered patterns of activity with agapeistic ones, he will be allowing us to share in his own life and thus will be facilitating the achievement of an objective quality of being which is of great worth. Now, of course, to avoid begging the question at issue, we must assume for the moment that the love God seeks to facilitate is a form of benevolence not necessarily involving the seeking of personal relationship. But, even so, the promised additional point follows. It is that if self-giving love has this special importance vis-à-vis our well-being, then given that we are often morally weak, we are even more obviously in a position to benefit from outside help—help of the sort made available by personal relationship with God.

Few religious writers would quarrel with this view. Their position is represented by Brian Hebblethwaite:

> Forgiveness, reconciliation, peace and justice sound much the same when advanced as ideals of life by theists and non-theists alike. But in fact these qualities and ideals of life turn out rather differently when they are experienced and embraced as effects of gratitude, grace and the divine indwelling. . . .
>
> The whole question of their practical realizability is different. Men need the resources of God's indwelling grace and inspiration if these values and ideals are to be realized humanely. . . . The major-

ity of people need a power not themselves that makes for righteous-
ness.[5]

Basil Mitchell and Robert Adams argue similarly:

> It is, above all, the love of God which serves both as a motive and as
> a reason for the love of neighbor. We should love him because he
> first loved us; and we should love others because he loves them. It is
> this theme preeminently which explains how it is *possible* for a man
> to turn away from anxious self-concern and identify himself with
> the interests of others, however uncongenial those others are, and
> even if it runs counter to the prevailing ethos of his society.[6]

> If one both loves God and trusts in God's love, this will issue in an
> inner peace or sense of security. And this, as many religious thinkers
> have argued, will free one to take a lively interest in God's creatures
> for their own sake—to enjoy his gifts with un-self-conscious grati-
> tude and to love one's neighbor. Here a love for God, combined
> with faith in him, provides an atmosphere of gladness and security
> in which a love for the creature can be encompassed.[7]

That a personal relationship with God would contribute ethically
to human well-being seems to me, for reasons of the sort here
mentioned, to be beyond dispute.

Turning now to the possible *experiential* benefits of such a relationship, I suggest that a similar judgment is warranted. Here we
are dealing not with moral character brought about through one's
actions, but with the quality of one's inner life—not with what one
does or becomes, but with what *happens* to one. Consider, for example, the peace or sense of security mentioned by Adams, the joy
that may come from the conviction that one is rightly related to
what is ultimately real, the self-enrichment experienced in worship, the experience of God's loving presence. As Hebblethwaite

5. Brian Hebblethwaite, *The Ocean of Truth* (Cambridge: Cambridge University Press, 1988), pp. 15–16.

6. Basil Mitchell, *Morality: Religious and Secular* (Oxford: Clarendon Press,
1980), p. 145.

7. Robert Adams, "The Problem of Total Devotion," in Robert Audi and William Wainwright, eds., *Rationality, Religious Belief, and Moral Commitment* (Ithaca,
N.Y.: Cornell University Press, 1986), p. 184.

suggests, it is arguable that even the experiential aspects of our relationships with other human beings would be significantly enhanced by relationship with God: "Where the other is seen as a child of God, and where human interpersonal relation is believed to find its own true fulfillment in conformity to and inspiration by the . . . love of God who made us, love occurs in a different dimension and takes on other transcendent qualities."[8] These things clearly are benefits in their own right; even if they did not strengthen us ethically, experiential features like these would contribute greatly to human well-being.

So far we have noted certain ethical and experiential benefits of personal relationship with God. There are, however, two more (closely related) senses in which such relationship may be said to contribute to human well-being. First, a personal relationship with God must also be viewed as adding value to human life by virtue of what it is *intrinsically*. To be personally related to unsurpassable goodness is a great good in itself. Second, the one who has committed herself to God and is growing in personal relationship with God will come to see ever more clearly that this is so (i.e., will see that relationship with God adds value to life by virtue of what it is intrinsically), and thus will desire for its own sake to enter ever more deeply into communion with God. In allowing this to take place, God is fulfilling the desire of the individual, and hence the individual will be happy—her well-being will be increased. She will be so even if she does not *seek* to be happy. Indeed, her not seeking personal relationship with God for the sake of the happiness it may produce is a necessary condition of her being happy in this way.[9]

The considerations I have adduced show that personal relationship with God would indeed enhance human well-being; hence we might expect a perfectly loving God, concerned for our well-being, to make such relationship possible for us. It must now be noted, however, that—as the argument of the previous paragraph already suggests—a proper understanding of "God loves human beings" requires us to view God as valuing (and so seeking) the

8. Hebblethwaite, *Ocean of Truth*, p. 15.
9. I am grateful to Richard Swinburne for drawing these points to my attention.

personal relationships in question not merely because they would be good for us but for *their own sakes* as well. This is persuasively argued by Adams, who sees the denial of this view as involving a confusion over the relation of agape and eros:

> The contrast between Agape and Eros is popularly seen as a special case of the contrast between altruism and self-interest. . . . [This] contrast between altruistic and self-interested desires is legitimate and useful. But it has too often been treated as a dichotomy. . . .
>
> The mistake, in trying to force love into the dichotomy of self-interest and altruism, is a failure to recognize a desire for a relationship for its own sake as a third type of desire that is not just a combination or consequence of desire for one's own good and desire for another person's good. . . .
>
> Thus identification of Eros with self-interested desire for personal relationship is in error; and so is the identification of Agape with benevolence. The ideal of Christian love includes not only benevolence but also desire for certain kinds of personal relationship, for their own sake. Were that not so, it would be strange to call it "love". It is an abuse of the word "love" to say that one *loves* a person, or any other object, if one does not care, except instrumentally, about one's relation to that object.[10]

As Adams notes, his view apparently agrees with the biblical understanding of Divine love:

> God's love for us is surely seen as involving a desire for certain relationships between God and us, for their own sakes and not merely as good for us. . . . He desires our worship and devotion. . . . No doubt it would be possible to interpret all of this on the hypothesis that God desires to be related to us only because it would be good for us. But I think that is implausible. The Bible depicts a God who seems at least as interested in divine-human relationships as in human happiness per se.[11]

If Adams's claims are correct—and it seems to me that they are—we must say that not only the one who acts benevolently without

---

10. Adams, *Virtue of Faith*, pp. 187–188.

11. Ibid., p. 189. Adams's view that eros is included in the Divine agape finds parallels in the writings of contemporary theologians. See, for example, Hendrikus Berkhof, *Christian Faith*, Sierd Woudstra, trans. (Grand Rapids: William B. Eerdmans, 1979), p. 124.

seeking personal relations, but also the one who seeks personal relations *only from benevolence*, fails to achieve the fullness of love. And so God, if he exists and is perfectly loving, must also desire personal relationship with us for its own sake.

This is, it seems to me, an important point. For it allows us to claim with full assurance that even if our *well-being* would be as well served for a time by the existence of a state of affairs entailing the absence of personal contact with God, God would not on that account be deterred from seeking personal relationship with us. His valuing of friendship for its own sake would in every case *prevent* him from actualizing the state of affairs in question.[12] By reflecting on our own friendships with other human beings and on the judgments we are inclined to make with respect to their value as we grow in them, we can see a little of the intrinsic value God (if he exists) might be expected to find in personal relationship with us. But it is only a little. God, infinitely more knowledgeable and capable of love than we, will, we may expect, see ever so much more of value in personal relationship with us—the beings he has (in biblical terms) fashioned in his own image—than we can see ourselves.

I have been defending the claim that the proper explication of "God loves human beings" must include the proposition "God seeks to be personally related to us." But two very important questions about this claim have yet to be addressed: (1) What is the extension of "us" here? Does this expression refer to all human beings or only to some? (2) Would a perfectly loving God seek to be personally related to us *only at some future point*, perhaps after death, or already in this life? I will treat these questions in turn.

(1) Although some theologians in times past have seemed to favor a contrary view, virtually all contemporary writers would say that if God's love is a perfect love, it must extend to everyone equally—nothing less than unlimited love in this sense would be worthy of God. Consider, for example, the following passages, chosen at random:

---

12. Except, perhaps, insofar as the latter was viewed as an *equally* great good in itself or as the necessary condition of such a good.

One thing is sure, that there is no theological justification for setting any limits on our side to the friendliness of God towards man.[13]

Since God is the one God of all beings, he can be no respecter of persons. His love is not marked by favoritism towards this individual or that but embraces the whole of mankind.[14]

The Divine love is limitless. . . . [It] extends to all creatures impartially. While it is fairly absurd to speak of degrees of love, it is true that in loving all things without restriction, God's love is unsurpassable; no other love could extend so far and be so indefectible.[15]

The view defended by the theologians cited seems clearly correct: if God is perfectly loving, he must give himself wholly to his creation, and to his whole creation. Does this imply, however, that God seeks to be *personally related* to all human beings? It would seem that it does, for perfect love, we have said, involves the seeking of personal relationship, and God, as we have just claimed, must be said to love everyone. But are all human beings *capable* of personal relationship with God? It would seem that the vast majority are, at least to some degree. For, presumably, to be capable of personal relationship with God at a time, one must be in possession at that time of the cognitive and affective equipment required to hold religious beliefs and exhibit such attitudes as trust, gratefulness, obedience, and worship; and this excludes few of us. Indeed, given this understanding, the majority of us are in most of the stages of life, from early to late, capable to some degree of personal relationship with God.[16] And if some human being, for whatever

---

13. Karl Barth, *God, Grace, and Gospel*, J. S. McNab, trans. (Edinburgh: Oliver and Boyd, 1966), p. 50.

14. Wolfhart Pannenberg, *Theology and the Kingdom of God* (Philadelphia: Westminster Press, 1969), p. 118.

15. Keith Ward, *Rational Theology and the Creativity of God* (Oxford: Basil Blackwell, 1982), p. 142.

16. For example, even individuals who have cognitive and affective powers that are still developing (children) or impaired (the mentally handicapped) may surely sometimes be said to have a capacity, however limited, for belief in God, gratefulness to God, and so on. Indeed, as the New Testament writer suggests, children are often the ones who provide our best examples of trusting, grateful, worshipful attitudes in relation to God (Matthew 19:13–15; 21:16). Of course, there comes a point when we would wish to say that a capacity for such attitudes does not exist.

reason, environmental or genetic, seems at some time utterly incapable of personal relationship with God, we cannot rule out the possibility that God, if he exists and is perfectly loving, will at some future point in that individual's life, or in the hereafter, provide him with the capacities required for this and other forms of well-being. So, I suggest, we may suppose that God seeks to be personally related to all human beings, for all may, at some time or other, be given some degree of capacity for such relationship. But to avoid the possibility of objection, let us say that God, if perfectly loving, seeks to be personally related to those human beings who at some time evince some capacity for such relationship. This is compatible both with the view that all human beings at some time enter into personal relationship with God and with the view that some never do. And surely it represents the least that we can say. Since love involves the seeking of personal relationship, if God is perfectly loving and creates an individual with a capacity for such relationship, he must surely seek to help him exercise it.

(2) This brings us to our second question. Would a perfectly loving God seek to be personally related to us only at some future point, perhaps after death, or already in this life? The correct answer, it seems to me, is "already in this life." For the points I have just made, if legitimate at all, would seem to support as well the further claim that God seeks to bring about a personal relationship with himself for human beings capable of such relationship *at all times* at which they are so capable, and hence not only in the hereafter but in this life as well. As Marilyn Adams puts it:

> For each created person, the primary source of meaning and satisfaction will be found in his/her intimate personal relationship with God. This relationship will also be the context in which a created person can be best convinced of his/her worth, because it is the place where God's love for the individual is most vividly and intimately experienced. Christians naturally see it as to everyone's advantage to enter into this relationship as deeply as one can in this world, as soon as possible.[17]

But this point is not reached as quickly as my fairly complicated *description* of this capacity might seem to suggest.

17. Marilyn McCord Adams, "Forgiveness: A Christian Model," *Faith and Philosophy*, 8 (1991), 291.

Now Adams is writing from within the Christian tradition, but I would suggest that what she and other Christians "naturally see" to be true ought to be more widely held. A personal relationship with a loving God could, as she writes, only enhance my well-being at any time at which I exist and, we might add, would not detract from—indeed, would contribute to—my deepest well-being and the well-being of others. For if there is a God, my deeper well-being lies in a deeper relationship with him. And because of its ethical contribution, such a relationship could, it seems, only result in the enhancement of the well-being of others. We might go on to point out once more that God would, at any time, desire personal relationship with us for its own sake as well. A loving God, we might expect, would bring us into existence *so that* he might enter into fellowship with us—for our sakes, but for its own sake too. We have, then, reason to suppose that there is *no* time at which some human being is to some extent capable of personal relationship with God but at which God does not wish the potential represented by that capacity to be realized.[18] God may create beings *without* such capacity, but if the beings he creates have it, then, at any time that they have it, to the extent that they do, we may expect that he will wish them to exercise it.[19] In this sense also, God's love must be unlimited.

Now to this, someone may be inclined to object as follows: "Although there is no reason for God to refrain from relating personally to us at some time at which we are capable of such relationship, there is no reason for him *not* to do so, and he therefore very well *might* do so. More specifically, God need only do what he is *obligated* to do, and relating personally to human beings is not among his obligations."

It seems to me, however, that all talk of obligation is out of

18. The fact that it is at some time a *limited* capacity does not imply that God does not wish it to be exercised, for he may have—and if religious claims about freedom are correct, *has*—created us this way so that we may have the opportunity of *growing* in personal relationship with himself as a result of our own free choices.

19. Perhaps God will also allow some to *lose* the capacity for a relationship with him or to suffer a diminished capacity because of, for example, the free actions of others. I am thinking here of those unfortunate individuals who have been deprived and/or abused in childhood and so are suspicious of everyone, incapable of trust in man or God. (This fact may, of course, itself constitute a problem of evil, but it is not the one that concerns us here.)

place here. Even if God may legitimately be said to have moral obligations (and some would deny this), the objector must still face the fact that it is not the nature of obligation-fulfillment but of *love* that we are exploring. Love *transcends* obligation. It is spontaneous and supererogatory, and naturally seeks the well-being of its object in relation to itself. This is true even of human love at its best. Parents who love their children fully do their best to ensure that it is always possible for their children to draw on the resources of personal relationship with them. If we add to this that love seeks personal relationship for its own sake, it seems that we have good reason to make the all-inclusive claim in question.

A qualification must, however, be entered here. For a personal relationship of the sort in question is not something God can bring about on his own: God may wish to be personally related to me, but if I choose not to respond to his overtures, personal relations will not exist between us. Indeed, there is reason to suppose that an emphasis on freedom is *itself* essential to the explication of Divine love. Love, as John Macquarrie puts it, involves "letting-be, a respect for the otherness, freedom and individuality of the beloved."[20] And as John Hick points out, freedom is essential to personal relationship: "In a [personal] relationship we apprehend and treat the other person as an autonomous mind and will, a responsible and self-directing consciousness with views and rights of his own which must be consulted and respected—in short, as another *person*."[21] Hence it may seem that our claim should be that God will bring it about that it is at all times possible for us to relate personally to him *if we so choose.*

The point about freedom, however, requires us to go farther still. For a loving God, out of respect for our freedom, might well allow us to shut him out altogether—not only to fail to respond to his overtures, but also to put ourselves in a position where these were *no longer noticed.* Such resistance of God would, of course, be culpable, for it would involve shutting out one whom we had seen to be our creator, and perfectly good, as well as the culpable activity of self-deception: in exercising our freedom in this way, we would be bringing it about through our own actions and/or omis-

20. John Macquarrie, *In Search of Humanity* (London: SCM Press, 1982), p. 180.
21. John Hick, *Faith and Knowledge,* 2d ed. (London: Macmillan, 1988), pp. 128–129.

sions that what was once seen was seen no longer. But if God is perfectly loving, and treats us as persons, he will, we may suppose, permit even this extent of freedom over against himself. Hence the clarified claim should read as follows: God will bring it about that, unless we culpably put ourselves in a contrary position, it is at all times possible for us to relate personally to him if we so choose. Or to put it more formally,

> $P1$ If God exists and is perfectly loving, then for any human subject S and time t, if S is at t capable of relating personally to God, S at t is in a position to do so (i.e., can at t do so just by choosing to), except insofar as S is culpably in a contrary position at t.[22]

Our discussion so far, then, suggests that we have good reason to affirm $P1$. In the absence of our own attempts to bring it about that a contrary state of affairs obtains, a perfectly loving God must surely bring it about that we are in a position to relate personally to himself. But some will no doubt feel that this claim requires more in the way of defense than I have given. It may be thought, for example, that I am asking for the beatific vision in this life. But the "personal relationship with God" referred to here is not to be viewed as identical with the beatific vision, although it might *culminate* in such an experience. As my use of the word "culminate" already suggests, the relationship I am thinking of is to be understood in developmental terms. Were it to obtain, it would admit of change, growth, progression, regression. It might be shallow or deep, depending on the response of the human term of the relation. This is, of course, what we would expect if the relationship is conceived as a relationship between God and beings caught up in the toil and vicissitudes of earthly life. Such a relationship *belongs* in this life: now, in the midst of earthly pain and conflict, is when we require Divine guidance, support, consolation, and forgiveness. In light of this, as well as of the other points we have adduced, I would suggest that there is indeed reason to suppose that a being

22. It is important to note that "capable of" and "in a position to" are here understood in such a way that someone might be *capable* of a personal relationship with God at a time—have the requisite cognitive and affective machinery—without being in a position to *exercise* her capacity at that time and so enter into the relationship.

who did not seek to relate himself to us explicitly in this life—who elected to remain elusive, distant, hidden, even in the absence of any culpable activity on our part—would not properly be viewed as perfectly loving.

Let us conclude this section by inspecting briefly the theological credentials of this view. We may do so by looking at the notion of "salvation." Salvation is often said to be something human beings *attain* or may seek to attain. But this language of attainment, when applied to salvation, is potentially misleading. In focusing our attention on the eschatological goal, it may obscure the fact that the process presupposed by the attaining of that goal, and indeed the events that initiate such a process, are also referred to by religious writers in salvific terms. "Salvation" in theology not only refers to the eschaton but also has application in the preeschatological life of the believer. The faith by which one begins upon the religious way is held to facilitate a personal relationship with God and deepened relations with others in the *here and now*. Thus, if we are to employ the language of attainment appropriately, we must say that salvation is an attainment partially realized in the present that may, as a result of activity in the present, be ever more fully realized. Or, to put it another way, the ultimate attainment that the hoped-for eschatological events represent is not discontinuous with the attainments of the present but is a fuller, deeper, perfected version of them. Grace Jantzen sums it up nicely:

> Salvation is not (or at least not primarily) about our future destiny but about our relationship to God and the gradual transforming effect of that relationship in our lives. . . . If religious experience is centrally the sense of the loving presence of God, gradually helping people to reorient and integrate their lives in accordance with their love for him, is this not precisely what salvation is? Salvation must, surely, be religious experience if anything ever is: not in the sense of being a single climactic experience . . . but in the sense of a gradual opening of all life, all of experience to the wholemaking love of God.[23]

Hence theologians, too, seem committed to the affirmation of *P*1.

23. Grace Jantzen, "Conspicuous Sanctity and Religious Belief," in William J. Abraham and Steven W. Holtzer, eds., *The Rationality of Religious Belief* (Oxford: Clarendon Press, 1987), pp. 128–129.

Some Epistemic Implications

If the preceding claims about what a loving God would do are correct, then given an uncontroversial intervening premise, certain interesting conclusions about theistic belief must follow. I will now attempt to clarify these.

The intervening premise I have in mind is foreshadowed in my earlier reference to the awareness of God. It states that a personal relationship with God entails belief in Divine existence, that is, entails a disposition to "feel it true" that God exists.[24] This claim seems obviously true. For I cannot love God, be grateful to God, or contemplate God's goodness unless I believe that there *is* a God. An adequate description of such attitudes and actions entails reference to belief in propositions such as the following: "God is the source of my being"; "God loves me"; "God is to be praised." And clearly, one can only believe propositions such as these if one believes that God exists.[25]

It is important to note that my point here is a logical one. There is something logically amiss in the suggestion that I could display attitudes and perform actions of the sort in question without being disposed to feel it true that God exists. It is not as though someone who cannot be grateful to God or praise God because she does not believe there is a God could do so if only she *tried* a little harder. Such attitudes and actions are not just contingently difficult but *logically impossible* for one who does not believe that God exists.

Since one cannot add to one's beliefs just by choosing to (since belief is involuntary), it follows that while in a state of nonbelief I am not in a position to relate personally to God. But then, given

24. I am here following L. J. Cohen, who defines "belief that *p*" as "a disposition to feel it true that *p*" ("Belief and Acceptance," *Mind*, 98 [1989], 368). Cohen's definition conforms quite closely, I think, to actual usage. It is at any rate very helpful in pinpointing what I am claiming to be logically presupposed by personal relationship with God. (More is said on the topic of the nature of belief later in this section.)

25. As Adams puts it, "it is our highest good to be related in love to God, and . . . we have to believe that he exists and loves us in order to be related to him in that way" (*Virtue of Faith*, p. 20). Adams's claim (as well as mine) echoes a much older claim: "anyone who comes to God must believe that he exists" (Hebrews 11:6, New International Version).

*P*1, we can infer that God will seek to bring it about that I am never in a state of nonbelief. More exactly, we can infer that

> *P*2 If God exists and is perfectly loving, then for any human subject *S* and time *t*, if *S* is at *t* capable of relating personally to God, *S* at *t* believes that God exists, except insofar as *S* is culpably in a contrary position at *t*.

For if God will bring it about that (insofar as I am capable and unless I resist) I am always in a position to relate personally to him, and if the latter state of affairs obtains only if I always believe that God exists, it follows that God will bring it about that (insofar as I am capable and unless I resist) I at all times believe that God exists.[26]

Let us now try to get a little clearer about the content of *P*2. What, more specifically, does belief involve? And what would God do to facilitate belief in his existence (call this the belief that G)?

Beginning with the first question, we may note that the concept of belief is a "graded" concept: varying degrees of belief that *p*—of disposition to feel it true that *p*—seem possible.[27] I may believe *p* weakly or firmly; I may have a weak or a strong disposition to feel it true that *p*. While I believe both that I am presently in Calgary, Canada, and that the distance between Calgary and Oxford, England, is 5,000 miles, the former belief is stronger than the latter. Even though both of the propositions in question are felt by me to be true—are constitutive of what I feel to be so about the world—I am more willing to give credence to the idea that I am wrong about the second than to the idea that I am wrong about the first.

26. It might be held that belief is not just necessary but also *sufficient* to put one in a position to enter into personal relationship with God, since anyone who has the relevant emotional and intellectual capacities *and believes* can, just by choosing to, contemplate God's goodness, cultivate a loving and trusting attitude toward God, and so on. But then, it might be concluded, *P*2 is in fact *equivalent* to *P*1. I have considerable sympathy for this claim, but it is not necessary, for our purposes, to endorse it. And the weaker claim, which *is* required, is quite obviously true.

27. The view of belief as "graded" is discussed by Alvin Goldman in *Epistemology and Cognition* (Cambridge, Mass.: Harvard University Press, 1986). See esp. p. 324. Goldman rejects the graded notion of belief in favor of a *categorical* one, according to which the onset of belief marks the complete victory of one contender over all others. My view, it will be noted, is a sort of compromise position.

This understanding of belief as graded may, however, seem to present a complication for my argument. For does not a personal relationship with God presuppose *firm* belief? If belief is graded, must we not say that not only belief, but belief of a *certain degree of strength* is necessary for a personal relationship with God?

Such a concession would indeed complicate matters, but I do not think it is required. For however weakly I believe, I am still, by definition, disposed to see the proposition in question *as true*. As far as I am concerned, it still reports the way the world is in relevant respects. There is, in other words, a categorical element in belief. If I believe *p*, I must be disposed to feel it true; and if I am not so disposed, I no longer believe it. However weak or strong the belief, if it *is* a belief, it finds a place in my worldview; and although I may be aware of alternatives to what I believe, these will, to varying degrees, remain in the background. If alternatives intrude too much, I must come to be uncertain whether *p* is true and so cease to believe. A closely related point is that in believing *p*, I do not usually think much about the fact *that I am believing* p. There is commonly a shift at the moment of belief formation from thinking *about* the proposition, its epistemic status, and so forth, to thinking *in terms* of it. And this must also be true of weak belief, for otherwise it could not be belief at all. If these arguments are correct, the contrast between weak and strong belief that *p* is not accurately described as a contrast between, for example, feeling it true that (probably) *p* and feeling it true that (certainly) *p*. If I believe that *p* occurrently, I have the thought *that* p, not thoughts about evidence. (Or at any rate, if I have thoughts of the latter sort, they are not mistaken for my thought that *p*.)

What all of this would seem to indicate is that we need not concede that belief of a certain (presumably quite high) degree of strength is necessary for personal relationship with God. Even a weak belief that God exists is compatible with gratefulness, love toward God, trust, contemplation, and the like, for even a weak belief involves a disposition to feel it true that G. If I feel, however weakly, that it is true that there is a God, I may be moved to praise him and to struggle with him in prayer in ways that would be ruled out were I to, for example, be *uncertain* whether G was true.

Now, of course, perhaps God would wish that I *normally* believe firmly. Weak belief, whether I am conscious of it or not, may carry with it a certain measure of stress, and this may affect the relationship. But, on the other hand, God might have reasons for leaving me for a time in a state of weak belief and, given that firm belief is not required for a personal relationship with God, might very well do so.[28] At any rate, relationship-related considerations do not provide nearly as strong a presumption in favor of the contrary view as they would if firm belief were necessary. I will therefore continue to speak of God wishing to facilitate belief, meaning by this *some degree or other* of a disposition to feel it true that G.

We must now take up the second question mentioned above: What will God do to facilitate belief in his existence? I would suggest, as a first approximation, that God would provide *evidence* that is sufficient to produce belief.[29] For if belief is involuntary, then, if I am to believe that G, there must be something or other apart from my own choice—some evidence—on account of which I feel it to be true that G. Now it may be objected that God could simply bring it about that it seems to me strongly that he exists—where the "strong seeming" is something analogous to what produces (for most of us) such beliefs as the belief that $2 + 2 = 4$ —instead of providing evidence. But on the broad understanding I am here assuming, "evidence" refers to anything that can serve as a ground of belief, and so not only to propositions that provide the basis for deductive and inductive inference but also to nonpropositional, experiential evidence in which belief may be directly (noninferentially) grounded. Hence the objector's point can be accommodated. For presumably, if it seems strongly to S that p is true, S may point to *that experiential circumstance*—the circumstance of it seeming strongly to S that p is true—as the ground of his belief.[30] More

---

28. And conversely, God might at times (as we will see) have reason to facilitate a stronger belief.

29. What I say here is meant to apply both to the initial acquisition of belief and (should it be retained) to its persistence.

30. This view is defended by Alvin Plantinga. See his "Reason and Belief in God," in Alvin Plantinga and Nicholas Wolterstorff, eds., *Faith and Rationality* (Notre Dame: University of Notre Dame Press, 1983), pp. 78–79.

generally, there is nothing to prevent God, on our understanding of "evidence," from bringing it about that I have certain experiences instead of providing an *argument* that has G as its conclusion.

This is not yet the whole story, however. For it is compatible with what we have said so far that I be led to believe on inadequate grounds, and this is surely not to be expected: God, we might expect, would provide evidence that *adequately supports* belief. Let us now look at this a little more closely. Why should we have this expectation? The answer, it seems to me, must be given in terms of the requirements of resistance and the nature of God. We have said that God would bring it about that it is only if S has put herself in a contrary position culpably that S is not in a position to relate personally to himself. If this is true, then, clearly, God would not take actions to facilitate belief that left open the possiblity of *inculpable* resistance. And so he would provide adequate evidence, for if the evidence was not adequate, S might very well come to see it as such and inculpably reject it.

Perhaps it will be replied here that God as omnipotent could easily prevent me from ever viewing the evidence he provided *as* poor (even when it was). But were God to take this route, he would systematically deceive us by bringing it about that whenever the (actually inadequate) evidence was examined, it was viewed as adequate; and this seems incompatible with his perfect goodness.[31] This point, indeed, provides us with an independent reason for supposing that the evidence provided would be adequate. For a perfectly good God would not permit his intentions to be fulfilled by deceitful means. And so, it seems, he would not permit me to believe that G on grounds I viewed as adequate, but that did not adequately support that belief. We might go farther and point out that even if I did *not* explicitly consider my grounds or the support they provided, God would still deceive me by

---

31. The qualification "whenever the evidence was examined" is to be carefully noted. S may believe *without* reflecting on her evidence and without articulating to herself exactly how it provides support for G or how *much* support it provides (how probable G is rendered by it). If we did not suppose this, we would have to say that individuals who do not have the capacity for such reflection and evaluation (e.g., small children) could not believe that G; and this is an implication to be avoided. I am indebted to William Alston for drawing the need for some such qualification to my attention.

bringing it about that they were inadequate. For in that case, my degree of firmness in believing (whatever it was) would not correspond to the degree of support provided by the evidence; and so— although I would not believe a false proposition about the evidence—God would have brought it about that I was, so to speak, living out a lie. We may therefore conclude that if God provides me with evidence, intending thereby to produce belief in his existence, it will be evidence that not only is sufficient to produce belief but also adequately supports it.

If now we consider what sort of evidence would provide the degree of objective support required here, I think we must say *probabilifying* evidence—evidence that renders G probable.[32] As William Alston has argued, it is only if a ground renders a claim probably true that the formation of belief on that basis would be "desirable from the epistemic point of view."[33] But there is another reason too: it is just not possible for anyone who considers the evidence on the basis of which she believes to continue believing unless it seems to her to render the proposition in question probably true. For suppose S offers the following description of her mental state: "I feel that G is true—that G conforms to the way the world is. But the arguments for G known to me (i.e., the public evidence) do not seem to me to favor G: neither individually nor cumulatively do they seem to me to show G to be more probable than its denial. Nor do I have any *private* evidence—any hunch or feeling or experience—that favors a contrary view." This description seems clearly contradictory, and the contradiction is one that S could hardly fail to see:

(1) I feel G to be true and I do not feel G to be true.

32. I do not wish to be taken as suggesting that God would ensure that his existence was probable on the *totality* of the evidence that exists—whatever that might be—or on the *public* evidence available—that is, on the set of propositions that provide the premises for arguments in natural theology. All we have seen reason to suppose (and all that the arguments immediately below suggest) is that God would bring it about that his existence was probable on S's evidence; and this evidence, as we have seen, might well include not only propositions of the sort mentioned above but certain of S's experiences too.

33. William Alston, *Perceiving God: The Epistemology of Religious Experience* (Ithaca, N.Y.: Cornell University Press, 1991), p. 74.

Hence the claim that one could consider one's evidence and continue to believe while not holding it to render the proposition one believed probable entails that S could believe a contradiction. But this does not seem to me to be something anyone could do. Hence that claim is false. But if it is false, we do indeed have additional reason to suppose that the evidence God would provide would be probabilifying evidence. For only that way could God ensure (without deception) that anyone who examined her evidence continued to believe.[34]

Perhaps it will now be objected that while probabilifying evidence is necessary, it would not be sufficient. Someone might argue for this as follows: "For those who consider the evidence, only the belief that the evidence renders G *very* probable would be sufficient to produce the belief that G. And so there could be a situation in which God provided probabilifying evidence and S saw it as such, but in which S *did not come to believe*, or in which S came to see the evidence on which she believed as probabilifying and forthwith *ceased* to believe. To avoid this, God would have either to deceive S into supposing the evidence to be stronger than it was or to provide stronger evidence. But obviously, if perfectly good, God would not choose the former route. Hence he would choose the latter. But then we cannot rest content with the claim that God would provide evidence that rendered his existence probable. We must, instead, say that he would provide evidence that rendered his existence *very* probable."

In response to this objection, I would suggest that we have good reason to reject the claim about belief on which it depends. We might first point out, with Richard Swinburne, that it is "tidier" to suppose that belief will exist as soon as the probability of the proposition believed is perceived as greater than 0.5 than to identify the

---

34. I would add here that on my view, any claim to the effect that S holds that G is not more probable than not-G and yet (irrationally) believes that G is most charitably interpreted as ignoring *private* evidence held by S to favor G, or as confusing belief with acceptance (a commitment to *act-as-if* some proposition is true which does not necessarily involve belief that the proposition is true). It is of course also possible for S, through self-deception, to lose the belief she once held that G and not-G are at epistemic parity and *come* to believe that G is true. But I can make no sense of the suggestion that S could *at one and the same time* hold both that G is not more probable than not-G *and* that G is true.

point at which belief arises with some (inevitably arbitrary) value of probability between 0.5 and 1.[35] But other reasons might also be adduced. Suppose I believe that G has a probability of 0.6. Then I believe that the world is to some extent in favor of G, and (it seems) I will have at any rate a *weak* disposition to feel it true that G. It is clear that I may have such a disposition when the perceived probability is less than 1—as the objector himself admits, if I view G as *very* probable, I believe that G—so why should I not believe weakly when the probability is taken to be 0.6? Of course, if I consider the evidence to be evenly balanced, I will be uncertain whether G is true. But if I see G's probability as greater than 0.5, it seems natural to suppose that I believe it to some extent.

This claim can call in its defense an argument of Nicholas Wolterstorff concerning (what he calls) human "belief dispositions." Wolterstorff suggests, following Thomas Reid, that "at any point in our lives we each have a variety of dispositions, inclinations, propensities, to believe things."[36] He provides a number of examples:

> What accounts for our beliefs, in the vast majority of cases anyway, is the triggering of one or another such disposition. For example, we are all so constituted that upon having memory experiences in certain situations, we are disposed to have certain beliefs about the past. We are all disposed, upon having certain sensations in certain situations, to have certain beliefs about the external physical world. Upon having certain other sensations in certain situations, we are all disposed to have certain beliefs about other persons. Likewise we are all so constituted as to be disposed in certain circumstances to believe what we apprehend people as telling us.[37]

And a little farther on, he writes: "In addition to the features of our constitution thus far mentioned, we are all so constituted that upon judging some proposition which we already believe as being good

35. Richard Swinburne, *Faith and Reason* (Oxford: Clarendon Press, 1981), p. 5.
36. Nicholas Wolterstorff, "Can Belief in God be Rational?" in Alvin Plantinga and Nicholas Wolterstorff, eds., *Faith and Rationality* (Notre Dame: University of Notre Dame Press, 1983), p. 149.
37. Ibid.

evidence for another proposition not yet believed, we are disposed to believe that other proposition as well."[38]

In the spirit of Wolterstorff's argument we may wish to claim that when someone takes a proposition to be probable—even marginally so—a belief disposition is triggered and the individual comes to (in some degree) feel the proposition to be true. We might even speculate that there is an evolutionary reason for this. Perhaps it is necessary that we have dispositions of this sort if we are to have, in Swinburne's words, a "map or view of the world" which can guide our actions.[39] Whatever the case, there seem to be introspective grounds for supposing that we do have such dispositions. And if we do, the belief that G is probable is indeed sufficient for the belief that G. Hence the argument that suggests it is not can safely be rejected.

Now all of this (as suggested above) is of course subject to the qualification at the end of $P1$ and $P2$, namely, that God will at all times leave it open to us to resist his facilitative endeavors—to resist the actions he takes to put us in a position to relate personally with himself. Transposing this into the key of the present discussion, we must say that S will remain free to bring it about that he is in a position incompatible with belief (and so no longer in a position to relate personally to God) by opposing the evidence that God provides. Since such resistance would be culpable, it follows that S would remain free to culpably bring about the loss of belief.

Taking this point (and the clarificatory points above) into account, we may now express $P2$ more fully as follows:

> $P2'$ If God exists and is perfectly loving, then for any human subject S and time t, if S is at t capable of relating personally to God, S at t believes that G on the basis of evidence that renders G probable, except insofar as S is culpably in a contrary position at t.[40]

38. Ibid., p. 150.

39. Richard Swinburne, *The Evolution of the Soul* (Oxford: Clarendon Press, 1986), p. 122.

40. It may be said that given the way $P2'$ is phrased, we may argue not only from reasonable nonbelief to the nonexistence of God, but also from reasonable (but inadequately grounded) *belief*. For $P2'$ states that all will believe on *good evi-*

$P2'$ represents my clarified estimate as to the sort of epistemic situation a perfectly loving God would seek to facilitate. If there is a perfectly loving God, S, unless prevented by her own culpable activity, will at all the times in question find herself in possession of evidence that renders G probable and will in some degree believe that G. If such a situation were to obtain, S could only fail to believe that G on good evidence culpably, and so (given my definition of "reasonable") G would be beyond reasonable nonbelief for S. What $P2'$ states, therefore, is that if a perfectly loving God exists, our situation will be one in which God's existence is beyond reasonable nonbelief for all who are capable of a personal relationship with God at all times at which they are so capable.[41] For the sake of ease of reference and stylistic variation, I will hereafter refer to such a situation as one in which God's existence is beyond reasonable nonbelief, or as one in which there is evidence sufficient for belief, or as "a strong epistemic situation in relation to theism." A weak epistemic situation in relation to theism I will take to be a situation in which God's existence is *not* beyond reasonable nonbelief—where, for one or more human beings capable of a personal relationship with God at one or more times at which they are

---

dence, and is it not obvious that many actual believers do not? This point may be conceded, but it does not cast into question the approach I am taking. For the claim of the one who argues from inculpable (but poorly grounded) belief to the nonexistence of God—who emphasizes that a loving God would provide good evidence—*depends on* the claim (and arguments for the claim) that God would provide evidence *at all*. The success of my argument, in other words, is a necessary condition for the success of any argument from inculpable (but poorly grounded) belief. To put it yet another way, the claim under consideration is really a conjunctive claim—"God will provide evidence, and the evidence God provides will be good evidence"—the first conjunct of which must be supported by an argument of the sort provided in this book. If this argument does not succeed, there is no reason to suppose that the other will. And if it *does* succeed, the other will be superfluous.

41. It may be objected that this conditional is not in fact equivalent to $P2'$. For as we have seen, S could be fooled into believing that poor evidence was good and so might very well find that G was beyond reasonable nonbelief for her—might find that she could not reject it without resisting what she took to be good evidence—without it being the case that G was in fact rendered probable by her evidence. I will simply assume, however, that what is *meant* by "G is beyond reasonable nonbelief for S" is "S can only fail to believe that G *on good evidence* culpably," in which case the equivalence holds.

so capable, evidence of the sort in question is not available. In other words, on my definition "a weak epistemic situation obtains" is simply the *negation* of "a strong epistemic situation obtains."

In bringing the chapter to a close, I will briefly consider two objections that might be brought against the argument of this section. According to the first, although it is necessary to believe that God exists in order to be in a position to relate personally to him, such belief is not all that is needed. One must also believe various other religious propositions, such as "God was in Christ, reconciling the world to himself." But then (the objector may claim) I am committed to arguing not only that $P2'$ is true, but also that various $P2'$ counterparts (which refer to these other propositions) are true, and this may considerably lessen the appeal of my view: the claim that God would be interested in ensuring that all human beings at all times are apprised of the truth of all these propositions is, to say the least, a large claim. Hence (he may say) we can argue as follows: The view that God might reveal any one of the propositions in question entails a similar claim in respect of all the others. But the general claim is unacceptable. So any of the more specific ones—including, in particular, the claim concerning G—is also unacceptable.

I answer as follows. It seems that if I believe that G, I may, by responding appropriately to this belief and to belief in the various propositions I see to be clearly entailed or rendered probable by G, turn it into faith and so (if there is a God) enter into personal relationship with God. Specifically, if I come to believe that there is a perfectly loving God, I will also believe such propositions as that I owe my existence to God, that my well-being lies in relationship with God, that other individuals are loved and valued by God, that I too should seek to act toward them in loving ways. And individuals who hold such beliefs are clearly in a position to act upon them by thanking and praising God, praying to God, cultivating a loving disposition towards others, and so forth. In other words, acquiring the belief in question *does* seem to put a person in a position to relate personally to God—at least if we assume (as the discussion in the first section of this chapter surely allows us to do) that God, if he exists and is perfectly loving, is disposed to respond in appropriate personal ways to the activities of such a believer.

Now no doubt there are, if there is a God, many other interesting and important religious truths not clearly entailed or rendered probable by the proposition "God exists," but I do not see that awareness of these is essential to a personal relationship with God if such a relationship is construed (as it is here) in developmental terms. Belief in the existence of a perfectly loving God, on the other hand, is clearly necessary to get one started in such a relationship: without it, as we have seen, explicit Divine-human reciprocity is ruled out. So I do think it appropriate to focus on belief in God's existence as we are doing. After this belief is acquired, many others may follow in due course. But if God exists, and if the individual has responded appropriately to his belief in God's existence, the acquisition of each such additional belief will be an event *within* the relationship and not a prerequisite for it.

I have been arguing that if God exists and is perfectly loving, humans will be given access to evidence sufficient for belief in God's existence. The second objection to this claim I will consider is a theological objection. Many recent theological writers, sensitive to the presence in our world of nontheistic religious traditions, as well as of morally sincere individuals who are nonetheless nonreligious, have claimed that there is no reason why persons who fail to believe that there is a God should not achieve salvation, and (by implication) that even a perfectly loving God, concerned for our salvation, need not be concerned to facilitate belief for everyone. In light of my earlier comments on salvation (which included the suggestion that theological statements about salvation provide confirmation for my claims), this view may seem to require a response. I will briefly consider the claims of one of its foremost exponents, Karl Rahner.

Rahner develops the Catholic position that nonbelievers may exhibit *implicit* belief. Those who do, he (notoriously) calls "anonymous Christians."[42] The following passage from the essay of that title expresses his view succinctly:

42. See Karl Rahner, "Anonymous Christians," in G. A. McCool, ed., *A Rahner Reader* (London: Darton, Longman, and Todd, 1975), p. 211. Further references to this essay will be made parenthetically in the text.

No matter what a man states in his conceptual, theoretical and religious reflection, anyone who does not say in his *heart* "there is no God" . . . but testifies to him by the radical acceptance of his being, is a believer. But if in this way he believes in deed and in truth in the holy mystery of God . . . then the grace of this truth by which he allows himself to be led is always already the grace of the Father in his Son. And anyone who has let himself be taken hold of by this grace can be called with every right an "anonymous Christian." [P. 214]

Elsewhere in the essay, "the radical acceptance of being" (which is also referred to as the acceptance of "transcendence" or of "limitless openness" [p. 213]) seems to be spelled out in terms of moral commitment: "We can say quite simply that wherever, and in so far as, the individual makes a moral decision in his life . . . this moral decision can also be thought to measure up to the character of a supernaturally elevated, believing and thus saving act" (p. 218). Rahner also speaks here of "loving humaneness" (p. 214), and suggests that "an atheist can be justified and receive salvation if he acts in accordance with his conscience" (p. 221).

In response to Rahner, we may point out that such claims seem to comport ill with views concerning God's love to which—as the following passages from "Anonymous Christians" show—he is also committed.

Love in its truly personal sense is . . . the ceding and the unfolding of one's inmost self to and for the other in love. [God wishes to enter] into unrestricted personal communion with man. [P. 134]

God makes a creature whom he can love: he creates man. He creates him in such a way that he *can* receive this Love which is God himself, and that he can and must at the same time accept it for what it is: the ever astounding wonder, the unexpected, unexacted gift. [Pp. 186–187]

Man should be *able* to receive this Love . . . ; he must have a congeniality for it. . . . He must have it *always*. He is indeed someone always addressed and claimed by this love. For . . . he is created for it; he is thought and called into being so that Love might bestow itself. . . . The capacity for the God of Self-bestowing personal Love is the . . . abiding existential of man as he really is. [Pp. 187–188]

These passages seem to make my point much more effectively than Rahner's. Indeed Rahner admits that in "explicitness," belief finds "its greatest support and confidence" (p. 214). So what should we say about the earlier claims concerning implicit belief? It would seem that in Rahner's case, as in the case of other writers who address this question, such claims presuppose either that God exists (which assumption would permit one to draw the conclusion that implicit belief, since it is in many cases the only form of "belief" possible, somehow falls within God's purposes), or that theologically acceptable arguments can be adduced to show that *despite* the support that exists for the contrary view, explicit awareness of God will be absent in many cases. But these assumptions are in this context at best inapplicable, and at worst question-begging—the first because we are exploring an argument *against* God's existence, and the second because we have not yet come to consider whether the support for $P2'$ (to which it alludes) can be overridden: we have only been concerned to *elucidate* that support. Certainly we cannot *assume* that that support will be overridden. We may conclude, therefore, that this second objection, like the first, does not take anything away from the considerable force of the argument for $P2'$.

Is a Strong Epistemic Situation in Relation to Theism Possible?

According to the argument of the previous chapter, there is reason to suppose that a perfectly loving God would ensure that the epistemic situation of humans in relation to theism was a strong one, that is, would bring it about that his existence was beyond reasonable nonbelief. But even if God apparently would wish to bring about such a state of affairs, perhaps it would not be possible (i.e., logically possible) for him to do so. If it would *not* be possible, then of course, any argument purporting to show that such a state of affairs will obtain if God exists collapses; for even an omnipotent God cannot do what is logically impossible for him to do. Hence it is important, in order to satisfy a necessary condition for the success of the prima facie case I am constructing, that some space be devoted to showing that the situation in question is indeed possible—that there is a possible world in which God brings it about that his existence is beyond reasonable nonbelief.

My procedure is as follows. In the first section of the chapter I briefly examine certain general considerations that might be held to show the situation in question to be impossible and offer certain considerations of my own that seem to me to provide at least initial support for the contrary view. In the second section I attempt to provide further and conclusive support for this view by describing in detail one way in which the possibility in question might be instantiated.

Opening Arguments

Some writers would no doubt be inclined to argue that it is *not* possible for God to put his existence beyond reasonable nonbelief, and that we can show this without examining particular examples of situations God could bring about. It might be argued, for example, that the state of affairs in question is ruled out by the fact of *human finitude*. Thus John Macquarrie:

> Contemporary theology probably reckons more seriously with the finitude of human existence than many theologians of the past have done. . . . To be finite is to live in risk and uncertainty, and that this is our life is clear to us from everyday experiences in which we have to commit ourselves to policies of action without complete knowledge of all the relevant circumstances and still less of all the consequences that will flow from the action. Our life in this world is not one that can be based only upon the certitude of knowledge—the man who tries to live this way, without risk, never really lives at all—but one that must go out in faith. This is true about the understanding of our life as a whole—we see it only from our limited standpoint and cannot know the ultimate truth about it. Thus to demand the guaranteed certitude of rational demonstration (that there is a God . . .) is to refuse to acknowledge one's own finitude.[1]

But our understanding of "beyond reasonable nonbelief" does not require that there be "certitude"; only that there be, in the absence of resistance, some degree of belief that G. Perhaps the former state would be difficult for finite beings to maintain (although certain fundamentalist groups seem to belie this); we must note that the latter does not seem at all like it in this respect. And while it might seem impossible for beings who are radically finite to be always convinced of the force of some "rational demonstration" of God's existence (although again there are apparent counterexamples), it is not at all obvious that probabilifying evidence of the sort that *my* argument requires must be such as finite beings like ourselves could not appreciate. Hence I suggest that the argument from finitude does not succeed.

1. John Macquarrie, *Principles of Christian Theology*, 2d ed. (London: SCM Press, 1977), p. 51.

A second argument that might be considered is an argument from *Divine transcendence*. Now not just any transcendence will do here. God may be very different from creatures, but so long as he is describable by *analogy* with ourselves, it is not obvious that his existence could not be put beyond reasonable nonbelief. This is brought out very clearly and forcefully by Swinburne in the context of a related discussion:

> God cannot be totally different if he is describable with words which we use to describe mundane things—e.g. "wise", "good", "powerful". If these words do have, however analogical, an application to him, God must be something like wise, good and powerful things on earth; and in that case kinds of arguments which are appropriate to prove the existence or non-existence of wise, good and powerful things in principle have application to proving his existence or non-existence.[2]

So the argument from Divine transcendence must claim that God is to be understood as *absolutely* transcendent—that talk about created things, including ourselves, does not have even an analogical application to him. Now if this view is correct, then it is hard to see how there could be evidence that probabilified God's existence or how God could meaningfully be described as acting so as to provide such evidence. But then, by the same token, it is hard to see how *anything* meaningful could be said about God. For this reason, I would claim, theists—who are after all committed to saying quite a lot about God—are not in a position to think of God as absolutely transcendent; and so this second argument is no more successful than the first.

Can we go any farther than this? Are there considerations that suggest God *could* put his existence beyond reasonable nonbelief? I think there are. The first of these is that the evidence actually available to individuals who inculpably fail to believe does go *some* way toward showing that there is a God. Individuals who doubt, for example, may nevertheless look upon such phenomena as the order manifested in the universe and religious experience as confirm-

2. Richard Swinburne, *Faith and Reason* (Oxford: Clarendon Press, 1981), p. 84.

ing to some degree the proposition that there is a God. And surely no one could reasonably deny that such phenomena do render the existence of God at least somewhat more likely than it would otherwise be. The second point (which will be seen to complement the first) is that our evidential situation is not the only one that could have obtained. This follows from the obvious truth that ours is not the only possible world. We can conceive of a great many ways in which our world might have been different. But then, surely, the *evidential situation of humans vis-à-vis God's existence* could have been different as well: every contingently existing thing in the world is relevant to the question whether there is a Creator, and so if the world changes, the evidence changes too.

These points, when taken in tandem, would seem to provide a certain amount of initial support for the claim under consideration. If we accept that the evidence actually available to individuals in our world goes some way toward showing that there is a God, and accept as well that there are innumerable ways in which the world (and ipso facto the evidence) could have been different, then it seems we have some reason to accept that there is a possible world in which *stronger* evidence is available—in particular, in which individuals are always in the presence of evidence sufficient for belief.

The Possibility of Religious Experience

What we have seen so far is that we have no obvious reason to suppose that God's existence could not be put beyond reasonable nonbelief and some initial reason to accept the contrary view. In this section, I attempt to provide the latter with conclusive support by means of a particular example—an example of a state of affairs that seems clearly possible, and that would, if it obtained, instantiate the state of affairs consisting in God's having brought it about that his existence is beyond reasonable nonbelief.

It may seem to some that God could quite easily put his existence beyond reasonable nonbelief by creating a world without evil (or with much less evil than ours contains), or by producing now and then spectacular and overwhelming events that could not reasonably be considered anything but counterinstances to true laws of nature. But this claim seems dubious. Presumably God could create a world without evil or with much less evil, but while this might remove an important obstacle to belief, it is not clear that it would make the required positive contribution to the epistemic circumstances of everyone concerned. In any case, I wish to show that a strong epistemic situation in relation to theism is compatible with the existence of much evil. Overwhelming miracles may also be possible, but miracles are by definition rare events, and so it is not easy to see how the sort of evidence they might provide could be generally and at all times available, as a strong epistemic situation requires. Furthermore, I wish to show that God need not overwhelm us in order to elicit belief, and to prove that the description of a state of affairs of the sort in question need not be theologically crude, as a description involving reference to Divinely produced spectacular events would no doubt seem to many to be.

A more fruitful approach, I suggest, would focus on the possible epistemic contribution of religious experience.[3] Experiential evidence, as we will see, could be generally and at all times available. It is also more likely to be religiously efficacious—to stimulate a religiously appropriate response. I may, if I am presented with a good argument or witness a spectacular miracle, conclude that there is a God, but if God is *present to me* in experience, my response (if I respond positively at all) is perhaps more likely to be the personal response a loving God would desire. Related to this is the point that it is only religious experience that makes possible the deepest forms of personal relationship between God and humankind.[4] Although perhaps not *necessary* for such relationship, religious experience must obviously enrich it and contribute to its flourishing.

Suppose, then, that the world is one in which all human beings who evince a capacity for personal relationship with God have an experience as of God presenting himself to them, which they take to be caused by God and which actually *is* caused by God present-

3. I do not assume that this is the *only* line of thought it would be profitable to pursue in this context, but, as I argue, it does seem an appropriate one.
4. On this point, see William Alston, *Perceiving God: The Epistemology of Religious Experience* (Ithaca, N.Y.: Cornell University Press, 1991), pp. 303–304. This impressive book is full of insights on our topic and has stimulated my thinking in a variety of ways.

ing himself to their experience. This experience, let us say, is non-sensory—an intense apparent awareness of a reality at once ulti-mate and loving which (1) produces the belief that God is lovingly present (and ipso facto, that God exists), (2) continues indefinitely in stronger or weaker forms and minimally as a "background awareness" in those who do not resist it, and (3) takes more partic-ular forms in the lives of those who respond to the beliefs to which it gives rise in religiously appropriate ways (for example, the be-liever who pursues a personal relationship with God may describe his experience as that of the *forgiving, comforting,* or *guiding* presence of God). Since the experience is had as soon as a capacity for per-sonal relationship with God exists, we may suppose that it occurs quite early on in the life of each individual, in particular, before any investigations as to the existence of God have been under-taken. We may further suppose that any investigations *subsequently* undertaken (at any rate by individuals who have not taken steps to hide from themselves the experience and its apparent implications for belief) fail to undermine, and indeed reinforce, the beliefs formed by this experience. In particular, those who encounter the problem of evil and other objections to theistic belief continue to believe that there is a God on the basis of their experience and take what they believe to be confirmed as they discover the *universality* of the experience and the *uniformity* of its descriptions—as they learn that reports of an experience very similar to their own have come from every time and place accessible to historical inquiry.

Let us now clarify one or two aspects of this description.

(1) The experiences in question are, as I have said, nonsensory, that is, not mediated by sensations of any sort. As Swinburne puts it in describing experiences of this kind, "The answer to 'What was it about your experience which made it seem to you that you were having an experience of God?' will be 'It just did. There were no visual, auditory or any other sensations which made it seem thus to me.'"[5] I do not mean to imply, however, that no religious experi-ences of a sensory sort are had by individuals in the world in ques-tion, or that if they are, none are caused by God.

(2) When I say that at the time in question humans have an expe-

---

5. Richard Swinburne, *The Existence of God* (Oxford: Clarendon Press, 1979), p. 252.

rience *caused by God being present to them*, I do not mean to suggest that prior to this time, God has not been lovingly present to human beings or that their experience is necessarily due to some special action of God at that time. Let us take up each of these points in turn. God, if he exists and is perfectly loving, is always present and lovingly disposed toward us, but it is only at a certain stage, when certain capacities are in place, that humans may become *sensitive* to the Divine presence. Just as the health of my optic nerve is necessary if distant objects—which are there all the time—are to cause me to *see* they are there, so it is that even though God, if he exists, is always and everywhere present, certain capacities are required if I am to become aware of God's presence—if God's being present is to cause me to *perceive* that God is present. And in the world I have described, these coincide with the capacities required for personal relationship with God.

Does this causation imply any special activity on God's part vis-à-vis the individuals in question? It seems to me that it does not. Suppose that the world I have described is actual and that Francine, an inhabitant of this world, becomes capable of personal relationship with God at time *t*. Although the state of affairs consisting in Francine's becoming aware of God's presence might obtain at *t* as a result of God's special intention at *t* that Francine should become so aware, this does not seem necessary. Given the state of affairs I have described, it may just as well be that the laws of nature which God has caused to operate are such that when the appropriate stage in Francine's development is reached, Francine, so to speak, "switches on" to the Divine presence. On this view, God is always lovingly disposed to Francine, and when certain developmental conditions are satisfied, she simply becomes aware of this, that is to say, the fact of God's being present to Francine becomes causally efficacious in the relevant way vis-à-vis Francine. Perhaps not much turns on which of these conceptions is accepted. But anyone inclined to accept a noninterventionist view of God should take note that my description does not rule it out.[6]

I turn now to a defense of my judgments as to the coherence of the description I have given and what it entails.

---

6. See Maurice Wiles, *God's Action in the World* (London: SCM Press, 1986) for a statement and defense of such a view.

The state of affairs I have described seems clearly possible: its description seems perfectly coherent. Surely it could be the case that all human beings with a capacity for personal relationship with God become aware of God's presence.[7] If it is suggested that only persons who already have a concept of God and a wider experience of life experience religiously, so that religious experience presupposes a period of preparation *following* acquisition of the capacity in question, we may reply that this is a contingent truth. An omnipotent God would be able to create us with the required mental furniture in place or, at any rate, would be able to bring it into existence at the time when the capacity for personal relationship with God was acquired. It has, indeed, often been held by theologians that the idea of the Divine is implanted in us by God. Now whether this is *true* or not, surely no one would deny that it is logically *possible*. But if so, the problem under consideration vanishes.[8]

What about the rest of the description? Is it coherent? It seems to me that it is. Belief could only fail to be formed in such circumstances if the subject was deterred by strong apparent counterevidence, and given the temporal priority of the experience as I have described it, this possibility is ruled out—that is, in the first instance at least, the subject's attention is focused on his experience and not on other evidence. And if the experience were universal and its descriptions uniform, and if it was ongoing in the lives of

---

7. Remember, we are *not* asking whether *actual* experiences of God have occurred or whether it is reasonable for persons who have *actually* had religious experiences to view them as providing contact with God. What we are asking is whether it should be deemed *possible* for God to bring human beings to awareness of himself.

8. Some might argue that while my points show that an *apparent* awareness of God could occur early on, we have no reason to suppose that anyone could *actually* recognize at this stage (or perhaps any other) the presence of a being exemplifying the collection of properties God is said to possess. But there is considerable support in the literature for the view that such attributes could be directly given in experience. See, for example, Swinburne, *Existence of God*, pp. 267–268; Gary Gutting, *Religious Belief and Religious Skepticism* (Notre Dame: University of Notre Dame Press, 1982), pp. 153–155; Alston, *Perceiving God*, pp. 17, 59–63; and George Mavrodes, *Revelation in Religious Belief* (Philadelphia: Temple University Press, 1988), pp. 104–109. Mavrodes defends the notion of "basic cognitive acts" analogous to basic physical acts. Earlier in his book (p. 94), Mavrodes makes what seems to me to be one of the central points here: "What kinds of experience there are [is] itself a matter of experience."

those who did not resist it, the judgment of experients with respect
to God's presence would (barring steps taken to remove belief)
surely be maintained indefinitely and, indeed, reinforced—even in
the face of evils such as our world contains. One's own experience
is a very powerful stimulus to belief; only under strong pressure
from outside forces will what is suggested by it be rejected.

Suppose, however, that some experients came to view evil (or
some other apparent counterevidence) as a threat. As we have seen,
there are degrees of experiential force and of belief, and so it would
be possible for the force of the experience in such circumstances to
be increased. God might allow the individuals in question to feel
his presence more strongly—or at least strongly enough to sustain
a certain degree of belief. Furthermore, if a state of affairs of the
sort I have described were to obtain, much of the additional evidence—in particular, the public evidence concerning the distribution and uniformity of this form of experience—would seem to
confirm the judgments of the individual with respect to her experience and its epistemic implications. This apparent confirmation,
together with what has already been described, would, it seems to
me, prevent the problem of evil or any other objection from overwhelming the subject's belief (provided, of course, that she did not
take steps to hide from herself her experience and this apparent
confirmation).[9]

Now even if the state of affairs I have sketched is a possible one,
it may be that its description does not entail the proposition in
question, namely (when completely spelled out), "God has
brought it about that for any subject S and time t, if S is at t
capable of relating personally to God, S at t believes that G on the
basis of evidence that renders G probable, except insofar as S is
culpably in a contrary position at t." In particular, it may be that
even if S *in fact* believes because of her evidence, including the
evidence of religious experience, that evidence does not render G
probable.

9. Perhaps it will be claimed that naturalistic explanations of the universality
and uniformity of the experience in question will cause S to doubt, at least occasionally. But given that religious experience can be forceful and that S would, as
mentioned below, have available to her an argument for *design* as an attractive
alternative to naturalistic explanation, this seems unlikely.

It seems to me, however, that the entailment does hold—at least if we allow for a little filling out of the description. What the experient comes to believe in the circumstances I have described is, we may assume, at least in the first instance *basic* for her. That is, the belief is supported by experience and not held for the reason that it is rendered probable by other propositions the subject believes. And utilizing terminology recently popularized by Alvin Plantinga and others, I think we can go on to say that it is *properly* basic, that is, "such that it is rational to accept it without accepting it on the basis of any other propositions or beliefs at all."[10] The subject's experience, in the first instance at least, is the only relevant evidence she has. Given that the experience is intense, it is perfectly proper for her to believe that God is present to her (and ipso facto, that God exists) and to believe this in a basic way. What follows *after* is, of course, another matter, but anyone looking back on such an experience would, I think rightly, wish to say that in the circumstances, the proposition believed by the subject was indeed properly basic for her. Hence it seems right to say that in the first instance at least, the relevant evidence available to S is such as to render G probable: given the nature of belief, to say that it is rational for S to believe on her evidence commits one to saying that it would be rational for her, upon reflection, to view her evidence as probabilifying; and there is no distinction between this claim and the admission that her evidence *is* probabilifying. It also seems right to say that unless she deceives herself, S believes that G. The rejection of belief at this stage would clearly require resistance, and because of the absence of counterevidence, such resistance would clearly be culpable. As Swinburne puts it, "We find ourselves with involuntary inclinations to belief; in the absence of reasons against going along with such an inclination the rational man will do so."[11]

Having established that the subject's initial belief is adequately supported, we must of course go on, as I have noted, to ask about what comes after. Does the proposition in question, by remaining

10. Alvin Plantinga, "Reason and Belief in God," in Alvin Plantinga and Nicholas Wolterstorff, eds., *Faith and Rationality* (Notre Dame: University of Notre Dame Press, 1983), p. 72.

11. Richard Swinburne, "Does Theism Need a Theodicy?" *Canadian Journal of Philosophy*, 18 (1988), 292.

properly basic or in some other way, retain its strong support
when the subject comes to consider *other* evidence?

It seems to me that it may. Let us look first at the positive considerations. Of the relevant facts that are likely to come to S's attention subsequently, two are of particular interest. The first is the
universality of the experience: others have it too, and indeed virtually every individual S believes to be honest can testify to it. The
other (as might be anticipated) is the uniformity in the detail of its
descriptions. These facts serve to reinforce S's belief not only psy-
chologically but *epistemically* as well. Now it may seem that if this
happens, S must cease to believe in a basic way. But even if S takes
these considerations into account, he need not believe on the *basis*
of them. A more natural understanding is that S's beliefs about the
universality and uniformity of this kind of religious experience
cause him to trust his *own* experience more strongly, that is, to
believe more strongly—but still in a basic way—that God is present to him.

Suppose, however, that S does come to believe at least in part
on the basis of other of his beliefs. Perhaps the considerations mentioned cause him to recognize the increased support for the argument for design. Then we may wish to accept a less stringent definition of basicality, such as Swinburne's: "I shall call those
propositions which seem to a man to be true and which he is inclined to believe, but not *solely* on the ground that they are made
probable by other propositions which he believes, his basic propositions" (my emphasis).[12] On this definition, even if other of the
propositions S believes form part of his grounds for believing that
God exists, his belief may also be grounded in what he takes to be
his experience of the world, and so it can appropriately be said that
G is basic for him. In any event, not much turns on whether we
say S believes basically or not, so long as we can say that he does
continue to *believe*, and that he does so with the strong legitimacy
referred to earlier. And it seems clear that given the circumstances
described, we can say this. Because of his experience and the experiences of others, S continues to believe that there is a God and (I
am arguing) is *right* to do so: the facts of universality and uniformity mentioned earlier provide *confirmation* for his judgments.

12. Swinburne, *Faith and Reason*, p. 20.

This claim would appear to be strongly supported by several recent philosophical discussions of religious experience. Swinburne, for example, argues that in this context a "Principle of Credulity" applies: "(In the absence of special considerations) if it seems (epistemically) to a subject that x is present, then probably x is present."[13] His examination of suggested "special considerations" leads him to the conclusion that "a religious experience apparently of God ought to be taken as veridical unless it can be shown on other grounds significantly more probable than not that God does not exist."[14] But he adds that even an apparent perception of what *is* "on background evidence too improbable to believe . . . may become credible if backed up by positive evidence that the experience is genuine," such as "others' having corroborating experiences."[15]

Garry Gutting, in his discussion of religious experience, also mentions the value of corroborating experiences. Indeed, on his view, most of the weight must be placed here. He criticizes Swinburne's principle of credulity which, as he puts it, suggests "that the evidence of the experience is itself decisive unless there is some overriding consideration in our background knowledge," and argues that "an of-X experience in general provides prima facie evidence of X's existence only in the sense of supplying some (but not sufficient) support for the claim that X exists. For belief in this claim to be warranted the solitary of-X experience requires supplementation by additional corroborating experiences."[16]

The point about corroboration is supported from a different angle by William Alston, who has given a good deal of attention to the (actual) problem of religious diversity. Incompatible religious experiential claims, he allows, significantly reduce the force of the evidence provided by religious experience for religious believers in the actual world. More to the point, were we *not* faced with "such persistent incompatibilities," persons forming beliefs on the basis of religious experience "would feel much more confident" and "would be justified in so feeling." It can hardly be denied, according to Alston, that such incompatibilities as actually exist reduce

---

13. Swinburne, *Existence of God*, p. 254.
14. Ibid., p. 270.
15. Ibid., p. 271.
16. Gutting, *Belief and Skepticism*, pp. 148, 149.

the rationality of believing on the basis of religious experience "below what it would be if this problem did not exist."[17] The application to our argument should be obvious.

Now it will perhaps be argued, in response, that we have
reached this positive conclusion only by ignoring the possibility of
contrary evidence. *S*, we may expect, will also come upon various
objections to theistic belief in the course of her life. Perhaps most
troubling will be the problem of evil, and her own experience of
evil and knowledge of the evil experienced by others will only
make this problem seem more severe. Would not this work against
her experience of God? And if *S* for a short or longer time failed to
believe in the existence of a loving God because of her experience
of evil, would her failure to believe not be inculpable? Although it
may be tempting initially to do so, I suggest that we have no reason to accept this view. If the experience apparently of God were
strong enough and its corroboration by others' experiences evident—if *S* were to feel strongly that God was present to her (and
especially if it were to seem strongly to *S* that God was present to
her in comforting and sustaining ways), and if other individuals
known to *S* testified to very similar experiences—then if *S* were to
lose *even weak* belief in the face of evil, we would not correctly
attribute this to the force of contrary evidence having its proper
effect: we would, I think, have to conclude that *S* had taken a hand

17. Alston, *Perceiving God*, p. 275. The arguments of Swinburne, Gutting, and
Alston seem to involve the claim that the justification provided for religious beliefs
(in the actual world) by religious experience is analogous to the justification provided for sensory beliefs by sensory experience. This analogy argument is subjected to detailed criticism by Richard Gale, in *On the Nature and Existence of God*
(Cambridge: Cambridge University Press, 1991), chap. 8. But Alston has replied
to Gale by pointing out that the *important* analogies *do* hold: the belief-forming
practice in question is socially established; it has a "functioning overrider system";
no reasons for judging the practice to be unreliable are sufficient; and the practice
enjoys "a significant degree of self-support" (*Perceiving God*, p. 224). Hence, Alston concludes, it is rational for persons to form beliefs on the basis of religious
experience in the absence of specific overriding considerations. It seems to me that
whatever may be true of the actual world, were individuals in the possible world I
am describing to avail themselves of Alston's premises (as well as the many arguments he offers in their support), adding to them the important points I have been
emphasizing with respect to universality and uniformity—points unavailable to
Alston, which strengthen the analogy with sense experience—they surely would
be justified in drawing his conclusion.

in the process herself, engaging in self-deception out of bitterness, resentment, or whatever. Although we might in such circumstances feel a certain sympathy for S and view her actions as in a sense understandable, if we were apprised of all the facts, we would also view them as mistaken and wrong.

These points seem to me to show that in the circumstances in question, the relevant evidence available to S is not only initially, but at *all* times, such that, unless culpably deterred, S believes that G on evidence rendering G probable. In summary, it seems clear that the experiential evidence described here does provide the required support in the absence of overriding considerations, and that God could bring it about, for all S and for all t, that there are no overriding considerations.[18] We may therefore conclude that the proposition at issue is entailed by the description I have given. But that description is of a possible state of affairs. Hence the proposition itself represents a possible state of affairs. In other words, a strong epistemic situation in relation to theism is indeed possible.[19]

18. Anyone who thinks that this position is incorrect may add other evidence or postulate further Divine action, as appropriate. (For an interesting discussion of how religious experience may interact with other grounds of religious belief, see Alston, *Perceiving God*, chap. 8.) But for myself, I do not think such additions to the picture are necessary.

19. Note that I have not argued that God should bring to our attention *every* piece of evidence normally considered relevant to the question of God's existence. This would entail God making philosophers of religion of us all, and then the world *would* be in a sorry state! Rather, I have pictured a state of affairs in which every human being is given *at least* the evidence of experience described, and have argued that given any amount of subsequent inquiry, this would be sufficient, in the absence of resistance, to sustain belief.

[3]

The Reasonableness
of Nonbelief

Although there are possible worlds (such as the one described in the preceding chapter) in which a strong epistemic situation in relation to theism obtains, the actual world is not one of these. In our world reasonable nonbelief occurs. This, at any rate, is my claim in the present chapter. I begin by spelling out what is meant by this claim and giving several arguments in its defense. I then go on to consider some of the relevant views of contemporary theologians and philosophers of religion, as well as a possible objection suggested by this discussion.

The Claim: Explication and Defense

Let us take a nonbeliever to be one who fails (for whatever reason and in whatever way) to believe that there is a God. Even allowing for some flexibility in the interpretation of "God," it is clear that many human beings in the actual world fit this description. There are, first of all, individuals—primarily from non-Western cultures—who have never so much as entertained the proposition "God exists" (G), let alone considered the question of its truth or falsity. Second, there are those, from both Western and non-Western backgrounds, who are to some extent familiar with the idea of God, but who have never considered with any degree of seriousness whether it is instantiated. Individuals in these two categories exhibit what we may call *unreflective* nonbelief. They are to be contrasted with *reflective* nonbelievers—individuals who disbelieve or are in doubt about G as a result of reflection on its content and some attempt to discover whether it is true or false.[1] Those who disbelieve consider this proposition to be improbable or certainly false and so believe that not-G.[2] Individuals who are in doubt, on the other hand (to whose state I will be returning presently), are uncertain about the truth of this proposition, believing neither G nor not-G, typically as a consequence of believing that epistemic parity obtains between G and its denial.[3]

So much for the varieties of nonbelief.[4] What about *reasonable* nonbelief? In the Introduction, I suggested that reasonable nonbelief is in this context to be understood as exemplified by any instance of failure to believe in the existence of God that is not the result of culpable actions or omissions on the part of the subject. The claim that reasonable nonbelief occurs is therefore the claim that the nonbelief of at any rate some nonbelievers is not the consequence of their culpable actions or omissions—that it arises through no fault of their own and so they are not in any sense to blame for it. In defending this claim, I will be looking at one particular form of nonbelief—doubt—and attempting to show that it is sometimes inculpable. This is not to suggest that other forms of nonbelief are *not* inculpable. It seems clear enough that each type is inculpably exemplified, especially the first. But it will be convenient, for our purposes, to narrow the discussion to some particular form of nonbelief; and it will be interesting in its own right to learn that even where there *has* been reflection on G, and on the evidence in its favor, inculpable nonbelief may remain.

1. Given present concerns, the expression "is in doubt about G" is to be preferred to "doubts whether (or that) G." The latter is most naturally construed as "is inclined to disbelieve G," and this is not a meaning I wish to convey. Doubt is also sometimes understood in such a way as to be compatible with *belief*, and this too is a view from which mine must be distinguished. On the understanding assumed here, one who doubts neither believes nor disbelieves that G. To put it another way: doubt is identified with the point *midway* between belief and disbelief.

2. For the sake of simplicity, I include in the "certainly false" subcategory those who consider G to be incoherent or meaningless.

3. There will be more on "epistemic parity" later in the chapter.

4. No doubt more varieties of nonbelief could be distinguished, but these are the main ones and will suffice for our purposes.

So let us look more closely at the notion of doubt. As I have already indicated, it is here explicated in terms of uncertainty about the truth of some proposition (typically) generated by the belief that epistemic parity obtains between that proposition and its denial.[5] *Inculpable* doubt, therefore, obtains if such a belief is inculpably held. That is to say, for all S, if S inculpably believes that epistemic parity obtains between G and not-G, then S is inculpably in doubt about G.[6] This is, of course, only a start, but it does show that our first topic of discussion must be the concept of inculpable *belief.*

A careful and nuanced discussion of belief and epistemic rationality which includes a discussion of culpability and inculpability in believing can be found in Richard Swinburne's *Faith and Reason.* Swinburne distinguishes five kinds of rationality. The first kind (which he calls rationality$_1$) obtains if and only if S's "belief that p is probable, given his inductive standards and given his evidence. . . . A failure in respect of rationality$_1$ is a failure of internal coherence in a subject's system of beliefs, a failure of which the subject is unaware." But even if a subject's beliefs are internally coherent, says Swinburne, something may be lacking: the subject may not be "responding to the world in a justifiable way." He therefore introduces a second kind of rationality (rationality$_2$) which obtains if and only if S's belief that p is *properly* grounded in experience or reason and arrived at by the application of *correct* inductive standards. "Rationality$_2$ is a matter of conformity to objective standards which the believer may not recognize and may indeed explicitly deny."[7]

5. "Typically" is inserted here to allow for the possibility of doubt occurring without being caused by a parity belief (see note 6), *not* to suggest that a parity belief need not generate doubt. In my view, it must do so. Anyone tempted by a contrary view is referred to the discussion of belief in Chapter 1, second section.

6. As this formulation indicates, I am not assuming that S's inculpably holding a parity belief is a *necessary* condition of S's being inculpably in doubt. To suppose that it is would be, as William Alston has pointed out to me, unduly restrictive, forcing us to say that individuals incapable of a parity belief (e.g., small children) cannot be in doubt. That such a belief constitutes a *sufficient* condition for inculpable doubt is, in any case, all that is required for our purposes.

7. Richard Swinburne, *Faith and Reason* (Oxford: Clarendon Press, 1981), pp. 45, 46. References to this work in Chapter 3 will henceforth be made parenthetically in the text.

The distinction between rationality in these first two senses and rationality in senses (3), (4), and (5) is an important one. It is expressed by Swinburne in the following passage:

> The rationality of both rational$_1$ and rational$_2$ beliefs is a matter of the believer's response to present sensations and memories of the past and to apparently self-justifying truths of reason at the time in question. . . . However, we often feel that although a man is justified in holding a certain belief at some time, he ought to have looked for more evidence or checked his standards more thoroughly at earlier times. Had he done so, he might have beliefs which were better justified, more probable. And so, according to whether the failure at an earlier stage was a failure by the subject's own standards of which he was aware, a failure by the subject's own standards of which he was not aware, or a failure by correct standards, we have three further kinds of irrationality of belief. In so far as these possible failures have been avoided, we have three further kinds of rationality. [P. 49]

Filling this out, Swinburne writes that S has a rational$_3$ belief that p if and only if his evidence, inductive standards, and belief as to p's probability on the evidence have been, in his own view at the time, adequately investigated; a rational$_4$ belief if and only if his investigation was adequate by his normal standards; and a rational$_5$ belief if and only if his investigation satisfied *correct* standards (pp. 49–54). S's judgment as to when investigation is adequate, says Swinburne, will depend "on four beliefs of his: (a) about the importance of the issue, (b) about the closeness to 0 or 1 of the probability of his belief about the issue, (c) about the probability that investigation will achieve something, and (d) about whether he has other more important actions to do" (p. 53). And how much investigation is *in fact* adequate will depend on what is *in fact* true with respect to (a)–(d) (p. 53).

According to Swinburne, belief is culpable if it is irrational$_3$. He describes several ways in which such irrationality may arise: "First, there may be a culpable failure, of which the subject is aware, to collect enough true, representative, relevant evidence of good quality" (p. 50). S may through culpable *negligence* fail to gather enough relevant evidence or to check the reliability of the evidential propositions he is inclined to believe on the basis of experience or reason. Sometimes this may involve self-deception: S may look only for evidence that supports his own view and then deliberately forget the bias of his evidence sample. S's belief would also be irrational₃ and hence culpable, says Swinburne, if S recognized that his inductive standards had not been "subjected to proper criticism" (p. 50). And "the third reason why a belief can fail to be rational₃ is that the subject has culpably failed to check that, given his standards, the belief is made probable by the evidence" (p. 51). So, on Swinburne's view, irrationality₃, and hence culpability in believing, is a matter of negligence of which one is aware in evidence acquisition, the use of inductive standards, or in judging the probability of one's belief on the evidence one accepts. And this irrationality is compounded, he suggests, if negligence at any of these levels is of a sort that is deliberately self-deceptive—designed to produce in one a belief about one's evidence, one's standards, or the relevant probabilities that is recognized (at least initially) to be unwarranted.

So far, so good, we might say. But is it *only* if it is irrational₃ that belief is culpable? Swinburne thinks so:

> It is only irrationality in sense (3) which is culpable irrationality, for it results from the subject neglecting investigative procedures which he recognizes that he ought to pursue. Irrationality in senses (4) and (5) are a matter of objective discrepancy between the subject's actual investigative procedures and either those which he normally recognizes or really adequate investigative procedures; but in so far as the subject does not recognize these discrepancies, no blame attaches to his conduct. Irrationality in senses (1) and (2) arises from a failure to recognize certain things at the time in question—discrepancies within the class of the subject's beliefs in the case of irrationality (1), and unjustified evidence and incorrect standards in the case of irrationality (2). But either you recognize the things in question at the time or you do not. Recognizing is coming to believe; and if, as I have argued, belief is a passive matter, so too is recognition. No blame is attachable to you for things that happen to you, only for things that you do. [P. 54]

The principle suggested here is the following: "S is culpable in respect of some failure of hers if and only if her failure is voluntary." If Swinburne does accept this principle, the argument of the first part of the passage (which concerns irrationality in senses (3), (4), and (5)) can be filled out as follows: "Only voluntary neglect of one's epistemic obligations is culpable; unrecognized neglect is involuntary; therefore unrecognized neglect is inculpable." When it comes to irrationality in senses (1) and (2), where the failures in question are not failures of investigation which may be recognized or unrecognized, but failures of *recognition* (i.e., failures to recognize certain things at the time of belief formation), Swinburne again argues that since these failures are involuntary, no blame attaches to the subject in respect of them. And of course, since the very state of belief is involuntarily acquired, it would be inappropriate to blame the believer for this as well.

In my view, Swinburne is right on these points. It seems correct to say that only for voluntary actions could we ever legitimately be blamed. If S is to blame for something, S must have made some intentional contribution to it. Hence no one can justifiably be blamed for involuntary epistemic failures or for the very fact of belief. This argument has, however, been criticized in recent philosophical writing. In his article "Involuntary Sins," Robert Adams maintains that we are sometimes to blame for holding some belief even though believing is not under our (direct) control.[8] Adams's argument (as well as a similar argument of Plantinga) seems to be motivated by our tendency to say that individuals who hold *morally repugnant* beliefs (e.g., the belief that all Jews should be exterminated) are to be blamed for holding such beliefs even if they arose involuntarily.[9] But as Swinburne has convincingly argued, in reproaching people for such beliefs, we are either voicing our conviction that it is an objectively bad thing that such beliefs should be held (which is compatible with the believers themselves being blameless) or laying blame "for past omissions to act which allowed such attitudes to develop."[10] And as Plantinga admits, when

8. Robert Adams, "Involuntary Sins," *The Philosophical Review*, 94 (1985), 3–31.

9. For Plantinga's argument, see his "Reason and Belief in God," in Alvin Plantinga and Nicholas Wolterstorff, eds., *Faith and Rationality* (Notre Dame: University of Notre Dame Press, 1983), pp. 34–37. Plantinga is ambivalent, however. See esp. p. 36. (See also immediately below.)

10. Richard Swinburne, *Responsibility and Atonement* (Oxford: Clarendon Press, 1989), p. 34, n. 1.

blame is laid for morally repugnant beliefs per se, it may derive from neglect of the possibility that the individuals in question are constitutionally *defective* in some way and so not really subject to blame.[11]

For these reasons, I suggest we need not accept Adams's examples as indicative of the truth of his position.[12] And therefore the claim that we are only culpable for *voluntary* epistemic failures *leading up to* belief—in particular, for voluntarily neglecting proper investigative procedures—can be upheld. Applying this to the question of inculpable religious doubt, we obtain the following:

> S is inculpably in doubt about the truth of G if (1) S believes that epistemic parity obtains between G and not-G, and (2) S has not knowingly (self-deceptively or non-self-deceptively) neglected to submit this belief to adequate investigation.

Having decided upon a criterion of inculpable doubt, we must now consider the question of its application: How can we tell in individual cases that its conditions are satisfied?

It is not difficult to see how we might have reason to say of some individual that she believes that G and not-G are at epistemic parity, for she may tell us that she does and we may have no reason to doubt her word.[13] But it may be useful to look a little more

---

11. Plantinga, "Reason and Belief," p. 36.

12. Suppose, however, that Adams is right. Then, even assuming S is not to blame for any *voluntary* epistemic failure, if the belief that epistemic parity obtains between G and not-G is morally repugnant (and perhaps also if S's belief, as a result, say, of laziness, fails to be rational in Swinburne's senses (1), (2), (4), or (5)), we may impute blame to S and claim that his parity belief is culpable. Should this disturb us? It seems not. The belief that epistemic parity obtains between G and not-G is, to say the least, not obviously morally repugnant, and as we will see later, there are individuals who hold this belief but have investigated it with great care—individuals to whom the expansion of Adams's point in terms of laziness, even if it is a legitimate expansion, is therefore manifestly inapplicable. Thus, even if Adams is right (and I do not think he is), his arguments are in this context irrelevant and so may safely be disregarded.

13. I am of course appealing here to the principle of testimony, which, as Swinburne puts it, states "that (in the absence of special considerations) the experiences of others are (probably) as they report them" (*The Existence of God* [Oxford: Clarendon Press, 1979], p. 272).

closely at what is involved in holding this belief. As I understand it, one who believes that G and not-G are at epistemic parity believes that, given her evidence, she is not justified in holding either proposition to be more probable than its denial—that neither is, for her, *epistemically preferable* to its denial. Given this understanding, it may seem that what the parity believer believes is that G and not-G are equally probable, but this is not necessarily so: I may hold beliefs about G and not-G that entail the belief that neither is epistemically preferable to the other without believing that they are equally probable. I may, for example, believe that given my evidence, the correct values for the relevant probabilities (whether precise numerical or comparative) *cannot be determined*.[14] This belief entails the belief that neither G nor not-G is epistemically preferable to its denial, but it clearly does not entail the belief that they are equally probable. Therefore, in deciding whether some individual holds the parity belief, we must not only look for evidence that she believes G and not-G to be equally probable.

The second part of my criterion may appear to pose more difficult problems. How could we ever have reason to say, upon evaluating S's parity belief, that S has not knowingly neglected adequate investigation? How could this information be available to us?

It seems to me that in some cases there may *not* be enough relevant information available. But it seems equally clear that in certain circumstances a judgment in favor of the subject would be appropriate. Again, what S tells us of her investigation is not to be taken lightly. But we may also be witness to her investigation and see it to be an exemplary one. S may have given as much or even more time and energy to investigation than our beliefs about the issue's importance, probabilities in the field, the probability that investigation will achieve something, and S's other responsibilities suggest is adequate. If so (and provided that S's own beliefs on these matters of which we have knowledge do not suggest that more investigation is required), we will rightly judge that S has not knowingly failed to pursue adequate investigation.

It may seem to some that the question whether self-deception

---

14. As we will see, this is in fact the more common assessment.

has occurred will be especially difficult to answer in individual cases. But here, too, under certain conditions (which may well be present), we would have to rule in the subject's favor. S's conduct in other contexts, especially other epistemic contexts, is particularly important. Has he shown himself to be honest, a lover of the truth? Does he resist his wants when his head tells him he ought not to give in to them? We may also have reason to believe that S *desires* to have a well-justified belief that G or that not-G. If this is clearly so in some particular case, then (unless there is very strong evidence to the contrary) we may surely conclude that S is not self-deceived in arriving at a parity belief. For, given such a wish, S is much more likely to find ways of avoiding a parity belief than to find ways of acquiring one.

This suggests a more general point as well. If S desires a well-justified belief that G, or that not-G, he will arrive at a parity belief only *reluctantly* and, therefore, only if careful attention to the matter seems to him to leave him with no other option. Thus, if we have reason to believe that S wishes to have a well-justified belief that G, or that not-G, we have reason to believe not only that S is not self-deceived, but, more generally, that his investigation was a thorough one.

A final point about assessing parity beliefs as culpable or inculpable is that, where beliefs of this sort are concerned, we may also ask whether the propositions in questions are *controversial*—whether expert opinion is divided over which is true. If this is the case, it is likely that there is something to be said for each side's position and so likely that more cautious investigators will see this. In such circumstances, instances of honest doubt are to be expected. Now this is not to say that if G and not-G *are* controversial, every parity belief is automatically inculpable. However, such controversy, where it exists, provides us with useful additional information, allowing our judgment, when we are inclined to conclude on other grounds that S's parity belief is inculpable, to be more confident. If such information is not available, or if the contrary is clearly true, it is reasonable to be more tentative and cautious, and to ask for more of the sort of evidence described above before making a judgment. For then we have inductive grounds for supposing that a thorough investigation would lead S to the confident endorsement of either G or not-G.

It is time now to apply these considerations to the question whether inculpable doubt about the truth of G actually occurs. It is clearly true that many individuals satisfy the first of the conditions specified by our criterion, for, as a glance at the philosophical literature will show, many do believe that G and not-G are at epistemic parity—that neither of these propositions is epistemically preferable to its denial. (Of course, many nonphilosophers hold this belief as well.) The term commonly associated with this view is "agnosticism." The agnostic claims that it is impossible to judge on rational grounds that there is or is not a God. (She may have in mind the present state of the evidence, allowing that the epistemic status of G and not-G may change, or she may hold that a judgment is impossible in principle.[15]) Now clearly, if an individual believes that the evidence does not allow a judgment as to whether there is a God, she believes that neither G nor not-G is epistemically preferable to its denial—that is, she holds a parity belief. That there are persons who believe the former (i.e., agnostics) is a truism.[16] We may therefore infer with the highest degree of confidence that there are individuals who hold a parity belief.

The second condition specified by our criterion seems also to be satisfied in many cases. Many who doubt have investigated the question of God's existence with great care and concern for the truth over a period of years. To say of them that they have not knowingly failed to pursue adequate investigation is to say too little: if their doubt is inculpable at all, it is *strongly* inculpable, that is, their investigations are exemplary, even supererogatory, and match in quality those of the most scrupulous of their opponents.

Now it may be thought that I have neglected the possibility of self-deception. But although there are no doubt some cases in which we have reason to suppose that it has occurred, in many

15. See Anthony Kenny, *Faith and Reason* (New York: Columbia University Press, 1983), pp. 87–88.

16. Prominent contemporary examples include Anthony Kenny and Ronald Hepburn. See ibid., p. 85, and Ronald Hepburn, *Christianity and Paradox* (London: Watts, 1966), p. 1.

others we either do not have such reason or have good reason to suppose that it has not occurred. There are, in particular, individuals of whom we would have to say that if they have any desire at all with respect to this issue, it is to have a well-justified belief one way or the other. Their longing corresponds to that of Pascal:

> I look around in every direction and all I see is darkness. Nature has nothing to offer me that does not give rise to doubt and anxiety. If I saw no sign there of a Divinity I should decide on a negative solution: if I saw signs of a creator everywhere I should peacefully settle down in the faith. But seeing too much to deny and not enough to affirm, I am in a pitiful state, where I have wished a hundred times over that, if there is a God supporting nature, she should unequivocally proclaim him, and that, if the signs in nature are deceptive, they should say all or nothing so that I could see what course I ought to follow. Instead of that, in the state in which I am, not knowing what I am or what I ought to do, I know neither my condition nor my duty. My whole heart strains to know what the true good is in order to pursue it: no price would be too high to pay for eternity.[17]

In individuals such as the one represented here—who certainly exist—self-deception, if it occurred, would, it seems, be much more likely to produce *belief* than doubt.

As I suggested earlier, the fact that some individuals who doubt desire to believe also gives us an independent reason for saying that doubt is sometimes inculpable. For such persons, the parity view is only to be arrived at after all alternatives have been exhausted. We can infer from the fact that they strongly wish to settle the question for themselves one way or the other but nonetheless hold a parity belief that their investigation was thorough, and that their parity belief—although it may be mistaken—is not the result of negligence.

My final point in support of the view that inculpable doubt occurs is perhaps more obvious than any other I have made, namely, that the question of God's existence is *controversial*—a question over which expert opinion is divided. The individual who begins

17. Blaise Pascal, *Pensées*, A. J. Krailsheimer, trans. (Harmondsworth: Penguin, 1966), fragment 429.

an inquiry into God's existence is faced with a plethora of arguments both for and against. There is no easy way to sort through these arguments, and it is not obvious a priori that one side's arguments are deficient. From this it would seem to follow that we should expect what we in fact seem to find, namely, that scrupulous doubt occurs. Of course, as I suggested above, this information should not on its own lead us to conclude that such doubt occurs. But it seems to me that when taken in conjunction with other points I have adduced (which suggest that there are individuals holding parity beliefs who pass various tests of inculpability), it ought indeed to have this effect.

Some Contemporary Theological and Philosophical Views

I have argued that in the actual world inculpable doubt occurs. Many contemporary theologians appear to agree. Eberhart Jüngel, for example, writes that "the fundamental theoretical and practical changes of our so-called modern age have defined the contemporary awareness of the problem [of God] in a way which is especially unsettling for theology. One simply cannot ignore the fact that the dubiousness of talk about God has intensified."[18]

Perhaps the majority of theologians would go farther still and allow that inculpable *disbelief* occurs. Take, for example, the view of theologians at Vatican II, as reported by Karl Rahner:

> The council makes no reference to the traditional textbook view that positive atheism cannot be entertained for any considerable period of time by a fully developed person of normal intelligence without involving blame on his part. The Council actually *assumed a contrary thesis,* i.e. that it is possible for a *normal adult to hold an explicit atheism for a long period of time*—even to his life's end—*without this implying moral blame* on the part of such an unbeliever. [Emphasis in the original][19]

18. Eberhart Jüngel, *God as the Mystery of the World*, Darrel L. Coden, trans. (Edinburgh: T&T Clark, 1983), p. 4.

19. Karl Rahner, "Atheism and Implicit Christianity," in G. A. McCool, ed., *A Rahner Reader* (London: Darton, Longman, and Todd, 1975), pp. 221–222. Rahner himself, as the context indicates, was wholly in favor of this view.

Many theologians seem *themselves* to be less than sure about the epistemic preferability of theism. There is a tendency to describe the world as "religiously ambiguous."[20] John Macquarrie, referring to the dispute between theism and atheism, writes that "the world always remains ambiguous, and although people can argue as long as they like, tracing their rival patterns, the case will never be established conclusively, one way or the other."[21] Parallel claims are made by theologians influenced by the conceptual relativism of such writers as Thomas Kuhn.[22] James McClendon, writing about Christian and other world views, states that "there is not among these any which can be clearly established to be the superior of all the others."[23] And George Lindbeck, in a similar vein, argues that "there is no higher neutral standpoint from which to adjudicate their competing perceptions of what is factual."[24]

Lest anyone suspect that theologians are alone among Christian writers in this regard, it should be noted that many contemporary philosophers of religion—even quite conservative Christian philosophers of religion—appear to be making similar claims. Perhaps in most cases these claims do not presuppose Kuhnian assumptions, but the difficulties involved in establishing theism as epistemically preferable to atheism are clearly recognized. Thomas Morris, for example, has argued that "epistemically null or epistemically ambiguous conditions can reasonably be thought sometimes to obtain."[25] And elsewhere he appears prepared to acquiesce in the view that "this world of ours is at best religiously ambiguous to the

20. This phrase, as far as I know, originates in John Hick's writings. For more on Hick and religious ambiguity, see Chapter 5.

21. John Macquarrie, *Thinking about God* (London: SCM Press, 1975), p. 119.

22. See Thomas Kuhn, *The Structure of Scientific Revolutions* (Chicago: Chicago University Press, 1962).

23. James W. McClendon and James M. Smith, *Understanding Religious Convictions* (Notre Dame: University of Notre Dame Press, 1975), p. 117.

24. George Lindbeck, *The Nature of Doctrine* (Philadelphia: Westminster Press, 1984), p. 11.

25. See Thomas Morris, *Anselmian Explorations* (Notre Dame: University of Notre Dame Press, 1987), p. 203.

inquiring observer," suggesting that this view may pose an important theological problem.[26]

Many Christian thinkers, therefore, not only allow that those who hold a parity belief sometimes do so reasonably, but appear to hold this belief themselves. As I have argued, one who investigates the evidence can believe that G only if he believes that the evidence favors G—that G is epistemically preferable to not-G. And surely all the individuals mentioned would claim to have investigated the evidence *and* to believe that there is a God. So what should we make of this?

As it seems to me, what we must do to solve this problem is sharpen up an important distinction, already alluded to, namely, the distinction between public and private evidence. When writers of the sort I have referred to speak of ambiguity or parity (or put forward arguments that entail claims about ambiguity or parity), they are certainly referring to the *public* evidence—evidence which is in principle available to everyone equally, (typically) reported in the premises of the various theistic and atheistic arguments. But I suspect that in many cases their own personal experiences, which are at least in part private to themselves, are not included in this judgment. Many theologians, for example, would argue that reason for believing is in some sense provided by such experiences— that religious experience is in an important sense the ground of faith.[27] Now although discussion of these matters among theologians is not always as clear as one might like, it is natural, I suggest, to take individuals who make such claims to be (implicitly) judging, at least in part on the basis of their own experience, that God's existence is *probable*, and thus to be treating their experience as supplementary *evidence*. Although they consider epistemic parity to obtain at the public level, the private evidence available to them (I am suggesting), perhaps in conjunction with the public evidence, seems to them to render G more probable than not-G,

26. See the review by Thomas Morris of Anthony O'Hear's *Experience, Explanation, and Faith*, in *Faith and Philosophy*, 2 (1985), 316.

27. See, for example, Langdon Gilkey, *Naming the Whirlwind: The Renewal of God-Language* (Indianapolis and New York: Bobbs-Merrill, 1969), part 2, chaps. 3 and 4.

and thus, *all things considered*, they do *not* consider epistemic parity to obtain.[28]

That this is also the correct interpretation where the theistic beliefs of many Christian philosophers of religion are concerned is strongly suggested by their writings. Stephen Davis, who accepts the ambiguity view, refers explicitly to the distinction between public and private evidence and argues in favor of the rationality of believing on the basis of the latter when the former is inconclusive.[29] Some of the more recent arguments of John Hick, Alvin Plantinga, William Alston, and others on the relations between religious experience and the justification of religious belief also lend themselves to this interpretation.[30] The claim of these writers is that experiences apparently of God, although they may count for little when publically reported (because they only provide a basis for weak inductive arguments), may provide the *experient* with good grounds for belief in God.[31] It is argued that such experiences must be understood by analogy with sensory experiences and the justification of the corresponding beliefs by analogy with the justification of sensory beliefs. I would suggest that what this shows is that the philosophers in question may, however implicitly, be treating their religious experiences as relevant evidence, and may therefore (all things considered) be believing that there is a God while continuing to believe that the *public* evidence (including such propositions as "religious experiences have been reported in various parts of the world") is indecisive. As George Mavrodes writes, after giving voice to the skeptical feelings many have about accepting the

28. Indeed, we can *deduce* the claim that the individuals in question consider themselves to have private evidence from the following statements, all of which are true: (1) that anyone who investigates the support for G can only believe that G if she believes G to be more probable than not; (2) that the individuals in question believe that G; (3) that they believe the public evidence to support only a parity judgment.

29. Stephen Davis, *Faith, Skepticism, and Evidence* (Lewisburg, Pa.: Bucknell University Press, 1978).

30. See John Hick, *An Interpretation of Religion* (London: Macmillan, 1989), chap. 13; Plantinga, "Reason and Belief"; and William Alston, *Perceiving God: The Epistemology of Religious Experience* (Ithaca, N.Y: Cornell University Press, 1991).

31. It should be noted that Swinburne, who accepts a similar view, is not as pessimistic as many others about the value of religious experience as public evidence.

public evidence provided by the religious experiences of others as indicative of God's existence, "I think that there is something that we could have, and that we might have, something that is better than that testimony, more solid somehow, richer in epistemic significance than any mere testimony can be. . . . That richer thing . . . would be *an experience of our own*" (emphasis in the original).[32]

So where does this leave us? It seems clear that both theologians and Christian philosophers of religion in many cases view the public evidence as indecisive and so are ready to go at least this far with those who are in doubt. Nevertheless, as we have seen, they seem to fall back on private evidence which they do *not* consider to be indecisive, and so cannot be classified with the doubters. The only issues between these believing theologians and philosophers and individuals who are in doubt must therefore be the issues of the availability and interpretation of private experiences apparently of God. Now as we have seen, many writers (and especially theologians) seem prepared to concede the reasonableness of doubt and so appear to accept as reasonable the claims of those who say that they have no experiences of this sort or that such experiences as they do have are ambiguous.[33] Nonetheless, some writers—in particular, certain latter-day Calvinian philosophers of religion—seem prepared to argue that a form of private evidence *has* been made

32. George Mavrodes, *Revelation in Religious Belief* (Philadelphia: Temple University Press, 1988), pp. 152–153. Richard Gale has recently argued against this sort of claim (and so implicitly against my distinction between public and private evidence—at least as justification-relevant) in *On the Nature and Existence of God* (Cambridge: Cambridge University Press, 1991), pp. 287–288. According to Gale, it is a fundamental principle of epistemology that "a cognitive [i.e., evidence- or warrant-providing] experience's status as evidential is observer-neutral." But it is surely a necessary condition of warrant in this context that one be justified in believing that the experience *occurred*; and this at least is *greater* for the experient. In some cases it might, indeed, be *only* the experient who was justified in believing that the experience occurred. This would be so if observers had reason to believe the experient to be a deceiver when in fact she was not, and knew that she was not. In such a case, the experient would, other things being equal, be justified in believing on the basis of her experience even though others were not so justified. Gale's general principle is therefore false and so poses no threat to Mavrodes's claim or to my distinction.

33. On the possibility of such claims, see Ronald Hepburn, "From World to God," in Basil Mitchell, ed., *The Philosophy of Religion* (Oxford: Oxford University Press, 1971), p. 177.

available to *everyone*, and that where it has not brought about belief in God's existence, this is because of the sinful resistance of the nonbeliever.[34] We have, therefore, the following objection to the view I am defending: doubt is never inculpable because it is always a result of *sin*. It is to a discussion of this objection that I now turn.

The Calvinian Response

In his *Institutes of the Christian Religion*, John Calvin argues that none of us lacks an awareness of God:

> "There is within the human mind, and indeed, by natural instinct, an awareness of divinity." This we take to be beyond controversy. To prevent anyone from taking refuge in the pretense of ignorance, God himself has implanted in all men a certain understanding of the divine majesty. Ever renewing its memory, he repeatedly sheds fresh drops. Since, therefore, men one and all perceive that there is a God and that he is their Maker, they are condemned by their own testimony because they have failed to honour him and to consecrate their lives to his will.[35]

Calvin's view here is apparently shared by Alvin Plantinga. In response to the "Great Pumpkin" objection to his view that belief in God is properly basic (the objection that if belief in God is properly basic, so are many other beliefs we would wish to reject as irrational, such as the belief that the Great Pumpkin returns every Halloween), Plantinga writes that "the Reformed epistemologist may concur with Calvin in holding that God has implanted in us a natural tendency to see his hand in the world around us; the same cannot be said of the Great Pumpkin, there being no Great Pumpkin and no natural tendency to accept beliefs about the Great Pumpkin."[36]

Now for Calvin, an obvious corollary of the claim that God has implanted in us "a certain understanding" of divine things is that

---

34. This view, it will be noted, entails that a situation much like that described in Chapter 2 *in fact obtains*.

35. John Calvin, *Institutes of the Christian Religion*, Lewis Battles Ford, trans. (Philadelphia: Westminster Press, 1960), book 1, chap. 3, p. 43.

36. Plantinga, "Reason and Belief," p. 78.

those who claim to be ignorant of God are "condemned"; they have rejected God, knowing full well that he exists, and so are blameworthy. We might expect something similar to be a corollary of Plantinga's "natural tendency" doctrine. But he is not very clear about this. It may be that he holds, with Calvin, that those who do not believe in God "instinctively" are inhibited by their *own* sin, having, for example, deceived themselves. On the other hand, he may hold that those who fail to believe are inhibited by sin *indirectly* in that they have inherited and now express involuntarily dispositions and values inimical to belief. The latter view implies that those who fail to believe are not themselves culpable for it, and thus gives rise to no objection to my claim. Because of this unclarity, I suggest we look no further at Plantinga but move instead to consider the claims endorsed by certain of his Calvinian counterparts, who quite clearly do wish to suggest that nonbelief is due to the sin of the nonbeliever.

One such philosopher is Mark R. Talbot. In his recent article "Is It Natural to Believe in God?" Talbot argues that Christians are justified in asserting the contrary-to-fact conditional "Everybody would believe in God, if it weren't for sin," and that "even a non-Christian's experience makes that claim more probable for him than it would otherwise be." Talbot spends some time developing the notion of an "epistemic set," which he defines as "a disposition to have particular experiences, thoughts, beliefs, and so on, in particular situations." Using this to explicate Calvin's view, he writes: "To sense God's glory in his handiwork and to feel his majesty within us is, by this account, a matter of possessing reliable epistemic sets. Since he thinks we naturally possess these sets, anyone's not possessing them signals, according to Calvin, his having worked to dismantle or lose them." Talbot clearly endorses Calvin's view, so I think that by "if it weren't for sin," we can take him to mean "if it weren't for the personal sin of the nonbeliever." This is confirmed later in his essay when he states that "unbelievers" have some reason to believe that they are "resisting theistic belief" and that this resistance is "in various ways, blinding them."[37]

37. Mark R. Talbot, "Is It Natural to Believe in God?" *Faith and Philosophy*, 6 (1989), 166, 168, 161, 165, 168. As far as I am aware, Talbot's is the only piece of

For our purposes, it will be best to focus on Talbot's argument
for the claim that *Christians* are justified in asserting the contrary-
to-fact conditional in question: it seems to me to display all the
errors that those who attempt a "resistance" explanation of nonbelief tend to fall into. To do his argument justice, I must quote
Talbot at some length. The quotation divides fairly neatly into
three parts, and I will discuss it in stages corresponding to these.
The first part is prefaced by a brief discussion of Hume, who, according to Talbot, proposes for our belief what amounts to the
following contrary-to-fact conditional: "the laws of nature would
be observed to be perfectly regular, if it weren't for our limited
powers of observation."[38] Talbot then goes on to argue as follows:

A. Someone is justified in asserting such a conditional if and only if
    it seems true to her when she surveys all of her relevant experi-
    ence and belief. And, thus, asserting the uniformity of causal
    influence is, as it should be, justified for almost all of us.

B. But, then, Christians can be justified in asserting that everybody
    would believe in God, if it weren't for sin.
        For suppose someone is converted and then argues like this: "At
    conversion, I realized that, up to then, I had been sinfully resist-
    ing acknowledging what I am naturally inclined to believe,
    namely, that God exists, that he is my Maker, and that I ought
    to make his will the law of my life. Others tell me that they
    also, at conversion, realized this. Moreover, before I was con-
    verted, I wasn't clearly aware of my resistance because of the
    damage that sin had already done to my epistemic sets. There-
    fore, my experience—and that of these others—suggests that a
    sinner's judgment about moral and spiritual matters is unreli-
    able. And, therefore, my post-conversion experience justifies

---

writing in the contemporary literature of philosophy of religion devoted in its
entirety to defending the Calvinist view of nonbelief, and so I focus on it. Others
have defended this view more briefly or in passing; their arguments seem to me to
suffer from weaknesses similar to those I claim to find in Talbot's argument. See J.
Kellenberger, *The Cognitivity of Religion: Three Perspectives* (London: Macmillan,
1985), pp. 136–137, 159–160; George Schlesinger, "The Availability of Evidence
in Support of Religious Belief," *Faith and Philosophy*, 1 (1984), 426; Ronald J. Feen-
stra, "Natural Theology, Epistemic Parity, and Unbelief," *Modern Theology*, 5
(1988), 9–11.

38. *Talbot*, "Is It Natural to Believe?" 166.

my discounting such preconversion judgments and my accepting the claim that everybody would believe in God, if it weren't for sin."

C. How can anyone justifiably object to this?

No one can claim that the believer is unjustified in asserting this conditional because that believer's grounds do not convince him. That begs the question against belief by failing to come to grips with the believer's claim that if you don't find her reasoning convincing it may be because you are unregenerate and thus lack a reliable epistemic set. Nor can anyone insist that the believer must factor in, as evidence relevant to her asserting this conditional, his opinion challenging it. For then his judgment would necessarily weaken or falsify her assertion, which begs the question again. Nor will it do to say that adequate grounds for justifiable assertion, in circumstances like these, must guarantee the assertion's truth. For that applies a stricter standard to the believer than it is possible to apply to oneself.[39]

A. Talbot argues that someone is justified in asserting a conditional of the sort in question if and only if it seems true to her when she surveys all of *her* relevant experience and belief. This seems to imply that when individuals are considering whether they are justified in asserting such conditionals, the experiences and beliefs of persons other than themselves are not relevant. That Talbot accepts this is confirmed later when he argues that the Christian who is investigating the justifiability of asserting that nonbelievers are sinfully resisting belief in God need not consider any experiences or beliefs incompatible with her own. But how, we may ask, can such epistemic isolationism be justified? Does it not imply the repugnant conclusion that individuals are justified in asserting virtually anything, no matter how outrageous, so long as it seems to them that their experience supports it? Was not Hitler, on this criterion, justified in supposing that the Jews deserved extermination?[40]

39. Ibid., 167.
40. It may be replied that no contrary-to-fact conditional is here being asserted. But Talbot does not show there to be a justification-related distinction between conditionals and other propositions such that the former may justifiably be asserted under conditions of epistemic isolation whereas the latter may not. But if a conditional is desired, consider the following: "The Jews would worship me as a god were they not ignorant and worthless."

Talbot himself gives no argument for his claim. Perhaps he takes it
to follow from a proper understanding of the Humean analogue.
But if so, he is wrong. For Hume, in the passage Talbot quotes,
clearly (and correctly) suggests the relevance to his claim of the
researches of individuals who have, for example, shown the human body to be a "mighty complicated machine" which therefore
might well "appear very uncertain in its operation" while in fact
the laws of nature are "observed with the greatest regularity in its
internal operations and government."[41] And, furthermore, as Talbot himself notes, it is apparently part of Hume's suggested justification for belief in causal uniformity that virtually *everyone* is disposed to believe in it.[42] So there is no support from Hume. And no
other support is suggested. Indeed, the more it is examined, the
more Talbot's criterion for the justified assertion of contrary-to-
fact conditionals looks tailor-made to accommodate the *particular*
conditional "Everybody would believe in God, if it weren't for
sin." The only way Talbot's criterion escapes these criticisms is if
he includes under "relevant belief" what seems to the inquirer to be
the case upon carefully investigating the relevant experiences and
beliefs of *others*. But that this is not his intent seems clearly indicated by the next part of the quotation, to which I now turn.

    B. There are two ways of reading the argument of Talbot's hy-
pothetical convert, but on neither reading does it provide the necessary support for its conclusion. Indeed, this is true even if we
allow Talbot his epistemic isolationism. On the first reading
(which, given Talbot's earlier arguments, seems the more natural
one), "naturally inclined to believe" is to be understood as "inclined qua human being to believe," and "sinner" as "unbeliever."
Read this way, the argument begs the question: by asserting that
she is inclined qua human being to believe, the believer ipso facto
asserts this of *every* human being and so asserts that in the absence
of resistance or rebellion she and every other human being must
believe, which is to say that if there are those who do not believe,
this is to be attributed to resistance or rebellion on their part. On
this interpretation, the premise "I am naturally inclined to believe"
entails the argument's conclusion but is logically irrelevant to the

41. Talbot, "Is it Natural to Believe?" 166.
42. Ibid., 164.

enterprise of establishing it, since it presupposes its truth. Thus, on its first reading, the believer's argument begs the question.

Now of course, although even an epistemic isolationist must, if she wishes to *argue* from her experience to some conclusion, avoid fallacies like that of begging the question, perhaps she need not argue at all. It is at least initially puzzling why, given his criterion of justification, Talbot wishes his hypothetical convert to argue: what is to prevent her from simply asserting the conditional in question, full stop—perhaps together with a brief explanation that this is what she is inclined to believe? But it seems that Talbot does want to argue, and not simply to assert his conclusion at the outset. He implies, for example, that in his view the conditional in question is not entailed by the experience of the new convert, but that that experience instead provides certain nonconclusive *grounds* for believing it to be true. (See Part *C* of the quotation above, especially its penultimate sentence.) I suggest, therefore, that we look again at the hypothetical convert's claims in an attempt to find a reading of them compatible with Talbot's apparent argumentative intent. As it seems to me, the only possible such reading involves understanding the phrase "what I am naturally inclined to believe," not as "what I am inclined qua human being to believe," but as "what I in fact am inclined to believe" (or "what I actually believed all along") and the term "sinner," not as "unbeliever," but—and here a longer explication is unavoidable—as "one who resists acknowledging what he or she is in fact inclined to believe." Given these explications, the hypothetical convert has indeed got an argument, but unfortunately for Talbot, only an argument for the conclusion that anyone who (like herself) resists acknowledging what he or she is in fact inclined to believe would believe if it weren't for their resistance. The conclusion that *everybody* would believe in God if it weren't for resistance is wildly unrelated to the evidence the convert is actually in a position to adduce on the basis of her experience. Only if some premise about everyone being naturally inclined to believe is illicitly slipped into the argument could the universal conclusion follow. But then, as we have seen, the argument would beg the question.[43]

43. I have argued that the believer's experience gives her no good reason to affirm the conditional in question. If this is correct, then, a fortiori, the believer's

C. Talbot asks (with reference to the argument described under
Part *B* of the passage quoted above), "How can anyone justifiably
object to this?" The answer to this question should be clear by
now. But it will be useful to discuss briefly the particular objections Talbot goes on to consider and his responses to them. These
objections are (1) that the believer is not justified in believing the
conditional because her grounds do not convince the unbeliever,
and (2) that the believer, to be justified in her claim, must factor in,
as relevant evidence, the unbeliever's positive reasons for taking a
contrary stance. Now the rejection of (1) and (2) would seem to
follow directly from Talbot's "isolationist" criterion of justification, enunciated in Part *A* of the passage quoted above. But here
he offers an additional reason for their rejection, namely, that they
are question-begging. The argument for this claim in the case of
(1) seems to be as follows: "Given the truth of the believer's claim,
the unbeliever's unwillingness to accept the grounds that support it
is to be expected. By claiming that the believer is not justified in
accepting her claim because of his dissent, the unbeliever is therefore presupposing the probable *falsehood* of that claim (if it were
true, his dissent would not be relevant) and so is begging the question." But given our earlier discussion, this argument can quite
easily be rendered ineffective. For only a foolish unbeliever would
urge the relevance of his view that the believer's premises are false.
The proper point to make is the logically prior point that the believer's premises, *even if true*, fail *for reasons of logic* to support her
conclusion. Given the first reading of the believer's argument, no
real grounds have been presented (the argument begs the question), and given the second, the believer's grounds, such as they
are, do not lead validly to her conclusion. Understood this way,
the first objection does not beg the question. What the unbeliever
is drawing to the believer's attention are certain *logical* points. And
I presume that Talbot would not wish to go so far as to suggest
that if the believer's claim is true, even the unbeliever's views on
logic are incorrect. If this is right, it follows that the unbeliever's
dissent, if it derives from logical considerations of the sort in ques-

---

experience fails to provide the *non*believer with any appreciable reason for affirm-
ing the conditional, and Talbot's claim (ibid., 168) that it does provide such reason
is to be rejected.

tion, *should* provoke the believer to the realization that her claim lacks justification.

What about the second objection? This, as will be recalled, was that the believer must factor in, as relevant evidence, the unbeliever's *positive* reasons for taking a *contrary* view. Is this question-begging? Talbot's argument in defense of an affirmative answer seems to run as follows: "By claiming that the believer is not justified in making her claim unless she takes his reasons for accepting its denial into account, the unbeliever assumes that his reasoning is not unreliable. But given the truth of the believer's claim, the unbeliever's reasoning in this context *is* unreliable." Hence the unbeliever, in making his objection, presupposes the falsehood of the believer's claim and so begs the question." Let us suppose that the second premise here is true—that the unbeliever's reasoning in this context is unreliable if the believer's claim is true. Even then, we may show that Talbot's conclusion need not be accepted, for his first premise is false. (Or rather, it is false under the interpretation required to generate the conclusion.) The unbeliever clearly must not assume that his reasoning is "not unreliable" in the sense of "in fact reliable" when the proposition at issue entails the unreliability of his reasoning. Otherwise his argument is indeed question-begging. But why should we suppose that the unbeliever *needs* to assume this in order to claim that the believer is not justified in making her claim unless she takes his reasons for denying it into account? All he need assume is that it has not been *shown* that his reasoning is unreliable—that it is at the start of the investigation an *open question* whether the contrary-to-fact conditional at issue is true or not, and that his arguments are for this reason not justifiably viewed as less likely to be reliable than the believer's, and should therefore be taken into account." It is clearly compatible with *this* assumption that the believer's claim is true (for the unbeliever allows that his reasoning may be unreliable). Hence the un-

44. The context suggests that what Talbot means is that given the truth of the believer's claim, the unbeliever's reasoning is *of an unreliable type*, that is, that the unbeliever is *qua sinner* unreliable in his reasoning.

45. After all, it is not as though the reliability of the unbeliever's reasoning is less likely than it would otherwise be just by virtue of the *question* of its reliability being raised! At the *beginning* of investigation there is by definition no presumption in favor of either claim.

believer may press his objection without begging the question. And since there is good reason to suppose that Talbot's epistemic isolationism must be rejected, this objection succeeds. Talbot's believer cannot legitimately refuse to consider as relevant the reasonings of those who would deny her claim.

We have seen that arguments of the sort put forward by Talbot, which consider the relevance of the believer's experience, fail to provide even the believer with justification for the claim "Everybody would believe in God, if it weren't for sin." If we now reintroduce the considerations adduced in the first section of this chapter (and we must remind ourselves that in view of the untenability of epistemic isolationism and the failure of Talbot's response to the second objection above, even the believer must take these into account), we can see, I think, that honest inquirers have very good reason indeed to accept that not all failures to believe are due to the sin of the nonbeliever, and in particular, that inculpable doubt occurs. There is, for example, good reason to suppose that some who claim they have no private experiences apparently of God or that such experiences as they do have are ambiguous, and who have carefully examined the relevant arguments, finding them indecisive, have no wish to be in doubt. Indeed, there are doubters who have agonized long years over matters of faith, hoping that belief may come to them. Why, we may ask, should this be the case if all doubt is due to a sinful rejection of belief? Now it is perhaps not *impossible* that despite such strong positive evidence and the absence of any significant contrary evidence, all doubters have sinfully rejected belief, but given the circumstances, that claim is, to say the least, unlikely.[46] I suggest, therefore, that we are justified in rejecting it.

It is my conclusion, then, in view of all the arguments considered, that in the actual world reasonable nonbelief occurs. Many writers already accept this, and so I have no quarrel with them. And although some latter-day Calvinians may be inclined to argue in favor of a contrary position, their views are unsustainable.

46. An additional point is that if in the face of the evidence, believers confidently claim that all doubt is due to the sinful rejection of belief, they display the very fault they claim to find in the nonbeliever—moral insensitivity. On the unbeliever's alleged moral insensitivity, see Talbot, "Is it Natural to Believe?" 168.

A Summation of the Case

Let us pause for a moment to consider the path along which we have come. In the Introduction we saw that

(1) If there is a God, he is perfectly loving.

Exploring this idea of Divine love further in Chapters 1 and 2, we found considerable support for the following claim:

(2) If a perfectly loving God exists, reasonable nonbelief does not occur.

Most recently, in Chapter 3, it was shown that (2)'s consequent is false, that

(3) Reasonable nonbelief occurs.

But (3), in combination with (2), yields

(4) No perfectly loving God exists;

and from (4), together with (1), it follows that

(5) There is no God.

We have arrived, then, at an argument of considerable force from the reasonableness of nonbelief to the nonexistence of God.

In this final chapter of Part 1, I wish to consider more closely the *status* of this argument (call it *A*), and the conditions that must be satisfied if it is to be *rebutted*. We are, in other words, tying up some loose ends and setting the stage for Part 2. On the issue of status, my view is as follows. First, it seems clear that *A* commits no error of logic: given (1), (2), and (3), we may validly conclude (5). Equally clear, I suggest, is the truth of (1), and (3); these premises seem more than adequately supported by the arguments I have given in their defense. It follows that everything depends on (2)— if it is true, *A* is sound. So what is (2)'s status? As it seems to me, our arguments for (2) constitute at least *prima facie evidence* that it is true: the reasons detailed in Chapter 1 for supposing that God, if perfectly loving, will prevent the occurrence of reasonable non-belief are clearly sufficient to warrant the conclusion that he *will* do so unless an adequate defense of that claim's denial can be mounted. It follows that *A* must be viewed as sound unless such a defense can be given. There is, in other words, a presumption in favor of its conclusion which is defeated only if our support for *(2)* is defeated. We may think of our prima facie evidence for (2), therefore, as conferring on *A* itself the status of a prima facie case. This, at any rate, is how I will hereafter refer to it.

What, more specifically, must an argument against (2) show to be "an adequate defense of that claim's denial" and so, by extension, a rebuttal for *A*? To facilitate discussion of this question, I introduce the following stipulative definition: "*p* is plausible" = df. "*p* is such that there is at least as much reason to suppose it true as to suppose it false."[1] The stipulative nature of this definition must be carefully noted. By defining "plausible" in this way, I give to it a narrower and *weaker* sense than it is commonly given. But it will be convenient for us to have something less cumbersome than "such that there is at least as much reason to suppose it true as to suppose it false" to work with, and "plausible" is chosen for lack of something better.[2] Assuming this to be clear, I would suggest, as a

---

1. And more loosely, we may say, if *p* is plausible, that it is plausible to suppose that *p*, and, if the proposition "*x* is *y*" is plausible, that *x* is plausibly viewed as *y*.

2. It might seem that "*p* is plausible" = df. "*p* is as probable as not" would

first approximation, that we have a rebuttal for A of the sort required if and only if we have an argument that succeeds in showing the plausibility of (2)'s denial. If the denial of (2) is shown plausible, there is no longer a presumption in (2)'s favor or in favor of A's conclusion, (5), and so we are not justified in accepting A as a sound argument; if it is *not* shown plausible, the presumption remains, permitting us to conclude that A is, all things considered, sound. This plausibility condition, it is important to note, is relatively weak, for it entails that to provide a rebuttal for A we need show *no more* than that there is as much reason to suppose its central premise false as to suppose it true. Of course, if it could be shown *conclusively* that (2) is false, we would also have provided a rebuttal for A (for if the denial of (2) is proven conclusively, it is plausible), but this much is not required (we can show (2)'s denial to be plausible without proving it conclusively), although it *is* required if the problem of reasonable nonbelief is to be finally settled.

Let us look more closely now at the plausibility condition. What must we show if we are to establish the plausibility of (2)'s denial? To answer this question, we must know what are the conditions of (2)'s falsity. I suggest that (2) is false if and only if there is a state of affairs in the actual world which it would be logically impossible for God to bring about without permitting the occurrence of at least one instance of reasonable nonbelief,[3] for the sake of which God would be willing to sacrifice the good of belief and all it en-

---

have served as well or better here. But some of the propositions I will be considering seem *necessarily* true if true at all (e.g., propositions claiming that one state of affairs is a greater good than another), and there is some doubt as to the applicability of terms like "probable as not" to necessary propositions: such propositions are commonly viewed as having a probability of 1. Therefore, I have chosen to speak in terms of reasons for and against. This language, it seems to me, is clearly applicable to inductive evidence capturable by the probability calculus but is appropriate as well where arguments for and against the necessity of a proposition are concerned, since we *do* commonly speak of having reasons for believing some proposition to be necessary.

3. It must be a state of affairs whose existence *logically necessitates* the permission of reasonable nonbelief, for otherwise an omnipotent God could (and a perfectly loving God would) bring it about *without* permitting the occurrence of reasonable nonbelief.

tails.⁴ If both these conditions are met, premise (2) of *A* is false; if either one is *not* met, (2) (and so (5)) is true. From this conclusion, together with the foregoing points, it follows that the denial of (2) is shown *plausible* if and only if we can show to be plausible the claim that each of the conditions just mentioned is met.

What, more specifically, must we be in a position to say about a state of affairs necessitating the permission of reasonable nonbelief if it is to be plausible to suppose that God would for its sake sacrifice the good of belief (that the second condition mentioned above is met)? In discussions of the problem of evil, to which this discussion is clearly related, it is sometimes said that the good for the sake of which evil is permitted to occur must be a greater or *outweighing* good, that is, it must be such that the world is better with it and the corresponding evil than with neither.⁵ Other writers have suggested that the good state of affairs need only be an equal or *offsetting* good—in other words, such that the world would be at least as good with it and the corresponding evil as with neither.⁶ It seems to me that the latter, weaker, claim is the one we should accept. An outweighing good, while clearly sufficient, is not necessary. For if there *were* a state of affairs which required for its existence that God permit the occurrence of reasonable nonbelief

4. I say that it must be logically necessary that God *permit* the occurrence of reasonable nonbelief, meaning by this, not that it must be logically necessary that God bring about reasonable nonbelief, but that it must be logically necessary that God *bring about or allow* the occurrence of reasonable nonbelief. Only by confusing the denial of (2) (viz., "It is not the case that if God exists, reasonable nonbelief does not occur") with the stronger claim "If God exists, reasonable nonbelief occurs" could we be led to suppose that "permit" must here be read as "bring about." This point is an important one, for it implies that not only goods that require the actual existence of reasonable nonbelief (and so God's *bringing it about* that reasonable nonbelief occurs) are relevant here, but also goods that require for their existence only that God *allow* the occurrence of reasonable nonbelief (by, e.g., leaving it up to human beings to determine whether reasonable nonbelief will occur or not). Cf. the discussion of the Responsibility Argument in Chapter 7.

5. See, for example, Bruce Russell, "The Persistent Problem of Evil," *Faith and Philosophy*, 6 (1989), 122. As Russell points out (129), "good" and "good state of affairs" must in the context of discussions like this be construed fairly broadly. God might permit an evil to occur "to fulfill a duty or to satisfy some other deontological requirement," or to prevent "an even worse evil from occurring."

6. See William L. Rowe, "The Empirical Argument from Evil," in Robert Audi and William J. Wainwright, eds., *Rationality, Religious Belief, and Moral Commitment* (Ithaca, N.Y.: Cornell University Press, 1986), p. 229.

and which constituted an offsetting good, God might very well bring it about, and so might be kept from putting his existence beyond reasonable nonbelief.

Allowing this, however, introduces certain complications, which we must now sort out. For the operative phrase here *is* "might very well." We cannot suppose that if an offsetting good requiring the permission of reasonable nonbelief presented itself, God would automatically seek to bring it about. Because it was only offsetting (i.e., because its value would no more than equal the value represented by God's putting his existence *beyond* reasonable nonbelief), he might, but also might not. So we cannot say of the claim that God would bring about a certain (actually obtaining) state of affairs necessitating the permission of reasonable nonbelief that it is plausible when all we know is that the state of affairs is *plausibly* viewed as an *offsetting* good, for then we are, given the point just made, only in a position to say that it is plausible to suppose that God *might or might not* bring it about—from which it certainly does not follow that it is plausible to suppose he *would* do so. We must have *good reason* to suppose that the state of affairs constitutes an offsetting good before we can say that it is plausible to suppose that God would bring it about. If we have good reason to suppose this, we can straightforwardly say that God might or might not bring it about (and not just that it is plausible to suppose that he might or might not do so), which is to say that it is plausible to suppose that he *would*: we have just as much reason to endorse this conclusion as to deny it. On the other hand, if we know of the state of affairs that it is plausibly viewed as an *outweighing* good, we have all that we need. For if it is outweighing, we may be *certain* that God would bring it about;[7] and therefore, if it is plausible to suppose that it is outweighing, it is plausible to suppose that God would bring it about.

To sum up our discussion, then, the denial of (2) is shown to be plausible and so *A* is rebutted if and only if (i) it is shown *conclusively* that an *offsetting* good necessitating the permission of reasonable nonbelief exists, and/or (ii) it is shown to be *plausible* that

7. I, at any rate, will assume that we may be certain of this. In making this assumption, it will be noted, I am only making it easier for my argument to be rebutted.

an *outweighing* good requiring the permission of reasonable non-belief exists.[8]

I come now to an important objection to the claim that A constitutes a prima facie case for atheism which goes through if counter-vailing considerations are not uncovered. This objection is derived from an argument of Stephen Wykstra.[9] It can be developed as follows: "A critical assumption of this chapter's argument is that if it turns out that all the goods we know of do not provide a rebuttal for A, we may infer that God has no good reason to permit the occurrence of reasonable nonbelief, and so that premise (2) of A (and hence A's conclusion) is true. But while this assumption, or an analogous assumption, is appropriate in legal contexts, where the notion of prima facie evidence originates, it is manifestly inappropriate here. In legal contexts it may be assumed that if the defendant is innocent despite strong initial indications of his guilt, signs of this are likely to become apparent to careful investigators. But in the present case, things are very different. Because of the weakness of our moral vision and the shortness of our cognitive grasp, and because of God's status as the omniscient creator of all, we may say that if there are God-purposed goods corresponding to the evil we experience, they are likely to be *inscrutable*, that is, beyond our grasp. Hence the fact that we find no rebuttal for our argument (if we do not)—our evidence—is not more to be expected given that no God-purposed goods exist than otherwise: we have no reason to suppose that this would be any less likely to occur given that God-purposed goods actually exist than otherwise. But our evidence (supposing we have it) can justify the conclusion that no God-purposed goods exist only if it *is* more to be

8. Correspondingly, a rebuttal attempt of this sort *fails* if and only if (i) there is good reason to suppose that there is no necessary connection between the obtaining of the state of affairs in question and the reasonableness of nonbelief, and/or (ii) there is good reason to suppose that the state of affairs does not constitute an outweighing good and it is no more than plausible that the state of affairs constitutes an offsetting good.

9. See Stephen Wykstra, "The Humean Obstacle to Evidential Arguments from Suffering: On Avoiding the Evils of 'Appearance'," *International Journal for Philosophy of Religion*, 16 (1984), 73–93. See also Bruce Russell and Stephen Wykstra, "The 'Inductive' Argument from Evil: A Dialogue," *Philosophical Topics*, 16 (1988), 133–160.

expected given that no God-purposed goods exist than otherwise, for it is a basic principle of confirmation theory that some claim C is more probable than not given evidence *e* only if *e* is more to be expected, more probable, given C than given not-C. Hence our evidence does *not* justify it."

Now it might seem that to repel this objection we need only make a distinction between God-purposed and God-*justifying* goods. What we have been discussing in this chapter, it might be said, are the latter, and all we need for our argument is to show that if we find no goods that are even plausibly viewed as God-justifying, we can infer that no God-justifying goods exist. But then, it might be continued, our inference is secure against the Wykstra-style objection. For to block *this* inference, the objector would have to show not only that we might expect God-*purposed* goods to be inscrutable, but also that *non*-God-purposed goods of the requisite sort (which could exist even if God does not) might be expected to be inscrutable. Otherwise, it might be concluded, the objector must beg the question in favor of God's existence.[10]

But this reply will not do. As the reply itself suggests, the claim that there are *no* goods of the sort in question (i.e., no God-justifying goods) entails, inter alia, that there are no God-purposed goods, and so any evidence supporting the former claim must support the latter as well. But if the Wykstra-style objector is right, the fact of our inability to find the requisite goods (supposing it to be a fact) does *not* support the latter claim. Hence, if the objector is correct, it cannot support the former either.

So I think it is safe to assume that if the claim about the inscrutability of God-purposed goods is justified, the inductive inference in question is indeed blocked. But *is* it justified? As it seems to me, an affirmative answer faces some serious problems. We must, first of all, distinguish between the claim that there are possible goods that we cannot grasp and the claim that the permission of evil is logically *necessary* for the existence of such goods. It is the second claim that the objector is apparently saying will be true if

10. Bruce Russell has recently leveled just this sort of criticism against the original Wykstra argument. See Russell and Wykstra, " 'Inductive' Argument from Evil," 147–148, 154. For the reasons given immediately below, it does not seem to me to succeed.

there is a God, and it seems clear that it has much less in its favor
than the first. It is to be expected, perhaps, that a God would
know of kinds of goodness that are impossible for us to understand. But why should this lead us to suppose that evils like that of
the reasonableness of nonbelief, with which we are intimately ac-
quainted, in fact *serve* such goods if God exists? If there is a perfectly good and loving God, he has, in creating, sacrificed his own
interests and taken on ours. We can therefore infer with some confidence that the goods many evils serve, if God exists, are *human*
goods—goods related to our "salvation." But if so related, it seems
unlikely that they, or their relation to evil, should be impossible
for us to grasp. Goods of the latter sort we might expect to be
totally unrelated to the vicissitudes of human life.

Applying a point made by William Rowe, we might also point
out that the goods for the sake of which God would permit evil to
occur would likely be "goods that either are or include good experiences" of the human beings in question. God, we might suppose,
would not subject anyone to evil who was not to "figure significantly in the good" for the sake of which it was permitted. But
then we might expect to know of the goods evils serve, for "the
conscious experiences of others are among the sorts of things we
do know."[11]

We should consider, finally, the great *specificity* of the claim that
reasonable nonbelief will serve inscrutable goods if God exists. The
claim that there are *some* evils (we don't know which) that will
appear pointless if there is a God may not be clearly false, but
when it is made on behalf of the occurrence of reasonable nonbelief
in particular, we should be much less sanguine. Suppose that it is as
likely as not (despite criticisms like those mentioned above) that if
there is a God, at any rate some evils of human experience serve
inscrutable goods. How can we know, with regard to the occurrence of reasonable nonbelief, that it is a *member* of this class? Without independent information bearing on the question, we would
have to say, "Well, it *might* belong to that group, but then again it
might *not*." Hence the probability that reasonable nonbelief will be
apparently pointless if God exists would seem to be at most *half*

---

11. Rowe, "Empirical Argument from Evil," p. 244.

that of the proposition that *some* instances of evil will be so. But then, given that we can surely say no *more* than that the latter proposition is as probable as not, the probability of the claim that reasonable nonbelief will be apparently pointless if God exists is clearly too low for rational acceptance.

The Wykstra-style objection, therefore, appears not to provide any reason to suppose that the inductive inference in question is unjustified. Accordingly, should we turn up no consideration of the sort required, we might indeed be justified in concluding on that ground that none exists, and that premise (2) of *A* is true. It must now be noted, however, that even if this objection *were* shown to be correct, *A*'s claim to the status of a prima facie case would not be imperiled. For even if the evidence of our inability to find any goods of the sort in question does not permit the inference that there are none, and so we cannot draw *this* conclusion from the failure of the arguments of Part 2 or in *this* way show that (2) is true, we may still infer from the failure of these arguments that we have *no reason to deny (2)*; hence, given the point made earlier (from which the Wykstra argument has momentarily diverted our attention), should these arguments fail, we would still be in a position to conclude that (2) (and so (5)) is true. As I have argued, there is considerable reason to *affirm* (2), which establishes a presumption in its favor. Accordingly, if the denial of (2) is not shown to be at least plausible, we must accept the claim that (2) is true as much better substantiated than the claim that it is false, in other words, as more probable than not. Against this, it seems, Wykstra could have nothing to say. His argument (even if successful) does not provide any reason to believe that the relevant goods *exist*; it only provides reason to suppose that our inability to find them is not evidence that they do *not* exist, and the denial of the latter claim is not essential to my case.

This brings me to my final point. I have been claiming that unless a rebuttal for *A* can be provided—that is, unless it can be shown plausible to suppose that there are countervailing considerations of the sort characterized above—its conclusion, that God does not exist, goes through. I will be looking at various arguments that may provide such a rebuttal in Part 2. What I wish to point out is that our discussion in this chapter has clarified both

their proper role or function and their great importance. Those
who have criticized instances of such arguments have sometimes
suggested that it is *puzzling* that they apparently do not succeed
and that no explanation of the absence of clear evidence for theism
can apparently be given. If my claims in Part 1 have been correct,
however, and if there is indeed a prima facie case against theism of
the sort I have described, it is clear that a much stronger conclusion
than this must be drawn if no such argument can be shown to
succeed, namely, that there is no God.[12]

12. This, at any rate, is the case if our assumption that neither theism nor atheism is clearly better-evidenced than its denial is accepted. There will be more on
this in the Conclusion.

Part 2

The Force of the Argument

[5]

Moral Freedom and Its Requirements

So far in the book my concern has been to show that the argument from the reasonableness of nonbelief is a successful prima facie argument—that in the absence of countervailing considerations, the reasonableness of nonbelief shows the nonexistence of God. Now in Part 2 I take up the question whether any such considerations can be adduced. As was mentioned in the Introduction, not all of the considerations in the literature that are relevant to the answering of this question have been given a clear shape in the past or are applicable as they stand, and so my procedure is to clarify and adapt them as I go along. Questions of interpretation of course inevitably arise in a project of this sort, but I wish to make clear at the outset that my main aim is to get as many relevant arguments out into the open as possible, and to assess their force according to the criterion for rebuttal set out in Chapter 4. This is not to say that I do not attempt to determine, in individual cases, what writers have claimed, but where their intent is unclear, I move quickly to talk of "possible" arguments. For our purposes, it does not ultimately matter whether some argument is actually to be attributed to a writer or not. If it is an argument *suggested* by his writing which can be turned into a possible rebuttal, I will consider it. A corollary of this procedural point is that there is here no chronological ordering of arguments or detailed historical discussion. Where there is a reason for the ordering of arguments, it has more to do with logical relations holding among them than with any historical consideration.[1]

In this first chapter of Part 2, I consider arguments from the value of *moral freedom*. It is of course widely held that an appeal to this good is an essential part of any credible theistic response to the problem of evil, and so, given that the problem of reasonable non-belief can be construed as a special instance of this problem, it is perhaps not surprising that free will arguments have been deployed here as well. According to the writers whose arguments I will be considering—John Hick and Richard Swinburne—God is concerned to ensure that our moral freedom be preserved, and thus is, to the extent required for the preservation of this good, hidden from us.[2] Since a proper explication of "the extent required" seems, for both writers, to entail reference to the permission of reasonable nonbelief, their arguments are clearly relevant to our discussion. In assessing them, I will assume that the freedom said to be valuable is indeed a good for the sake of which God would, if necessary, permit reasonable nonbelief to occur. For it is itself a necessary condition of personal relationship with God, and quite apart from this, of great intrinsic value. But I will maintain that the permission of a weak epistemic situation in relation to theism is *not* required for the existence of this good, and that there is in consequence no successful free will defense against the problem of reasonable nonbelief.

---

1. I do not mean to imply that historical questions are irrelevant. If through careful investigation we discover that some historical figure x meant to say y instead of z, we may uncover a new argument. But there is obviously neither time nor space here for the sort of detailed historical investigation that might be useful. And in any case, by looking at all the arguments suggested by a person's writings, we stand a good chance of uncovering the argument actually intended, and so of missing none.

2. Hick's view on Divine hiddenness, which is well known and influential, is commonly understood to involve only an emphasis on the value of *cognitive* freedom, that is, freedom with respect to the acquisition of religious belief. But I will argue that this interpretation—although a natural one given what Hick has to say—is in fact mistaken. Hick is ultimately concerned for the preservation of our *moral* freedom, and so discussion of his argument belongs in this chapter.

Exposition of Hick's Arguments

Hick's claim, impressively developed in numerous writings, is that the world is "capable of being interpreted intellectually and experientially in both religious and naturalistic ways." It is a "religiously ambiguous" world.[3] This, apparently, is the state of affairs he has in mind when he claims that God, if he exists, has set us at an "epistemic distance" from himself.[4] From where we are, God's existence is anything but obvious. The third of Hick's famous claims in this connection is that this situation is logically necessary if our "cognitive freedom" in relation to God is to be preserved, and the fourth is that this freedom *must* be preserved if God's loving purposes for us are to be fulfilled.[5] These four claims—in particular, the last two—represent Hick's contribution to the discussion of our topic. Let us now examine them more closely.

Interpreters of Hick, no doubt influenced by his repeated use of the phrase "cognitive freedom," commonly suppose that his main concern is to show the importance of freedom in respect of the belief that there is a God. For example, Richard Swinburne, in his *Faith and Reason*, associates Hick's position with "the argument that if there were a proof of the existence of God which became known, those who heard it and understood it would have no option but to believe and in that case faith would not be meritorious." Responding to this argument, Swinburne writes that "meritorious religious faith is not a matter merely or at all of having a belief that there is a God (and other beliefs also)—what matters is how we act on our belief; what purposes, given that belief, we seek to achieve."[6] Similar criticisms of Hick (suggesting similar

---

3. John Hick, *An Interpretation of Religion* (London: Macmillan, 1989), p. 129. Further references to this work will be made parenthetically in the text.

4. See, for example, John Hick, *The Second Christianity* (London: SCM Press, 1983), pp. 47, 56. Further references to this work will be made parenthetically in the text.

5. See John Hick, *Evil and the God of Love*, 2d ed. (London: Macmillan, 1985), pp. 281–282, 287.

6. Richard Swinburne, *Faith and Reason* (Oxford: Clarendon Press, 1981), p. 86.

assumptions about his position) are put forward by Anthony O'Hear and (implicitly) by Frank B. Dilley.[7]

Not only do many interpreters of Hick take him to be primarily concerned with freely believing that God exists, many also read him as saying, more specifically, that what this freedom amounts to is the freedom to *choose* (directly) to believe (or not to believe) that there is a God. C. Robert Mesle, for example, in a recent article refers to Hick's view as the view that we are "[free] to make the voluntary cognitive choice to believe that God exists."[8] A similar interpretation is to be found in Robert McKim's "The Hiddenness of God."[9]

It seems to me, however, that neither of the interpretations in question—namely, that Hick is primarily concerned with freedom in respect of the belief that there is a God and, more narrowly, that on his view we are free to choose to believe or not to believe that there is a God—is obviously correct. If Hick did make the latter claim, his view would clearly be subject to the criticism that belief is involuntary. But despite his frequent use of expressions that seem at first sight to imply such a claim, I think it must be said that an explicit and unambiguous statement or defense of it is not to be found anywhere in his writings. On the basis of what *is* clearly stated, I would venture to say that our cognitive freedom, on Hick's view, is more a matter of the necessity of searching for God if we are to experience his presence and of the possibility of willfully removing theological questions from our purview, than of our freedom to choose to believe or not to believe that God exists. And it seems to me that he is primarily concerned not with the belief *that* there is a God, but with belief *in* God (i.e., religious commitment, involving love and trust) and with the preservation of our freedom in respect of *it*—a kind of freedom which he himself refers to as *moral* freedom. It is because of what he takes to be a

7. See Anthony O'Hear, *Experience, Explanation, and Faith* (London: Routledge and Kegan Paul, 1984), p. 239; and Frank B. Dilley, "Fool-Proof Proofs of God?" *International Journal for Philosophy of Religion*, 8 (1977), 21.

8. C. Robert Mesle, "Does God Hide from Us? John Hick and Process Theology on Faith, Freedom, and Theodicy," *International Journal for Philosophy of Religion*, 24 (1988), 99.

9. Robert McKim, "The Hiddenness of God," *Religious Studies*, 26 (1990), 150.

very close connection between the belief that there is a God and belief in God that he sometimes focuses on the importance of freedom in respect of the former.

This interpretation, of course, requires elucidation and defense. I will begin with the point about Hick's notion of cognitive freedom.

It is Hick's talk (apparently in connection with the acquisition of theistic belief) of "cognitive decisions" and "acts of interpretation" which seems to suggest the view that belief in the existence of God is under our direct voluntary control.[10] He writes in *Faith and Knowledge* that "our knowledge of God . . . is not given to us as a compulsory perception, but is achieved as a voluntary act of interpretation."[11] And in *An Interpretation of Religion* a similar view is expressed: "Faith as interpretation is . . . a cognitive decision in face of an intrinsically ambiguous universe" (p. 159).

We need not look far, however, to note that there appears to be some confusion in Hick's account over exactly what this "act of interpretation" or "cognitive decision" amounts to; in particular, over whether it is truly voluntary. For example, in *Faith and Knowledge* (p. 102) he defines "interpretation" as a "recognition," "attribution," or "perception" of "significance" (a significance attaching, in the religious case, to the world as a whole). These terms (with the possible exception of "attribution") suggest that interpretation is involuntary, but, despite the apparent incongruity, Hick refers in the same breath to interpretation as an "*act* of recognition" (p. 102, my emphasis).[12]

10. Some writers not only may be influenced by Hick's talk of cognitive decisions and the like, but may *infer* from his claim that religious belief must not be forced upon us that, on his view, such belief should be (and is) under our (direct) voluntary control. That this would be an illicit inference is clear; the view in question should not be the only one to occur to someone questing about for alternatives to intellectual coercion. Hick himself, as we will see, takes a less directly voluntarist stance, but one compatible with the claim that we are not forced into belief.

11. John Hick, *Faith and Knowledge*, 2d ed. (London: Macmillan, 1988), p. 121. Further references to this work will be made parenthetically in the text.

12. Perhaps in order to soften the incongruity, Hick suggests that recognition may be correct or incorrect, but this seems odd, to say the least. Later in the same work, however (e.g., p. 115), it is clear that he is vacillating between a theologically committed and an ontologically neutral account.

It is worth pointing out that this confusion seems all-pervasive of Hick's discussion of interpretation in *Faith and Knowledge*, which refers to recognition (or attribution) of significance as operative not only at the religious level but at every level of our experience. Religious significance, he writes, is only the "highest and ultimate order of significance." We may speak, in addition, of "natural" and "ethical" significance (p. 113). And "in the case of each of these three realms, the natural, the human, and the divine, a basic act of interpretation is required which discloses to us the existence of the sphere in question, thus providing the ground for our multifarious detailed interpretations within that sphere" (pp. 107–108).[13] But the voluntarist position suggested here is apparently denied a few pages later:

> We cannot explain . . . how we are conscious of sensory phenomena as constituting an objective physical environment; we just *find ourselves* interpreting the data of experience in this way. . . . Likewise we cannot explain how we know ourselves to be responsible beings subject to moral obligations; we just *find ourselves* interpreting our social experience in this way. . . . The theistic believer cannot explain how he knows the divine presence to be mediated through his human experience. He just *finds himself* interpreting his experience in this way. [Pp. 118–119, my emphases]

This passage, it is interesting to note, is reproduced in its entirety in Hick's most recent work, *An Interpretation of Religion* (p. 214).

So where does this lead us? I would suggest the following modest result. Although Hick wants to use libertarian language in describing interpretation ("choice," "act," "decision," etc.), he falls into involuntarist forms of speech time and again. It is not clear

---

13. It may seem to some that this quotation, with its interesting distinction between a "basic" act of interpretation which, so to speak, gets us started, and more detailed interpretations which presuppose it, holds out a way of harmonizing the (seemingly) incompatible emphases in Hick's account. Perhaps the *basic* act of interpretation is voluntary even if the others are not. This way of resolving the problem is ultimately unsatisfactory, however. For Hick often recognizes no such distinction, speaking of all our interpretive activity, both basic and nonbasic, in involuntarist language (see, for example, *Faith and Knowledge*, pp. 110, 111, 114–115).

that interpretation is on his view voluntary at all, and therefore, even if belief formation (including formation of the belief that there is a God) *is* being identified by him with interpretation, it does not clearly and unambiguously follow that belief is, on his view, under our voluntary control.

We must now note, however, that upon closer examination, Hick's view seems to be that interpretation and belief formation are *not* to be identified, since the latter is a *result* of the former. This is indicated most clearly in *An Interpretation of Religion*:

> *Propositional* faith [i.e., belief] rests upon . . . a distinctively religious mode of experiencing the world and one's life within it. And I suggest the *interpretive activity upon which this depends* should be equated with faith in its most *fundamental* sense. [P. 159, my emphases]

> How can religious experience be both powerfully convincing, leaving no room for doubt, and also an exercise of cognitive freedom in response to ambiguity? The answer is that *these phrases refer to different stages*. Behind all conscious experience there lies a phase of unconscious interpretive activity and it is here that, in the case of religious experience, the free response to ambiguity occurs. In the conscious experience the ambiguity has been resolved in a distinctively religious . . . way, and the resulting experience itself may have any degree of intensity and of compelling quality. [P. 170, n. 9, my emphasis][14]

We should also note that, as these quotations already suggest, belief in the existence of a Divine reality is on Hick's view given in and along with religious experience, from which it would seem to follow that he views such belief as *involuntary*. Other passages from the same work provide additional support for this interpretation:

14. In this passage, it will be noted, the "cognitive decision" is said to be *unconscious*, and this is added reason to suppose that on Hick's view, the primary "act" of interpretation is not to be identified with the formation of belief, for belief (as he implies) is given in and along with religious experience, and "experience" is earlier defined by him as "a modification of the content of consciousness" (*Interpretation of Religion*, p. 153).

> What it is reasonable for a given person . . . to believe depends in large part upon . . . his or her information or cognitive input. And the input that is most centrally relevant in this case is religious experience. [P. 211]

> Theistic belief arises, like perceptual belief, from a natural response of the human mind to its experiences. All that we can say of a form of natural belief, whether perceptual, moral, or religious, is that it *occurs* and *seems to be firmly embedded in our human nature*. [P. 214, my emphases][15]

> The observation that propositional faith is subjectively firm belief corresponds to the powerfully convincing character of much religious experience, leaving no room for doubt. [P. 159]

What our investigations reveal, therefore, is the following: (1) Even if the "act" of interpretation were, on Hick's view, identical to the formation of belief, the conclusion that belief is, on his view, a voluntary matter would not clearly follow, since he is ambivalent about the voluntariness of interpretation. (2) Belief is in fact said by Hick to *follow* interpretation—it is the indirect result of interpretation—so that even if the latter *is* to be construed as voluntary, it does not follow that the former is. (3) There is independent textual evidence for the view that, whatever may be true of interpretation, Hick considers belief to be *in*voluntary (the output of religious experience).

We have reason to suppose, then, that Hick does not hold the view that we are free to choose to believe (or not to believe) that there is a God. But while this helps us avoid a common misunderstanding of Hick's view of cognitive freedom, it does not tell us what the correct understanding is. He obviously thinks that we are in some sense free with respect to belief and that this freedom is in some sense connected to religious interpretation, but how we are free and how this is related to interpretation we have yet to determine.

To see what the proper understanding is, we must, I think, turn to such passages as the following:

15. In the first part of this passage, Hick is describing a *possible* view, but the context clearly indicates that he endorses it.

In order to know our environment aright . . . we have to interpret it aright. . . . We are thus endowed with a significant measure of cognitive freedom. Our powers of apprehension are improved and extended not by eliminating but by deliberately perfecting their interpretive phase. We must often exert ourselves in relation to a suspected or reported or half-apprehended aspect of reality in order to become more fully aware of it. What we can know depends in consequence, to an important extent, upon what we choose to be and do. [Faith and Knowledge, p. 122]

The point being made here seems to be that cognitive freedom involves the possibility of choosing, not to experience in a particular way or to believe in the existence of the reality in question, but to be *open* to its existence, to carefully and honestly follow up on any *suggestion* of its existence we may find in our experience. The point appears again a little later in Faith and Knowledge, except this time with a more explicit reference to what we may choose *not* to do:

Our rejection of moral obligations which we are unwilling to accept does not typically take the form of a blank refusal to do what we see to be right, but rather of an evasion at the prior stage of cognition, the turning of a blind eye to the moral facts of the situation. We try to exclude from our minds an obligation which is beginning to dawn unwelcomely upon us. . . . This wilful moral blindness is an exercise of cognitive freedom. The line on which we make our stand is the outer defence of our personality, the frontier of awareness. . . . This frontier of the personality, which each man controls for himself, safeguards his personal integrity and liberty in relation to those aspects of the environment which would lay a *claim* upon him. We have the primary cognitive freedom to recognize or reject the credentials of any imperative which claims authority over us. [Pp. 126–127]

What is important here, of course, is Hick's application of this point to the realm of the religious. In Faith and Knowledge he puts it this way: the recognition of God is contingent on our "desiring to enter into relationship with him" (p. 134). The same understanding is evident in other writings. In his Arguments for the Existence of God, Hick states that "the individual's own free receptivity and responsiveness play an essential part in his dawning consciousness of God."[16] In *The Second Christianity*, the knowledge of God is said to depend on our "willingness" to live in God's presence (p. 48). And most recently, in *An Interpretation of Religion*, Hick speaks of the exercise of cognitive freedom in terms of "the individual's innermost choice of openness to the divine presence" (p. 159).

What a close examination reveals, then, is that cognitive freedom, on Hick's view, consists in the fact that if we are to know God, we must first take certain steps in his direction, and that if we do not wish to know him, we can always shut him out. Openness, willingness, searching (and their contraries)—these represent the volitional element with which Hick is concerned. (He connects them to the notion of a "propensity" which may be encouraged or thwarted, but this is perhaps dispensable.) Openness to God and a willingness to live in his presence give rise to religious experience and to belief; as he writes in *The Second Christianity*, "we can . . . come to know God by a free response to the ambiguous indications of his existence, a willingness to know him which then crystallizes into the experience of being in his presence" (p. 48). Our freedom to determine whether belief is acquired is therefore indirect, consisting in our ability to allow or not to allow ourselves to come to experience the world as mediating God's presence and purpose.[17]

With this understanding of cognitive freedom in mind, we must now ask (moving on to the second part of my interpretation) why Hick considers it to be important. As I noted earlier in the chapter, Hick claims that cognitive freedom is necessary if God's loving purposes for us are to be fulfilled. *Why* is it necessary?

It seems to me that to make sense of this claim we must look more closely at what Hick has to say about belief *in* God—about the trusting, loving, obedient *response* of the believer to his aware-

16. John Hick, *Arguments for the Existence of God* (London: Macmillan, 1970), p. 114.
17. One of the merits of this interpretation of Hick is that it makes sense of his repeated endorsement of Pascal's claim that God "so regulates the knowledge of Himself that He has given signs of Himself, visible to those who seek Him, and not to those who seek Him not." (The reference to Pascal is found in, e.g., Hick, *Faith and Knowledge*, p. 141.)

ness of God's existence. Many of Hick's interpreters, as we saw, take him to be primarily concerned with the preservation of our freedom with respect to the belief *that* there is a God. But far from being irrelevant or of secondary importance, as this would suggest, belief *in* God is at the heart of Hick's concern.

Of critical importance in this connection is what Hick says about the nature of persons and personal relationships; in particular, what he says about the conditions necessary for a personal relationship with God. In order to bring this out clearly, I will quote at some length from *Faith and Knowledge*:

> The infinite nature of the Deity requires him to veil himself from us if we are to exist as autonomous persons in his presence. For to know God is . . . to know the One . . . in whose will lies our final good and blessedness . . . , whose commands come with the accent of absolute and unconditional demand. . . .
>
> Clearly, to become aware of the existence of such a being must affect us in a manner to which the awareness of other human persons can offer only a remote parallel. . . . [The believer's] life must become consciously reorientated towards a Being infinitely superior to himself in worth as well as in power. There is thus involved a radical reordering of his outlook as must be undergone willingly if it is not to crush and even destroy the personality. . . . Only when we ourselves *voluntarily* recognize God, desiring to enter into relationship with him, can our knowledge of him be compatible with our freedom, and so with our existence as personal beings. . . .
>
> If man is to be personal, God must be *deus absconditus*. . . . He desires, not a compelled obedience but our uncoerced growth towards the humanity revealed in Christ. [Pp. 133–135]

Summing it all up a few pages later, Hick writes: "The reason why God reveals himself indirectly—meeting us in and through the world as mediating a significance which requires an appropriate response on our part . . .—is that only thus can the conditions exist for a *personal* relationship between God and man" (p. 140).

It would seem, therefore, that Hick is primarily concerned not with cognitive freedom but with *moral* freedom—freedom with respect to belief *in* God. Our love, trust, and obedience must be freely given; otherwise God's intention to relate to us as persons cannot be fulfilled. But this should not be taken to imply that he views cognitive freedom as unimportant. Quite the contrary: "Cognitive freedom . . . has a negative function, namely to *protect* our finite freedom and autonomy" (*Interpretation of Religion*, p. 162, my emphasis). As the passages quoted above already suggest, there is, according to Hick, a very strong *connection* between belief that and belief in, such that if one acquires the former, one *must* (in some sense of "must") also acquire the latter. Anyone who came suddenly to believe that God exists as a result of God's presenting himself to her experience would on account of fear and astonishment automatically conform to what she perceived as God's will. Cognitive freedom is therefore, as Hick sees it, a *necessary condition* of moral freedom. For we could not be forced to believe that there is a God and yet remain free to respond or not to respond to this belief.

The following passages also provide support for this interpretation:

> To know God is to know oneself as standing in a subordinate relationship to a higher Being and to acknowledge the claims of that being upon the whole range of one's life. The act of will or the state of willingness and consent by which one adopts the religious mode of apperception is accordingly also an act of obedience or a willingness to obey. Thus although belief in the reality of God, and a practical trust and obedience towards him, must be distinguished in thought, they occur together and depend closely upon one another: *fides* and *fiducia* are two elements in a single whole, which is man's awareness of the divine. [*Faith and Knowledge*, pp. 143–144]

> God, if he is known to exist, can only be known as the One who makes a total difference for us. For he is known as infinitely higher than we, in worth as well as in power, and as having so made us that our own final self-fulfillment and happiness are also the fulfillment of his purpose for us. *I cannot know that such a being exists and be at the same time indifferent to him.* [*Second Christianity*, p. 48, my emphasis]

Since Hick, as these passages indicate, considers belief in to *follow* from belief that, his emphasis on the latter, which we have traced, and on freedom with respect to it (cognitive freedom), is perfectly compatible with my claim that he is *ultimately* interested in the

former, and in freedom with respect to *it* (moral freedom). As the
following more formal reconstruction of it shows, the movement
of his argument is a *backward* movement from the importance of
moral freedom to the necessity of cognitive freedom:

(1) If we were deprived of moral freedom in relation to
God—forced to obey God, to commit ourselves to him—
personal relationships between ourselves and God could
not exist.

(2) God wishes us to enter into personal relationship with
himself.

(3) So God will not deprive us of our moral freedom in relation to himself. (From (1) and (2))

(4) Anyone forced to experience (and to believe in the existence of) God is ipso facto forced to *obey* God, and so is
deprived of moral freedom in relation to God.

(5) Hence God will *not* force us to experience and to believe
in the existence of God, but will leave us with a measure
of freedom in this respect, that is, cognitive freedom.
(From (3) and (4))

Our answer to the question "Why, on Hick's view, is cognitive
freedom essential to the fulfillment of God's loving purposes for
us?" must consequently be the following. Cognitive freedom is
theologically necessary because only if it is in place can those who
experience the presence of God and commit themselves to him be
said to be morally free in relation to God. God, by making experience of himself contingent upon a demonstrated disposition to believe in his existence and live in his presence, creates a situation in
which those who experience God and find themselves obeying
God are by definition individuals who have shown themselves
willing to *be* in this position. In this way their moral autonomy,
and therefore the possibility of genuinely personal relationships between themselves and God, are preserved.

So how does all of this bear on our discussion? Do Hick's points
provide a possible rebuttal for the prima facie case of Part 1? Well,
given his famous claim about the connection between cognitive
freedom and *religious ambiguity*, mentioned at the outset of this dis-

cussion, I think Hick would endorse the following expansion of his argument:

(6) Cognitive freedom requires that the world be religiously ambiguous.

(7) God will therefore create a religiously ambiguous world. (From (5)and (6))

(8) If God's existence is beyond reasonable nonbelief, the world is not religiously ambiguous in the required sense.

(9) Therefore, if God exists, his existence is *not* beyond reasonable nonbelief. (From (7) and (8))

Hick would likely concede to my argument prima facie force, admitting the (initial) strangeness of the suggestion that support for theistic belief could possibly stand in the way of explicit personal relationship with God when belief is itself a logically necessary condition of such relationship. But he would argue that since the early availability of good evidence for theistic belief would have the effect of removing our cognitive and so our moral freedom in relation to God, and since this would *rule out* the possibility of personal relationship with God, it is necessary for the realization of such relationship that evidence *not* be provided as soon as a capacity for it exists. Belief must rather be something we come to *over time* as a result of the exercise of moral freedom in investigation.

Hick's Challenge: A Critique

Let us move on now to a discussion of objections that can be raised against Hick's account.[18] As I pointed out in the preceding

18. One criticism of Hick I will not consider is that he reaches his conclusion only by focusing too narrowly on religious experience. Hick himself has distinguished between theoretical proofs and religious experience, arguing that only the latter could remove human freedom (*Arguments for God*, pp. 105–107), and so would seem clearly to be open to such an objection. But as I argued in Chapter 2, there seems to be some reason to suppose that, were God to put his existence beyond reasonable nonbelief, he would do so by means of religious experience. And so it will be important to see whether Hick's argument succeeds when stated in those terms.

section, the "involuntariness of belief" objection, which seems on a surface reading to be an objection to which Hick's account is susceptible, in fact reflects only a misunderstanding of it. There are, however, other objections that cannot so easily be turned aside.

The first of these is directed at Hick's claim that openness to God is sufficient for religious experience. It would seem that some who earnestly seek to know God do not have experiences (apparently) of him. Regardless, therefore, of whether Hick's claim is based on psychological or theological considerations or both, it would appear to be false.

Suppose, however, that Hick is right on this matter and that there is a "constant correlation" between a willingness to know God and religious experience. As a second objection points out, religious experience is not always coercive in the sense of creating the "situation of a person who *cannot help* believing in the reality of God."[19] Some of those who have religious experiences—even of those willing to know God—find them *ambiguous* and remain in doubt as to the existence of God. Again, although it might seem strange from a theological perspective that a willingness to know God should be followed by a religious experience too weak to produce belief (and this perhaps explains why Hick makes the connection between experience and belief a tight one), it does seem that this sometimes occurs.

Let us, however, grant for the sake of argument that here too Hick's view can be successfully defended—that a willingness to know God leads inevitably both to religious experience *and* the acquisition of belief. The most fundamental objection to Hick is that his claims with regard to the *need* for such a prior willingness if our experience of God is to be compatible with our moral freedom (premises (4) and (5) of his argument) are false, and that he has therefore provided us with no reason to suppose that religious experience must be withheld by God until it is shown. Even if our situation were to be of the sort described in Chapter 2, one in which belief *is* (at least in the first instance) the product of religious experience and religious experience is available as soon as a capacity for personal relationship exists, it is not at all clear that individ-

19. Hick, *Arguments for God*, p. 114.

uals who came to believe would not be cognitively and morally free.

In support of this, it can be argued, first of all, that there are indirect ways in which a newly acquired belief can be *resisted*. One can, if one finds the moral implications of a belief distasteful, avoid acting upon it (moral freedom) by taking steps to remove one's active awareness of it or to lose it altogether (cognitive freedom). That we are capable of self-deception is, as we saw in the previous section, recognized by Hick, but he seems to think that it could only operate *prior* to the formation of belief: once belief is formed—at any rate, belief in the existence of God—it cannot be successfully resisted. But there seems no reason to suppose that our powers of self-deception are as restricted as this. It seems possible to shut out an *already formed* belief—even belief in God's existence—as well as to fail to acquire it in the first place. As Anthony Kenny writes in response to a similar view (to that of Hick's) about knowledge, "it is all too easy to shut one's mind to what one knows."[20] Where motives for self-deception exist (and they seem not to be lacking in the religious case), an initial inclination to believe can be overcome, for example, through looking at the evidence for and against again but selectively, and then taking steps to forget having done so. This is all the more obviously possible where (as in the circumstances described in Chapter 2) the evidence does not render the proposition in question *certain*; any small margin of negative probability can be blown all out of proportion if one has the requisite motives.

I have argued that moral commitment need not follow upon the formation of theistic belief because such belief can be successfully resisted, but it is interesting to note that even if one does not take this option and theistic belief is *retained*, moral commitment need not follow. Hick's claim (premise (4) of his argument) with regard to the connection between believing and obeying—between cognitive and moral commitments, belief that and belief in—is untenable. As Terence Penelhum writes, in direct opposition to Hick's view: "I *can* 'know that such a Being exists and be at the same time

20. Anthony Kenny, *Faith and Reason* (New York: Columbia University Press, 1983), p. 77.

indifferent to him'—if I lull myself with sufficient persistence."[21]
Penelhum suggests that such "lulling" (self-deception, this time,
with respect to the *moral implications* of belief) could take the following forms:

> One way . . . might be to join an undemanding church organization
> that let him [i.e., one who believes that there is a God but wishes to
> avoid the moral implications of this belief] participate in cozy and
> received practices that could serve as a specious sign of involvement
> and lull him into complacency. This is . . . the sort of conventional
> Christianity which Kierkegaard attacks most heatedly. Another way
> would be to adjust his understanding of the moral demands to
> which he saw he was subject so that they did not interfere much
> with his worldly preferences. This is the sort of behaviour Pascal
> ascribed, no doubt unfairly, to the Jesuits of his day.[22]

Penelhum has suggested another reason as well for thinking that
theistic belief, even if retained, would not render us morally unfree: "Perhaps, what makes faith voluntary is not that its grounds
are inconclusive, but that even if they are conclusive, men are free
to deceive themselves and refuse to admit that they are. Faith
would be the outcome of a willingness to admit this, and faith and
knowledge need not then be exclusive at all."[23] In other words,
given that it is possible to deceive ourselves with respect to both
theistic belief and its moral implications, we are (meritoriously)
exercising both cognitive and moral freedom if, *instead* of giving in
to the temptation to deceive ourselves, we respond in the *right* way
to our beliefs.

There are, therefore, two ways in which cognitive and moral
freedom may be exercised even by one who retains theistic belief:
(1) She may deceive herself about the moral implications of her
belief. (2) She may, instead of actualizing the very real possibility
of self-deception with respect to either theistic belief or its moral
implications, embrace these beliefs gladly, willingly acting upon

21. Terence Penelhum, *God and Skepticism* (Dordrecht: Reidel, 1983), pp. 111–
112.
22. Ibid., p. 110.
23. Terence Penelhum, "The Analysis of Faith in St. Thomas Aquinas," in Terence Penelhum, ed., *Faith* (New York: Macmillan, 1989), p. 132.

them in religiously appropriate ways. These points, together with my earlier point about self-deception with respect to theistic belief itself, suggest that a range of moral choices would remain open to one provided with good evidence for theism.

How might Hick respond to these arguments? It seems to me that he would be inclined to say that they hold only if we assume that belief is arrived at inferentially, through *argument*, that things are different where belief is the product of religious experience, since it is impossible to ignore and remain unaffected by the latter.[24] My arguments, he might say, are especially unconvincing if we presuppose a situation of the sort described in Chapter 2, in which *all* have *forceful* religious experiences as soon as the relevant capacities are in place. Indeed, it would likely be his view that my arguments in Chapter 2 *undermine* those presented here. For (he might suggest) in arguing that God should bring it about that individuals have ongoing religious experiences and so (continuously) evidence sufficient for belief, I have ipso facto argued (however inadvertently) that God should be *so* close as to prevent a genuinely free response.

To this I would respond, first of all, with a reminder of what we have already seen, namely, that the sense of God's presence, as I suggested in Chapter 2 and as Hick himself states in *An Interpretation of Religion*, need not always be "sharply focused," but could after its initial impression continue as "a general background awareness" (p. 154). As such, it would not be inordinately intrusive—incapable of being ignored or overridden. Hence self-deception seems possible even when belief is the product of experience. I have, in fact, deliberately made certain elements of the Chapter 2 description flexible to *allow* for this. The evidence of experience there described is at all times sufficient to sustain a *measure* of belief and so clearly need not be always forceful. As I have described the experience, it is strongest when the legitimacy of belief genuinely seems threatened. Hence there is no reason to suppose that God must be vividly sensed as present in situations where, for example, the moral implications of belief with respect to some particularly difficult action are recognized. A related point, but one which

24. On this (alleged) difference, see Hick, *Arguments for God*, pp. 105–107.

builds on what has already been said, is that even in a situation of the sort described in Chapter 2, individuals would still be required to deal with what Penelhum calls "the exigencies and distractions of worldly existence."[25] Specifically, the *evil* which is so much a part of human existence (and which, as we have shown, could very well coexist with convincing evidence of God) would even in such circumstances make self-deception or a grudging obedience a live possibility and render meritorious a willing response. For there is no reason to suppose that persons who believed under such circumstances would feel less in the way of pain when serious illness befell them or escape altogether the emotional havoc caused by, for example, a death in the family.[26]

As far as I can see, the only way Hick gets his point, given these considerations, is if he assumes that the religious experiences in question are overwhelming—ones in which God is present to us *unmistakably* and *continuously*—in such a way as to take our (moral) breath away. He does in fact suggest at times (when arguments of the sort I am advancing are seen as needing to be addressed) that this *is* the only alternative to our actual situation of ambiguity. In *God and the Universe of Faiths*, for example, he writes that

> given . . . the human situation as we observe it, we form the theological hypothesis that the meaning of human existence . . . is that God is creating finite personal beings, with a real freedom over against himself, who may thus enter into personal relationship with him. Suppose that such beings had been brought into existence in the immediate "presence" of God. . . . They would not in that case have had any real autonomy and freedom in relation to God. In order then to possess such freedom they had to be created at . . . an epistemic distance. . . . They had to be brought into being in a situation in which they are not automatically conscious of God. . . . Now our actual human situation . . . fits these specifications.[27]

And in *Faith and Knowledge* he suggests that the only alternative to ambiguity is God revealing himself to us "in the coercive way in

25. Penelhum, "Faith in Thomas Aquinas," p. 132.

26. To avoid begging the question, I suggest we understand these afflictions as ones that are not caused or preventable by human action, that is, as instances of natural evil. But natural evil is, I think, quite enough.

27. John Hick, *God and the Universe of Faiths* (London: Macmillan, 1973), pp. 95–96.

which the physical world is disclosed to us" (p. 134). But this view must be rejected, for it suggests that any slight change in our actual situation with respect to the distribution and forcefulness of religious experience would place us in the immediate presence of God, and this is clearly false. Hick himself (at other times) recognizes that it is false. Indeed, he argues that it is precisely to avoid this sort of proximity to the Divine that we are created as part of a physical universe in the first place:

> The physical universe is a divine creation, determined by a purpose which has deliberately made it an autonomously functioning sphere in which its creator is not evident. . . . Its function in relation to ourselves is to enable finite personal life to exist in its own creaturely world. The Creator is so disproportionate to his creatures, as the infinite being over against finite beings, that the two cannot exist in the same sphere. If they were to run on the same rails of physical existence there would be no room left for the creature! Therefore God, who is not a physical entity but Spirit, has created man within and as part of a physical universe in which he can live his own proper creaturely life. For only if man is a free being existing in his own sphere at a distance from his Creator can he make a free response of faith and worship to that Creator. [*Second Christianity*, p. 105]

This suggests that only in *another* life could we experience the direct presence of God (and Hick seems unsure at times whether experience of God will be unmediated even then; see *Faith and Knowledge*, p. 187, and *Interpretation of Religion*, p. 179). In this life, because of the physical "screen" between ourselves and God, we cannot expect our experience to be of that kind:

> The ordinary person's religious awareness here on earth is not [a vision of God in solitary glory]. He claims instead an apprehension of God meeting him in and through his material and social environments. . . . In short, it is not apart from the course of mundane life, but in it and through it, that the ordinary religious believer claims to experience, however imperfectly and fragmentarily, the divine presence and activity. [*Faith and Knowledge*, pp. 95–96]

The passage quoted earlier, therefore, presents us with a false choice. God, according to Hick, *cannot* be revealed in the way in

which the physical world is disclosed to us. It is always "possible
for our minds to rest in the world itself without passing beyond it
to its Maker."[28] If, as Hick suggests, it is only in the direct presence
of God that we would be morally unfree, and if, as he also states,
we can never be in the direct presence of God in this life, it follows
that we could never be morally unfree in this life, no matter what
form our experience of God might take. Of course, Hick may be
wrong here. There may well be forms of religious experience that,
even in this life, would make self-deception impossible and render
us morally unfree. But clearly experiences of this sort do not constitute the sole alternative to our actual situation. God's presence
need not be overwhelming to be persuasive. Religious experiences
strong enough to remove the possibility of *reasonable* nonbelief
need not be so overwhelming as to "crush our autonomy." Only a
quite unjustified insistence on more evidence than is needed or a
lack of imagination concerning the manner of its provision could,
it seems, lead anyone to suppose otherwise.

Hick, then, would appear to have an argument that cannot be
successfully defended. In particular, it does not provide the required rebuttal. There is no reason to suppose that, were God to
put his existence beyond reasonable nonbelief, our cognitive and
moral freedom would be infringed, for there is no reason why we
should not exercise cognitive and moral freedom by rejecting God
or responding appropriately to him *after* this. For all that Hick has
told us, a personal relationship with God would still be possible
even if such a situation were to obtain.

A Variation on the Hickian Theme

Hick's arguments, as we have seen, suggest that improvements
in our epistemic situation of the sort described in Part 1 would
entail the loss of cognitive and moral freedom in relation to God.
Given such improvements, theistic belief would be forced upon us,
and we would be forced as well to serve God. Fear and stupefac-
tion would produce automatic conformity to what was perceived
as God's will. A subtly different approach (but one leading to a

28. Hick, *Evil and Love*, p. 282.

similar conclusion) is taken by Richard Swinburne. Swinburne argues, not that forceful religious experience, in particular, would
paralyze or shatter human personality and autonomy, but that any
too-clear indication of God's existence would render obedience to
God eminently *prudent and rational*, removing temptation to do
wrong, and hence removing the freedom we now possess to form
our own characters for good or ill through our *responses* to temptation (in Swinburne's terminology, the freedom of a genuine choice
of destiny).

Now this notion of "self-constitution" is clearly related to some
aspects of Hick's discussion, but Hick does not give much attention to a concept central to Swinburne's discussion, namely, that of
free will *limited by desire*. Like Hick, Swinburne holds that humans
are free in a sense not compatible with determinism—that is, they
"act intentionally," and how they act is "not fully determined by
prior states of the world"—but, unlike Hick, he makes much of
the point that this freedom is and must be limited if a genuine
choice of destiny is to be possible. "Man has to struggle to act
rationally in a situation of temptation." Yet, significantly, "if man
does have very limited free will, he seems also to have the power
to grow in the extent of his freedom, to decrease the influence over
himself of natural inclinations." And, according to Swinburne, it is
in this capacity and in its corollary, the capacity to allow natural
inclinations to have their way, that a choice of destiny lies. Such a
choice therefore *requires* limited freedom. God, who is perfectly
free, does not and could not have a choice of destiny. Seeing the
good, and having no contrary desires, he must inevitably pursue it.
The freedom that humans actually possess, that is, limited freedom, is the freedom they *must* have if they are to have the choice
of whether to "return to the level of the beasts or to move in the
direction of divinity."[29]

It is this notion of the necessity of limited freedom for a genuine
choice of destiny that provides the basis for Swinburne's explanation of our epistemic situation. On his view, if God's existence
were clear and evident, the desires for lesser goods essential to free-

29. Richard Swinburne, *The Existence of God* (Oxford: Clarendon Press, 1979),
pp. 153, 154, 157, 159.

dom of this sort would be overridden by strong desires to conform to God's will. This possibility did not come up in our discussion of Hick. There it was possible to assume quite straightforwardly—because nothing in Hick's argument suggests otherwise—that humans would, given clear evidence of God, continue to have desires for bad actions and, thus, strong motives for self-deception. Swinburne's argument suggests that the structure of human desire systems would *change* and, hence (implicitly), that such motives would be greatly weakened. It is by virtue of this point, apparently unnoticed by Hick, that Swinburne's view requires separate treatment.[30]

Swinburne's argument appears in *The Existence of God* as well as in a more recent article titled "Knowledge from Experience, and the Problem of Evil."[31] In each case the situation envisaged is one in which human beings become aware of the fact that there is a God through his speaking to them at regular intervals. In *The Existence of God* Swinburne spells out what he takes to be the implications of such a situation as follows:

> The existence of God would be for them [i.e., human beings] an item of evident common knowledge. Knowing that there was a God, men would know that their most secret thoughts and actions were known to God; and knowing that he was just, they would expect for their bad actions and thoughts whatever punishment was just. Even if a good God would not punish bad men further, still

30. Hick puts so much emphasis on the need for freedom that he fails to note that *unlimited* freedom would be as much a problem as no freedom at all—that it would rule out the sort of difficult and gradual development toward personhood that he, like Swinburne, considers to be of great value. Because of this, he is prevented from seeing the possibility of a "prudential" argument of the kind Swinburne advances. There is also an independent reason for supposing that he fails to see this, namely, that he distinguishes between theoretical proofs and religious experience, arguing that only the *latter* could remove human freedom (*Arguments for God*, pp. 105–107). If he had seen the possibility of a prudential argument, he would surely not have insisted on this distinction. For, clearly, proofs could indicate the path of prudence as well as religious experience, and (assuming that prudential reasons would have the force assigned to them by the Prudential Argument) would therefore remove human freedom just as effectively.

31. Richard Swinburne, "Knowledge from Experience, and the Problem of Evil," in William J. Abraham and Steven W. Holtzer, eds., *The Rationality of Religious Belief* (Oxford: Clarendon Press, 1987).

they would have the punishment of knowing that their bad actions were known to God. They could no longer pose as respectable citizens; God would be too evident a member of the community. Further, in seeing God, as it were, face to face, men would see him to be good and worshipful, and hence would have every reason for conforming to his will. In such a world men would have little temptation to do wrong—it would be the mark of both prudence and reason to do what was virtuous. Yet a man only has a genuine choice of destiny if he has reasons for pursuing either good or evil courses of action; for . . . a man can only perform an action which he has some reason to do.[32]

And in the article mentioned above, Swinburne puts the argument in the following way:

I would regard my every movement as overseen by an all-knowing and perfectly good being, namely a God who would therefore wish me to be good, and value me and so preserve me, insofar as I was good. The reasons for being good would be virtually irresistible: a genuine choice of destiny would not be open to me, at least given that men are as rational as they now are. If men were given a much greater inbuilt depravity than they now have their choice would still be open. By depravity I mean strong desires to do what is correctly believed to be evil. But then such extra depravity would itself be a great evil.[33]

A central notion here is that of temptation. By "temptation" Swinburne means a "felt desire" or "natural inclination" to do what is seen to be evil (all things considered), which "it needs an effort of will" to stop one from acting upon. On his view, if we knew of God's existence, we would not be faced with temptation.

32. Swinburne, *Existence of God*, pp. 211–212.
33. Swinburne, "Knowledge from Experience," p. 157. Swinburne's point in these passages was anticipated by Kant: "For suppose we could attain to scientific knowledge of God's existence, through our experience or in some other way. . . . Then in this case, all our morality would break down. In his every action, man would represent God to himself as a rewarder or avenger. This image would force itself involuntarily upon his soul and his hope for reward and fear of punishment would take the place of moral motives. Man would be virtuous out of sensuous impulses" (*Lectures on Philosophical Theology*, Allen W. Wood and Gertrude M. Clark, trans. [Ithaca, N.Y.: Cornell University Press, 1978], p. 123).

in this sense, for such knowledge would bring with it strong reasons for not doing evil—reasons stemming ultimately from desires for our well-being, for example, the desire not to be punished. Prudential reasons of this sort would in such a situation swing us strongly in the direction of good action—it would require little in the way of an act of will to master desires to do evil—and so a genuine choice of destiny would not be open to us.[34]

Before I assess the force of this argument (as well as that of another, apparently independent, argument for the "no choice of destiny" conclusion to be found in the first passage quoted above), two points should be noted. First, what Swinburne hints at in the first passage (by saying *little* temptation) but does not bring out is that, even in the state of affairs he has described, desires to perform actions seen to be wrong would not simply *vanish*; although such desires would, if he is right, be rendered inefficacious by all the reasons available for not doing evil (reasons stemming from strong prudential desires), they might be expected to persist. As Swinburne himself writes in *The Evolution of the Soul*, "the agent still finds himself ready geared to do the action, even when he believes it immoral," and "it is the fate of humans that the inclinations to act needed for enjoyment still move towards action (make the action easier, more natural to do) when the agent believes the action overall bad."[35]

Examples bring this out. If I strongly desire to go to the university bookstore to buy a volume that has just come out on the shelves but recognize that in so doing I will fail to prepare adequately for an important lecture, my desire for the lesser good will not simply disappear. I will do what I see as the better act (if I do it at all) somewhat reluctantly, still feeling the pressure of my contrary desire. This example can be made more directly relevant to the present discussion as well. If I am told by someone who has taken it upon himself to keep the book of which I desire a copy out of the hands of the reading public that he will cause me serious bodily harm if I go to the bookstore, and if I am certain that the threat will be carried out if I do go, I will likely not go to the

34. Swinburne, *Existence of God*, p. 157.
35. Richard Swinburne, *The Evolution of the Soul* (Oxford: Clarendon Press, 1986), pp. 106, 107.

bookstore. But it does not follow that my *desire* to go will simply vanish. It will at most be rendered inefficacious, and even as I choose not to go in order to avoid bodily harm I may feel the twinge that accompanies frustrated desire. What follows from this is that when Swinburne says "little temptation," he is best interpreted as suggesting not that felt desires to do what is wrong would in the situation in question be simply *eliminated*, but that one's overwhelming inclination would be to do what is right, so that whatever felt desires one might have to do wrong would be rendered inefficacious.

Another point which should be noted in this connection is that, on Swinburne's view, having a desire involves seeing the satisfaction of that desire as in some way a good thing, and so involves having a reason for satisfying it: "An agent's having a desire to do some action is always a reason for his doing it." This implies that in the situation Swinburne describes, if contrary desires persisted, as we have seen they would, human beings would continue to have reasons for doing bad actions, although, if he is right, reasons overwhelmed by other reasons for *not* doing bad actions.[36]

As I mentioned earlier, there seems to be a second argument as well in the passage quoted above from *The Existence of God*. I find it in the sentence following the "little temptation" claim, which states that a man "only has a genuine choice of destiny if he has reasons for pursuing either good or evil courses of action; for . . . a man can only perform an action which he has some reason to do." It is implied here that in the situation described, humans would have no reason for performing bad actions, and that in order to have a genuine choice of destiny, they must be *capable* of both good and bad actions. The argument suggested by these claims is the following:

> (10) A person can only perform an action if he has some reason to perform it.

> (11) If no reasons existed for performing bad actions, persons would be incapable of them. (From (10))

36. Ibid., p. 115.

(12) If God's existence were evident, persons would have no reasons to do bad actions.

(13) So in such a situation bad actions couldn't be done. (From (11) and (12))

(14) But both good and bad actions must be possible if persons are to have a genuine choice of destiny.

(15) Therefore, in a situation of the sort in question, no one would have a genuine choice of destiny. (From (13) and (14))

But given my interim points above, it is clear that on Swinburne's own principles, premise (12) of this argument must be rejected. Desires to do bad actions would not simply vanish even in a situation of certainty of the sort Swinburne describes, and so there would always be reasons for doing bad actions (although perhaps reasons overwhelmed by contrary reasons). Thus, if we assume that Swinburne's points about desire and reason are correct, this second argument for the conclusion that a genuine choice of destiny would in a situation of certainty not be open to human beings is unsound. I do not have any difficulty with this assumption, and so I think the argument *is* unsound.

As it seems to me, a more challenging argument is Swinburne's first argument, described above, which, put a little more formally, runs as follows:

(16) In the situation in question, persons would have strong prudential reasons for not doing wrong.

(17) Because of the strength of these reasons, it would require little in the way of an act of will to do what was right— there would be little temptation to do wrong, contrary desires would be easily overcome.

(18) Where there is little temptation to do wrong, persons lack a genuine choice of destiny.

(19) Therefore, in the situation in question no one would have a genuine choice of destiny.

The situation referred to here is, as we have noted, one in which God's existence is "clear and evident," and so one in which humans know for *certain* that there is a God and in which whatever reasons humans take themselves to have for doing good actions they consider themselves to *certainly* have. A situation in which the evidence available is sufficient for belief (i.e., as we have seen, probabilifying) is, however, not of this sort, and it is the *latter* situation that must be shown to be problematic if the prima facie case of Part 1 is to be rebutted. To assess the force of Swinburne's argument in the context of our discussion, therefore, we must take it to refer to evidence sufficient for belief, and ask whether it is plausibly viewed as sound when construed this way.

For the sake of argument, let us, for the moment, concede to Swinburne the truth of (18). This leaves (16) and (17). Are these premises plausibly viewed as true? Is it plausible to think of the reasons in question as ones that humans would, given evidence sufficient for belief, consider themselves to have (i.e., as *pertinent*)? And are they plausibly viewed as strong enough to overwhelm desires for bad actions (i.e., as *efficacious*)? The reasons in question are, it seems, primarily reasons deriving from the belief that God preserves human beings insofar as they do what is right, and more specifically, that bad actions will be punished by God. Are these reasons pertinent? And would they be efficacious? Let us begin with the second question.

Unfortunately, Swinburne is less than clear (in the passages concerned) on how the relevant notion of punishment is to be understood. Does it, for example, imply punishment for each bad action at the time at which it is performed, or only punishment in the distant future, perhaps after death? And what is the nature of this punishment? Bodily harm in the here and now or hellfire in the hereafter or a progressively deteriorating quality of character leading to eventual annihilation or. . . ?[37] Clearly, to know whether the reasons associated with punishment would be efficacious, we need to know more about the form that punishment might be expected to take. Swinburne comments: "whatever punishment is just." But this leaves the question wide open. Human beings, it seems, might very well conceive of God as justly lenient in the moment of de-

---

37. This is the view Swinburne seems to support in more recent writing. See his *Responsiblity and Atonement* (Oxford: Clarendon Press, 1989), pp. 180–184.

sire, and of punishment as, at worst, an afterlife affair, and hence find themselves in a situation of temptation after all, and with a genuine choice of destiny.

Suppose, however, that the punishment expected would be punishment in the here and now, in the form of some sort of bodily harm correlated with each bad action (perhaps something analogous to a severe electrical shock). This, it seems, would have quite a strong deterrent effect. But would all temptation to do forbidden actions be removed? Swinburne suggests that given such a state of affairs, performing a bad action would amount to "deliberately bringing harm upon oneself," and that few of us are ever tempted to do this.[38] But, clearly, one who performed a bad action in such a situation would be acting on exceedingly strong desire, and so her action would first of all be an action performed in *satisfaction of desire*. To say that it would be an action of deliberately bringing harm upon oneself obscures this fact. Desires may remain even when one sees overriding reason not to satisfy them and may exercise an influence disproportionate to the weight one is inclined to give them when dispassionately considering reasons for and against action.[39] In any case, given evidence sufficient for belief instead of proof, one who is under the influence of desires for what is "correctly believed to be evil" is likely to seize upon the margin of possible error: believing, but not certain of God's existence, or of punishment, she may well move, through self-deception, from the belief that God exists and will punish bad actions to (i) the belief that God likely or as likely as not does not exist, and so that punishment is unlikely, or only as likely as not, or (ii) the belief that God will not punish after all, but will be tolerant of lapses from correct behavior.[40] If self-deception *is* still open to individuals, then

38. Swinburne, "Knowledge from Experience," p. 157, n. 10.

39. Swinburne seems to think (see the last point of the second passage quoted above) that our desires are not in fact of this character; that they would be so only if God gave us "a much greater inbuilt depravity" than we in fact have. But this rests on a judgment about the rationality of human beings which the empirical evidence does not seem to me to support. There will be more on this later in the section.

40. Of course, the subject may also deceive himself into thinking that the action he desires is not after all so bad and that punishment is for *this* reason unlikely, or

clearly they are still in a position to yield to bad desires and so retain a genuine choice of destiny.

Let us suppose, however, that these points can be answered and that fear of punishment *would*, in the circumstances in question, overwhelm contrary desires, greatly reducing temptation to do wrong. It seems clear that Swinburne's premise (17), when interpreted in terms of punishment, *requires* that the circumstances be circumstances of this sort (viz., ones in which the punishment expected is punishment in the here and now, correlated with each bad action). For as soon as we weaken the notion of punishment, all the points I have been making—about the continuing, often disproportionate, influence of desires, for example—come back with redoubled force, and the notion that temptation would no longer exist is rendered implausible. As soon as punishment is pushed off into the future, rendered less immediate and concrete, the force of any desires I may have to *avoid* punishment is reduced. It always requires an act of will to give up short-term goods in favor of longer-term interests. If punishment is seen as something in the future, its deterrent effect must be greatly reduced. Then, in addition, various further forms of self-deception become possible. The agent may, for example, be inclined to reason as follows: "It is not if I give in to *this* desire that God will punish me, perhaps even annihilate me, but only if I persistently, to my life's end, give in to such desires. But of course, I do not intend to give in tomorrow, or the next day . . .; only today. So I may perform this action without fear of being punished." I suggest, therefore, that it is only if an individual believes that God's policy on punishment implies that a failure to do good actions will in the *here and now* result in bodily harm or loss of life, that the motivating effect of his belief can be plausibly viewed as great. Only then would good actions involve little effort. If the reasons associated with punishment are not given such a strong interpretation, they cannot legitimately be viewed as efficacious.

---

that his desires are overpowering and so he is *not responsible* for his action. These sorts of self-deception are possible even where there is *certainty* about God's existence and policies. Swinburne does not seem to me to take adequate account of them.

Let us now turn to the first question mentioned above, concerning Swinburne's premise (16). Are the reasons we have mentioned—reasons associated with punishment—plausibly viewed as *pertinent?* Are they reasons that, given evidence sufficient for belief, human beings would in fact consider themselves to have?

It seems to me that these reasons are clearly not pertinent *when given the strong interpretation required.* Why should God's goodness be taken to imply that he will harm us severely each time we do wrong? It seems much more reasonable to suppose that persons met in experience by a loving God would come to believe (correctly) that God desired their deepest well-being, and that they would, in consequence, be left without a clear belief about the ultimate implications of resisting the good or with the belief that God would never refuse anyone a second chance (or, at the very most, with the belief that only after persistently, over a long period of time, rejecting the good, the likelihood of well-being in the hereafter would be greatly diminished). Even if the expectation of punishment in the strong sense *were* prevalent in some quarters at first, upon further experience and reflection the understanding of humans might be expected to mature and deepen (as it has in the actual world under much less favorable epistemic conditions) to the point where such views were universally rejected. Further, those who (unreasonably) expected severe punishment to follow each bad action would soon note that those who did not have this expectation, and so occasionally fell into temptation and did bad actions, were not immediately severely punished. As in our world, the wicked would prosper, and all would soon come to the realization that, in the short term at least, the wicked could be expected to continue to prosper.

The Swinburnian case fails, therefore, when stated in terms of punishment. The plausibility of premise (17) is incompatible with that of (16); that is, to be plausibly viewed as efficacious, reasons associated with punishment must be interpreted in such a way as to be clearly no longer *pertinent.* But perhaps Swinburne is less interested in emphasizing the possible effects of punishment than the passages quoted above seem to suggest, and so we must ask whether there is some other way of understanding the prudential reasons in question, and whether they are plausibly viewed as both

pertinent and efficacious when so understood. One such alternative
construal would involve giving more emphasis than we have so far
to a phrase appearing in the second passage, which affirms that
God, as perfectly good, will *value* (i.e., "think well of") human
beings *insofar as they are good.*[41] Developing this idea, Swinburne
may argue as follows: "All of us already have desires to be well
thought of by other persons, in particular, by other *good* persons.
We strive to do actions that will cause these others to hold us in
high regard. Of course, other human beings do not observe everything we do, and so it is possible to perform bad actions and still
be esteemed by them, but insofar as doing certain good actions is
required for them to think well of us, we desire to perform them.
If now we came in contact with *God* and so came to believe in
God's existence—in the existence of a being at once unsurpassably
good and aware of *all* our actions and thoughts—this would give a
particular *focus* to the aforementioned prudential desires, resulting,
in effect, in a greatly increased desire to do good actions in *every*
circumstance. Desiring to be well thought of by God, whom we
knew to be aware of all our actions and thoughts, we would have
little temptation to do evil. It would be *easy* to do the good in
every situation, and so we would be left without a genuine choice
of destiny."[42]

What should we say in response to this? Can premises (16) and
(17) of Swinburne's argument both be accepted as plausible when
the prudential reasons in question are reasons associated with Divine *approval*, instead of reasons associated with punishment? Start-
ing this time with the question of pertinence, I would suggest that
Swinburne's case again faces difficulties. It is, first of all, not
clearly true that all or most of us have the desire to be well thought
of by good persons as *opposed* to others. And so seeing God to be
unsurpassably good might not create in us any particular desire to
be well thought of by him. Suppose, however, that Swinburne is
correct on this point. A more important criticism is that the conception of Divine approval at the heart of his argument seems to

41. Swinburne has indicated in conversation that "think well of" is the meaning
(of "value") he intends.

42. I am grateful to Professor Swinburne for drawing this alternative construal
of his passages to my attention.

conflict with the notions most of us would naturally associate with perfect love—notions of equal regard and unconditional acceptance—and so seems to be one that individuals who came to believe themselves loved of God would reject. Now of course, presumably few would, upon encountering a perfectly loving God, deny that God *desires* humans to do good actions. (We might expect it to be noticed, for example, that an obvious feature of love is desire for the well-being of the beloved, and that human well-being, especially if God exists, is best served by good actions.) The notion of a God gladdened by our good actions and saddened by any deviations therefrom is no doubt a pertinent one. And we may suppose as well that God would be viewed by individuals as taking seriously human freedom and so as not willing to prevent humans from doing wrong actions when they choose to do so. But none of these beliefs implies that humans are (in what is apparently Swinburne's sense) *less well thought of* by God when they do bad actions. It is compatible with these beliefs that God, if he exists and is perfectly loving, views each human being as irreducibly valuable. And *this* view is one that Swinburne's notion of God thinking well of human beings insofar as they are good seems, on its most natural reading, to exclude.

Is there any other, more qualified, sense in which God may be said to value (think well of) human beings insofar as they are good, which individuals met in experience by a loving God would, plausibly, accept? Perhaps there is. Perhaps we can speak of God as approving of our *actions* insofar as they are good and, therefore, disapproving of what we do, and so in a sense (and indirectly) of *us*, if our actions are bad. But this notion, to be pertinent, will have to be spelled out in such a way as to be compatible with the view mentioned earlier, namely, that God, if he exists and is perfectly loving, accords to each of us a basic dignity and value which is not altered by our actions, good or bad. Otherwise, it is not a notion that we have any reason to believe persons met in experience by a perfectly loving God would accept.

Let us turn now to premise (17) and the question of efficaciousness. Under which, if either, of the interpretations we have distinguished can the prudential reasons in question—reasons associated with Divine approval—be plausibly viewed as strong enough to overwhelm contrary desire? Let us take, first of all, the strongest interpretation, according to which, if we fail to do good actions we will in the here and now be rejected or ignored by God, and viewed as inferior to other of his human creations. Supposing we were provided with evidence sufficient for belief and saw this as an entailment of our belief, would bad desires be overwhelmed? It seems not. The consideration in question must be plausibly viewed as giving rise to a very strong desire indeed before it can plausibly be viewed as rendering *easy* those actions we all otherwise must struggle to perform, and this requirement does not seem to be met.[43] If we take into account that God's existence would not be known for certain, that contrary desires *would* persist at least to some extent, that God would not be physically present, like other humans, and (as we saw in the preceding section) that even if God chose to reveal himself in our experience, he might well bring it about that the sense of his presence was diminished in moments of ethical deliberation, we must surely conclude that many good choices would remain difficult. It seems likely, for example, that since (as Swinburne's argument points out) we could continue to have the high regard of our peers while doing bad actions (even if *not* that of God), we would, under the pressure of contrary desire, often be tempted to ignore God and focus on pleasing human beings instead, thus making it possible to do as we wished. Even if this form of self-deception does not seem likely, others clearly are. I might convince myself that my bad actions would not be repeated tomorrow or the next day and that I would therefore not really fall out of favor with God by performing them. I might reason that God, having *made* me weak and subject to contrary desire, would understand and tolerate at any rate *some* departures from correct behavior. I might also convince myself that what I wished to do *was in fact legitimate*, appearances to the contrary notwithstanding, and so remain assured of God's favor for *this* reason. In any of these ways (and no doubt, there are others), I might convince myself that *both* the desire to be well thought of by God *and* desires for lesser goods could be satisfied, and so find ways of

---

43. Of course, not all of us find the same actions difficult, but all that is needed here is the assumption that *each* of us finds *some* actions difficult.

yielding to contrary desire *without* ignoring God. I suggest, therefore, that even given a strong interpretation, the reasons under consideration—reasons associated with Divine approval—are not plausibly viewed as efficacious: there seems good reason to suppose that given evidence sufficient for belief, they would not overwhelm contrary desire. And if this is true with respect to the strongest interpretation, it is true a fortiori where a *weaker* is concerned.

It seems, then, that the Swinburnian case is not successful. Of the reasons mentioned, some, to be plausibly viewed as efficacious, must be construed in such a way as to be clearly no longer pertinent, and others are clearly not efficacious under any interpretation. Since, as we have seen, there must be prudential reasons that are plausibly viewed as both efficacious *and* pertinent if the Swinburnian argument is to succeed, we may conclude that it does not succeed.

Two final points. First, in evaluating arguments of the sort considered here, we are not restricted to hypothetical examples. Their claims may also be tested by reference to "real life" situations in which people consider themselves to have experienced God and are convinced of his existence and sustaining presence, and of his moral demands. (Of course, it may be that their beliefs are mistaken. But how is that relevant? The question at issue has been "What effects might we expect assurance as to the existence of a perfectly good and loving God to have?" and so it is not the objective quality of the evidence these people have but the degree of assurance it affords *for them* that counts.) Now such people seem quite capable of doing what they believe to be wrong. They have temptations, that is, they are forced to struggle with desires for lesser goods, and occasionally yield to them. One might think in this connection of the corruption in the television evangelism industry: not all televangelists who end up corrupt started out that way. But perhaps a more appropriate example is that of St. Paul, who in Romans 7 writes, "I have the desire to do what is good, but I cannot carry it out. For what I do is not the good I want to do; no, the evil I do not want to do—this I keep on doing." Surely no one was ever more convinced on experiential grounds of God's existence and goodness than St. Paul. And yet, by his own admission, bad actions continued. This (and more generally, the fact that undeniably religious people evince weakness of will) provides my response to Swinburne with additional support.

Finally, it should be noted that even if premises (16) and (17) of Swinburne's argument *were* to be plausible, it would not clearly succeed as a rebuttal, since there are also reasons for rejecting (18). Premise (18) states that "where there is little temptation to do wrong [i.e., little temptation to fail in one's obligations], persons lack a genuine choice of destiny." But this seems false. Swinburne has neglected the connection between a choice of destiny and *supererogatory* action. Even if his claims are plausible where obligatory action is concerned (and I have argued that they are not), it seems that supererogatory action must escape the net: there is no reason for anyone to suppose, for example, that failure to perform supererogatory actions would ever be *punished* by God. But if this is the case, then even if persons would not in circumstances of evidence sufficient for belief be tempted to fail in their obligations, they might still desire not to perform supererogatory actions, and thus have the opportunity of progressively *overcoming* such desires through acts of will and, thereby, of *molding their characters for the good.* Even though they might not, in such circumstances, have the opportunity of returning "to the level of the beasts," they would still have a choice between moral mediocrity and moving "in the direction of divinity," and so a genuine choice of destiny would remain open to them.

[6]

The Importance of Inwardness

We saw in the previous chapter that the "free will" arguments offered by Swinburne and Hick fail to provide a rebuttal for the argument of Part 1. Evidence sufficient for belief would not shatter human autonomy or remove a genuine choice of destiny. In this chapter I consider arguments suggested by the writings of Pascal and Kierkegaard—arguments whose common claim is that a certain valuable sort of inward or subjective orientation (valuable because essential to the proper moral and religious development of human beings) requires for its existence that God's existence be obscure.[1] As in the preceeding chapter, the question that will guide our discussion is whether the arguments considered are successful when *adapted for our purposes*, that is, when treated as claiming that it is plausible to suppose that the good in question is such as a loving God would seek to bring about even at the cost of permitting the occurrence of reasonable nonbelief, and that its existence is plausibly viewed as incompatible with a strong epistemic situation in relation to theism. My conclusion is that the arguments that can be drawn from the writings of Pascal and Kierkegaard are *not* successful, when so construed.

Any investigation of our question would be derelict in its duty if

1. The "common claim" must, of course, be stated loosely to allow for different kinds and degrees of emphasis.

it did not consider the famous discussions of Kierkegaard and Pascal. But for the very reason of their fame, it may seem strange that my treatment of these discussions does not *precede* my treatment of Swinburne and Hick. However, as I pointed out at the beginning of Part 2, the structure of this second part of the book is dictated not by historical but by theoretical considerations. As it happens, some of the arguments considered here bear interesting relations to arguments discussed in the previous chapter. It will therefore be convenient to have the results of that chapter's discussion before us as we proceed.

Reasons for Divine Hiddenness in Pascal

To understand Pascal's doctrine of the Hidden God we must first recognize that on his view, God was not *always* hidden. There was a time, so his *Pensées* tells us, when the existence of God was evident to all: "I created man holy, innocent, perfect, I filled him with light and understanding, I showed him my glory and my wondrous works. Man's eye then beheld the majesty of God. He was not then in the darkness that now blinds his sight."[2] But man withdrew from God, and God's hiddenness was the eventual result. As the *Pensées* has it:

> He could not bear such great glory without falling into presumption. He wanted to make himself his own centre and do without my help. He withdrew from my rule, setting himself up as my equal in his desire to find happiness in himself, and I abandoned him to himself. The creatures who were subject to him I incited to revolt and made his enemies, so that today man has become like the beasts, and is so far apart from me that a barely glimmering idea of his author alone remains of all his dead or flickering knowledge. [Fragment 149, p. 77]

Pascal, then, accepts the historicity of the Fall. But there are two aspects of his view which, for our purposes, need to be made more

---

2. Blaise Pascal, *Pensées*, A. J. Krailsheimer, trans. (Harmondsworth: Penguin, 1966), fragment 149, p. 77. Further references to this work, in both text and notes, will be made parenthetically.

explicit. First, humans did not initially fall away from the knowledge of God; only from a *proper relation to it*. On Pascal's view, a consciousness of God was at first retained; the Fall consisted in an attempt to become *equal* with God. But the sequence of events that followed took human beings ever farther away from God, until *today* only a vestige of the original knowledge remains. Second, the claim "God is hidden by sin," where this is interpreted as "the apparent weakness of theistic evidence is simply a matter of human blindness," would be criticized by Pascal as incomplete, for on his view God himself contributed to the sequence of events just mentioned by "inciting" the creatures to revolt: the harmony of the created order (and, ipso facto, the evidence of its origin in God) was intentionally weakened.[3] Of course, humans have made things worse for themselves by not responding appropriately to the signs of God that *remain* in nature, and so there is a sense in which God's *continuing* hiddenness may be said to be (in part) the result of human blindness; but it should be recognized that on Pascal's view, the relative weakness of the evidence provided by the created order is fundamentally a function not of our blindness but of God's intentional withdrawal.

The theme of Divine hiddenness can be traced not only in passages of the *Pensées* which refer to the Fall but also in those dealing with the Incarnation. In agreement with the Christian tradition, Pascal held that God in the fullness of time responded to the Fall by opening a "way of salvation" (fragment 149, p. 79). But he writes that God's wish to redeem humankind did not lead him to give a clear revelation of himself—to attempt in this way an immediate return to the pre-Fall state of affairs. God *did* make contact with human beings, to be sure; but, in accordance with the policy of restraint suggested by his immediate response to the Fall and its repercussions on the created order, he came mildly—in a *hidden* way:

> If he had wished to overcome the obstinacy of the most hardened,
> he could have done so by revealing himself to them so plainly that

---

3. Hence Pascal writes, "All creatures either distress or tempt him [i.e., man] and dominate him either by forcibly subduing him or charming him with sweetness, which is a far more terrible and harmful yoke" (ibid.).

they could not doubt the truth of his essence. . . . This is not the way he wished to appear when he came in mildness, because so many men had shown themselves unworthy of his clemency, that he wished to deprive them of the good they did not desire. It was therefore not right that he should appear in a manner manifestly divine and absolutely capable of convincing all men, but neither was it right that his coming should be so hidden that he could not be recognized by those who sincerely sought him. He wished to make himself perfectly recognizable to them. Thus wishing to appear openly to those who seek him with all their heart and hidden from those who shun him with all their heart, he has qualified our knowledge of him by giving signs which can be seen by those who seek him and not by those who do not.

There is enough light for those who desire only to see, and enough darkness for those of a contrary disposition. [Fragment 149, pp. 79–80]

So God is hidden. Neither nature nor history proclaims him as loudly as it might, and in each case this is not in the first instance a matter of human blindness, but of God's intentional withdrawal or restraint.[4] Now we must ask, *why* is this the case? Why, according to Pascal, does God hide himself?

As we saw in the previous chapter, John Hick cites Pascal in support of his own view that human beings are required to seek God so that their *moral freedom* may be preserved. But it seems that Hick's interpretation of Pascal must be mistaken. For, as the second passage quoted above clearly indicates, Pascal accepts the traditional view that human beings were morally free (in Hick's sense) even in the *direct presence of God*, and that they exercised this freedom by rejecting God's rule. Now Pascal does say (in the last passage quoted) that a startlingly clear revelation would "overcome the obstinacy of the most hardened," but the obstinacy referred to seems to be obstinacy with respect to the admission of God's *existence*. In other words, what Pascal appears to be saying is that God could render us *cognitively* unfree. Given his earlier claims, however, it seems that he, unlike Hick, does not consider there to be a

---

4. As Pascal puts it, "all things combine to establish the point that God does not manifest himself to men as obviously as he might" (ibid., fragment 449, p. 168).

necessary connection between cognitive and moral freedom in this context. Hick's repeated appeal to Pascal is therefore misleading at best.[5]

So why does God hide himself? Another possible Pascalian answer, suggested by the last passage quoted above, is the Just Deserts Argument: "Human beings have shown themselves *unworthy* and so God has deprived them of the good of his presence, leaving them to their folly.[6] Divine hiddenness is no more than they *deserve*."[7]

But surely there must be more to Pascal's doctrine of the Hidden God than this. For the response this view attributes to God is all too human. It is, indeed, one that contravenes the Christian ethic, as Pascal seems himself to have recognized:

> As for those who live without either knowing or seeking him, they consider it so little worth while to take trouble over themselves that they are not worth other people's trouble, and it takes all the charity of that religion they despise not to despise them to the point of abandoning them to their folly. But as this religion obliges us always to regard them, as long as they live, as beings capable of grace which may enlighten them . . . we must do for them what we would wish to be done for us in their place, and appeal to them to have pity on themselves, and to take at least a few steps in an attempt to find some light. [*Pensées*, fragment 427, pp. 160–161]

If the Christian attitude of love should prompt Christians to a more charitable response, what must we say about *God*, of whose perfect love our own best love is but a dim reflection?

5. In any event, I have provided reasons (in Chapter 5) for rejecting Hick's Autonomy Argument and so will not need to consider it any further here.

6. As another fragment puts it, "Religion is so great a thing that it is right that those who will not take the trouble to look for it, if it is obscure, should be deprived of it" (*Pensées*, fragment 472, p. 180).

7. It might seem that a less strident and more persuasive version of this argument is also possible: "Humans have freely chosen to reject God, and it would be inappropriate for God to overrule this decision. So they have been left to themselves. God respects their freedom." But this argument suggests no reason for God to intentionally withdraw, to hide *himself*. It may be good for God to leave us in our blindness if this results from free choices, but why should he make things even *more* obscure? To this question, free will arguments do not seem to have an answer.

There are other reasons as well for supposing that Pascal may have had more in mind than is suggested by the Just Deserts Argument. As Terence Penelhum points out (and as, more generally, our discussion in the preceeding chapter should lead us to conclude), God can be hidden from human eyes even when, *objectively*, the signs of his presence are clear:

> If God hides himself in the face of human corruption he may hide himself from human beings who are in the presence of probative phenomena. . . . Their corruption might hinder them from heeding the presence of these phenomena. It might hinder them from drawing from these phenomena the conclusions they proved. And it might affect some of them so that they drew the conclusions but did so with such reluctance that they did not submit themselves to God and allow their knowledge of him to change their lives. In all these cases they would be responsible for God's remaining hidden from them, for they would be keeping faith at arm's length.[8]

As against the Just Deserts Argument, this point shows that if humans are indeed corrupt, God would not necessarily get any better revenge by hiding himself than by manifesting himself clearly. Of course, perhaps in a situation of the sort Pascal describes, in which God's existence is *overwhelmingly* manifested, it would be more difficult for us to keep God "at arm's length" (although, as his discussion of the Fall suggests, it may be that humans could eventually fall away from God even then). But why should such a situation be thought to be the only alternative to hiddenness? For these reasons, I conclude both that the Just Deserts Argument is inadequate and that Pascal, brilliant and charitable thinker that he was, may well have had some other explanation of hiddenness in mind.[9] But what might this explanation be? It seems to me that an answer to this question is latent in the following passages from the *Pensées*:

> If there were no obscurity man would not feel his corruption: if there were no light man could not hope for a cure. Thus it is not

8. Terence Penelhum, *God and Skepticism* (Dordrecht: Reidel, 1983), p. 109.
9. It will, in any event, be useful for our purposes to *assume* that he did, in order to see whether there are any arguments lurking in this neighborhood that might serve to rebut the prima facie case we are considering.

only right but useful for us that God should be partly concealed and partly revealed, since it is equally dangerous for man to know God without knowing his own wretchedness as to know his wretchedness without knowing God. [Fragment 446, p. 167]

[Christianity] teaches men then these two truths alike: that there is a God, of whom men are capable, and that there is a corruption in nature which makes them unworthy. It is of equal importance for men to know each of these points. . . . Knowing only one of these points leads either to the arrogance of the philosophers, who have known God but not known their own wretchedness, or to the despair of the atheists, who know their own wretchedness without knowing their Redeemer. [Fragment 449, p. 168]

"If I had seen a miracle," they say, "I should be converted." . . . They imagine that such a conversion consists in a worship of God conducted, as they picture it, like some exchange or conversation. True conversion consists in self-annihilation before the universal being whom we have so often vexed. [Fragment 378, p. 137]

He [i.e., man] must not see nothing at all, nor must he see enough to think that he possesses God, but he must see enough to know that he has lost him. [Fragment 449, p. 170]

God wishes to move the will rather than the mind. Perfect clarity would help the mind and harm the will.
   Humble their pride. [Fragment 234, p. 101]

One needs no great sublimity of soul to realize that in this life there is no true and solid satisfaction, that all our pleasures are mere vanity, that our afflictions are infinite, and finally that death which threatens us at every moment must in a few years infallibly face us with the inescapable and appalling alternative of being annihilated or wretched throughout eternity. . . .
   Let us ponder these things, and then say whether it is not beyond doubt that the only good thing in this life is the hope of another life, that we become happy only as we come nearer to it. . . .
   It is therefore certainly a great evil to have . . . doubts, but it is at least an indispensable obligation to seek when one does thus doubt; so the doubter who does not seek is at the same time very unhappy and very wrong. [Fragment 427, p. 157]

The view of Divine hiddenness suggested by these passages (when interpreted in the light of Pascal's remarks on the Fall and on the Incarnation) is the following: "The hiddenness of God has both a positive and a negative function, acting both as a *stimulus* and as a *restraint*. Negatively, it prevents us from responding to God in external, presumptuous ways, by effectively removing the possibility of (easily acquired) knowledge of God. This restraint was first imposed in the beginning, when, in order to put an end to human attempts to become equal with God, and to begin to reestablish the relationship on another footing, God withdrew from humankind and weakened the testimony of nature to his existence, introducing death and misery into the world. But it is good for us that it *remain* in effect, so that we are prevented from frustrating God's program of rehabilitation and restoration through yet *another* inappropriate response. The danger of such a response is clear. Witness the arrogance of philosophers who consider themselves to have found proofs of God's existence. They not only use such proofs to advance their own selfishly conceived intellectual ends, but have, in constructing them, failed to show proper respect for the great *difference* between God and humans. This suggests that, were true intellectual clarity to be restored, we would simply demonstrate once more our great capacity for presumption, ignoring the implications for behavior of our creaturely status and God's holiness, and, ipso facto, failing to acquire the very attitudes of contrition and humility required for the restoration of relationship with God. We would be led *away* from a proper relationship with God, rather than *toward* it. Now, of course, as has already been suggested, God wishes not only to prevent us from responding inappropriately to the knowledge of his existence (this would be compatible with *never* revealing himself), but also to provide opportunities for the acquisition of an *appropriate* self-conception and humility, so that a revelation may at some point be given and properly received, and a relationship with God restored. The hiddenness of God helps to promote this and so has not only a negative but also a *positive* function. By withdrawing, God hopes to awaken us to the wretchedness of life on our own, to stimulate a recognition of the barrenness of our existence in a corrupt God-forsaken environment, and to prompt us to search for God with due contrition and humility. We must be made to *feel* our corruption. God's hiddenness can help us to feel this. By doing so, it also helps us to admit our weakness and limitations, and the impossibility of earthly fulfillment. In short, it (paradoxically) points us Godward. Those who listen to the message and seek for God will not be disappointed, for God has left signs of his presence (in particular, of his presence in Christ as Mediator) which they will find. Of course, in accordance with God's general policy of restraint, these signs have been hidden. But this does not diminish their usefulness. Indeed, their usefulness is thereby increased. By providing hidden signs, God ensures *both* that those who do seek will find *and* that those who find will respond appropriately (i.e., inwardly,[10] with humility) and so enter into the relationship which was his wish for them from the beginning."[11]

If this interpretation of Pascal is correct, he has at least two additional answers for those who ask why God hides himself. The first, which I will call the Presumption Argument, claims that if God were *not* hidden, humans would relate to God and to their knowledge of God in arrogant and presumptuous ways, and that the possibility of developing the inner attitudes essential to a proper relationship with God would ipso facto be ruled out. The second, which I will call the Stimulus Argument, claims that God's hiddenness is required because it prompts human beings to recognize their true condition and thus helps to bring about the necessary inwardness, clearing the way for a revelation of God and a restored relationship with God. Both arguments allow Pascal to say that "it is

10. Pascal writes: "a purely intellectual religion would be . . . appropriate to the clever, but it would be no good for the people. The Christian religion . . . exalts the people inwardly, and humbles the proud outwardly" (*Pensées*, fragment 219, p. 99).

11. It may seem to some that there is an inconsistency in Pascal's view, as I have presented it. If human beings are as eager as he suggests to exploit the knowledge of God, will they not avidly *seek* for it? But Pascal has at least two answers to this. First, he can say that although humans would not wish to be rid of the knowledge of God were it *handed* to them, they are too caught up in selfish pursuits to seek it for themselves. Second, and more important, he can say that many of the signs God has left of himself are in the *Church* and its scriptures and (because of the nature of the Church's message) are not only indications of God's presence but at the same time *indictments of our wretchedness*. We do not wish to be told of our wretchedness and so, unless we have come to acknowledge it first, are not likely to recognize or pursue these signs (even though we may play with theoretical arguments). God, that is, in hiding the signs, has ensured that they are of such a sort that only individuals with a certain inward orientation will take to *be* signs.

not only right but *useful* for us that God should be partly concealed and partly revealed" (my emphasis), and so take him beyond the Just Deserts Argument.[12]

One of the virtues of the Presumption Argument, in particular, is that it provides Pascal with a response to arguments such as Penelhum's. Penelhum argues, as we saw, that God might very well remain hidden from corrupt human beings in a situation of good evidence, for, desiring to escape the knowledge of God, such individuals would likely engage in various sorts of self-deception and thus keep God at "arms length." Pascal's argument responds to such claims by questioning the assumption on which they depend, namely, that human beings would *wish to escape* the knowledge of God. On his view, corrupt humans would *not* wish to be rid of God, but rather would wish to compare themselves with him and compete with him, or use him for their own selfish purposes. If this view is correct, a situation of good evidence is *not* compatible with Divine hiddenness. Thus Penelhum's argument, although it may point up a weakness in the Just Deserts Argument when that argument is viewed in isolation, does not do so when it is taken together with the Presumption Argument; nor does it have any force against the Presumption Argument considered independently.[13]

It must now be noted, however, that even if the Stimulus Argument and the Presumption Argument, as so far developed, were to be judged sound, no answer to our problem would be forthcoming. All these arguments suggest is that God has a reason for withholding good evidence from those humans whose present actions and motives are such as to prevent them from responding to it appropriately. No reason is suggested for withholding evidence from those who do not fall into this category—from those, for example, who *have* felt their corruption and the emptiness of life without God and who have begun to search for God with proper motives. No reason is suggested, in short, for supposing that God would permit the occurrence of *reasonable nonbelief.*

12. For a recent discussion of Pascal that seems to follow him here, see Thomas V. Morris, "The Hidden God," *Philosophical Topics*, 16 (1988), 5–21.

13. And this is of course how we must consider the Presumption Argument, having rejected the Just Deserts Argument not only because of the force of Penelhum's criticism but also because of the implications of Christian charity.

Now it may be said that I am burdening Pascal with a problem which he did not consider to exist, that he considered it to be the case that all nonbelief is culpable and that those who recognize their wretchedness and respond with humility receive immediate satisfaction (i.e., find that God "appears openly to them"). This claim is mistaken, however. Pascal recognized, for example, that nonbelievers may search diligently but without success, as the following passages from the *Pensées* show:

Amongst those who are not convinced, I make an absolute distinction between those who strive with all their might to learn and those who live without troubling themselves or thinking about it.

I can feel nothing but compassion for those who sincerely lament their doubt, who regard it as the ultimate misfortune, and who, sparing no effort to escape from it, make their search their principal and most serious business. [Fragment 427, p. 156]

There are only two classes of people who can be called reasonable: those who serve God with all their heart because they know him and those who seek him with all their heart because they do not know him. [Fragment 427, p. 160]

This is what I see and what troubles me. I look around in every direction and all I see is darkness. Nature has nothing to offer me that does not give rise to doubt and anxiety. If I saw no sign there of a Divinity I should decide on a negative solution: if I saw signs of a Creator everywhere I should peacefully settle down in the faith. But, seeing too much to deny and not enough to affirm, I am in a pitiful state, where I have wished a hundred times over that, if there is a God supporting nature, she should unequivocally proclaim him, and that, if the signs in nature are deceptive, they should be completely erased; that nature should say all or nothing so that I could see what course I ought to follow. Instead of that, in the state in which I am, not knowing what I am or what I ought to do, I know neither my condition nor my duty. My whole heart strains to know what the true good is in order to pursue it: no price would be too high to pay for eternity. [Fragment 429, pp. 162–163][14]

14. It is hard to know what to make of this passage. If it is to be taken as autobiographical, it certainly contrasts sharply with other fragments in which Pascal seems quite confident of God's existence. Perhaps it represents a prior state of his self. Perhaps, on the other hand, it is meant to represent the *proper occupation* of

Because of such passages as these, it seems we must say that Pascal
accepted the existence of the problem I have mentioned, however
implicitly, and that he *either* had no solution to offer *or* had some
solution other than the ones we have hitherto considered *or* held
one or another or both of the arguments just distinguished—
namely, the Stimulus and Presumption Arguments—to be capable, suitably revised and extended, of accommodating it. These
would appear to be the interpretive options. The first option may
well be correct, but it is the least interesting, and so I will not
consider it further. The second may be right, but I do not think so:
I can find no independent, supplementary explanation in Pascal.
We are therefore left with the third option. In pursuing it, I will
indulge in maneuvers that may seem at times to find little warrant
in the text. But it must be remembered that I am, in the final
analysis, more interested in *possible* arguments (in what Pascal *could*
have said) than in determining exactly what the historical Pascal
meant to say.

That Pascal considered a period of diligent searching to be a condition of revelation is indicated by a phrase that occurs several
times in the *Pensées*. Here is one example: "God has appointed visible signs in the Church . . . [and] has . . . hidden them in such a
way that he will only be perceived by those who seek him *with all
their heart*" (fragment 427, p. 155, my emphasis; cf. fragment 149,
p. 80). What may, however, strike us about Pascal's use of the
phrase "with all their heart" is that given what he says about reasonable doubters in the passages quoted above, namely, that they
have sought with all their heart, even if his claim were to be accepted, he would be faced with essentially the same problem as
that referred to earlier—namely, the problem of explaining why
individuals who have met the standard set by God may nonetheless
fail to *meet God*. The claim that God will only reveal himself to
those who seek with all their heart may seem, therefore, to be
unhelpful (assuming Pascal is right about reasonable doubters),
even if justified.

---

the nonbeliever, namely, seeking, and so to contrast with indifference, which Pascal calls "monstrous" (fragment 427, p. 157). Whatever the case, it strongly suggests that Pascal considered "seeking without finding" to be part of the human
condition (although note the absence of any reference to the Christian revelation).

It seems to me, however, that Pascal need not be faced with this problem. For the phrase "with all their heart" is ambiguous. The purity of *desire*, of *motive*, of *intention* (and perhaps depth of *conviction* on matters such as one's wretchedness) to which it seems to refer can be seen as instantiated in one who, upon recognizing her unworthiness, is filled with remorse and, perhaps in prayer, expresses a desire to be properly related to God, *even if* she is subsequently deterred from pursuing her search by pride or selfish desires; or as instantiated only in one who, through long, persistent, unremitting searching, has a *deeply ingrained* attitude of humility and desire for the life of faith, one who is no longer at all likely to be deterred by lesser motives from pursuing a (proper) relationship with God. If the phrase "with all their heart" is indeed ambiguous in this way, Pascal can claim that the reasonable doubters to whom he refers do not necessarily seek for God "with all their heart" in the *second*, stronger sense of that phrase, and that it is this second sense that is intended when it is said that God will reveal himself clearly to those who seek with all their heart.

Whether Pascal saw this distinction or not, it is clearly one he could employ. That he would be *inclined* to employ it (more specifically, that when he says God will be revealed to those who seek with all their heart, he has in mind an attitude developed and expressed in the course of a long and toilsome search) is suggested by the following passage from the *Pensées*, in which it is said that obscurity can only provide the basis for an objection to Christian theism if the one who complains of it has engaged in a *very long* and *very thorough* search:

> The obscurity in which they [i.e., religious skeptics] find themselves, and which they use as an objection against the Church, simply establishes one of the things the Church maintains [viz., that God has hidden himself so only those who seek with all their heart will find him] without affecting the other [viz., that those who *do* genuinely seek will be satisfied], and far from proving his teaching false, confirms it.
>
> In order really to attack the truth they would have to protest that they had made *every effort* to seek it *everywhere*, even in what the Church offers by way of instruction, but without any satisfaction. *If they talked like that* they would indeed be attacking one of Christianity's claims. [Fragment 427, p. 155, my emphases]

But even if we assume that Pascal does not necessarily face the problem in question, and that he considers a long and thorough search and a deeply ingrained attitude of humility to be necessary for a clear revelation of God, we must still ask *how this latter claim is to be justified*. It is only if we can find an *argument* for it that we will have located the Pascalian answer to the problem of reasonable nonbelief.

As I suggested earlier, such an argument, if it exists, is likely to involve an extension of the Stimulus Argument or the Presumption Argument, or both. Do either of these arguments admit of extension? It seems to me that, quite obviously, both do. For Pascal can claim the following: "The knowledge of God is a gift that must be carefully given. Humans who have begun to search for God (and, indeed, those who have honestly searched for some time) may still be tempted, by virtue of their sinful nature, to fall back into older and less worthy patterns of behavior; in particular, they might very well relate externally and in a relationship-inhibiting way to any good evidence they were given. It is therefore important that God remain hidden until they have persevered over a long period and have developed a *deeply ingrained* attitude of humility and a desire for a proper relationship with God strong enough to overwhelm selfish desires. The hiddenness of God itself helps to bring this development about by continually bringing home to humans the poverty of a life without God and by continually prompting them to seek God humbly. God's hiddenness can therefore be understood in terms of *patience*. Although he wishes to be more deeply and intimately related to human beings (and, indeed, *because* he wishes this), God is willing to wait until good evidence will be religiously efficacious. It is only if he is patient that God can ensure that those who come to be aware of his presence are those willing to submit in the right way to what they see."[15]

This, then, is the explanation of reasonable nonbelief to which the arguments in the *Pensées* most naturally lead. Having got it out

---

15. One of the virtues of this interpretation is that it is able to make good sense of Pascal's repeated claim that in order to acquire a proper belief in God humans need first to diminish their *passions*, and that to diminish passion we must resort to *habit* (see fragments 119, p. 60; 125, p. 61; 418, p. 152; and 821, p. 274).

into the open, we are now in a position to see whether it stands up
to critical scrutiny. This will be my concern in the next section.

The Pascalian Solution: An Assessment

Before we move to a critical discussion of Pascal, two points
should be noted. First, in the context of our discussion, the notions
of Divine hiddenness and disclosure must be understood in terms
of the notion of evidence sufficient for belief: God is disclosed if he
has made such evidence available and hidden if he has not. Hence,
for the Pascalian explanation to succeed in this context, it must
show that it is plausible to suppose that a propensity for presumption is the reason why *evidence sufficient for belief* is not generally
available. This requirement makes the Pascalian's task more difficult than it would otherwise be. For claims about the dangers of
Divine disclosure (as we saw in the previous chapter) have much
more force when the notion of disclosure is given a *very strong*
interpretation (when, e.g., it is understood to involve reference to
an overwhelming manifestation of glory); and the interpretation to
which we are committed by the terms of the problem of reasonable nonbelief, as I have developed it, is clearly not of this sort.

Second, although it may seem that I have in describing the Pascalian's task just now neglected the role of the extended Stimulus
Argument, this argument is quite obviously a weak argument and
so may be dispatched here at the outset. In order for it to succeed
as an independent reason for supposing that God would remain
hidden (in the relevant sense), it must be plausible to suppose that
Divine hiddenness is necessary for humans to be stimulated to a
continuing awareness of their wretchedness. But this is not the
case. Indeed, a Divine revelation might do the job quite well. Now
of course, if the extended *Presumption* Argument is correct, such
direct methods might well be ruled out; and so we might be led to
conclude that the extended Stimulus Argument is at worst *dependent* on the extended Presumption Argument. But even this would
be too strong a conclusion. For it does not follow from the claim
that the extended Presumption Argument is correct that God must
hide in order to stimulate the awareness in question. Even if that
argument is correct, it might be sufficient for such an awareness

that, for example, *much evil* exist—in other words, there remain *indirect* methods of stimulating such an awareness which do not require Divine hiddenness.[16] I conclude therefore that the extended Stimulus Argument does not succeed and that the success of the Pascalian solution depends on the extended Presumption Argument. For this reason, I will be focusing on the latter.

Pascal's claim about the likelihood of a presumptuous response to clear evidence of God's existence may seem stronger than it otherwise would if we assume, as he does, that a historical "Fall" actually took place. If we assume this, we are in effect assuming that there is inductive evidence for the claim that, were God's existence to be revealed today, a presumptuous response would follow. But in light of the findings of disciplines like evolutionary biology and biblical criticism, it is hard to see how such an assumption could be successfully defended. Thus it would seem that we do not have the inductive evidence in question and, as a result, that Pascal's argument is deprived of (possibly) vital support from the very beginning.

But there is more that can be said on this score. For the pre-Fall state of affairs—a state of absolute intellectual clarity and without misery or death—seems to be, for Pascal, the paradigm of a situation in which God is not hidden.[17] Consequently (we may surmise), when he refers to Divine *disclosure*, he is inclined to think of, inter alia, a world without evil, *and the disastrous response of the first humans to life in such a world.* This interpretation, whatever its other merits, certainly helps explain why Pascal considered a presumptuous response to Divine disclosure to be so likely. For it makes *some* sense to suppose that if we knew of God's existence and were untroubled by evils which in the actual world bring home to us our limitations, we might develop an inflated self-conception and begin to respond to God in inappropriate ways. However, espe-

16. As I suggest immediately below, Pascal may assume that there *is* a necessary connection between evil and hiddenness. But I will argue that this view is incorrect.

17. This is perhaps to be expected since, as we have seen, God's hiddenness is, on his view, bound up with the corruption of nature and the introduction of misery and death. It is only natural to think of the *removal* of hiddenness as involving the removal of those phenomena that brought it about in the first place (cf. *Pensées*, fragment 149, pp. 79–80; fragment 449, p. 170).

cially without the classical doctrine of the Fall, Divine hiddenness and disclosure *need not* be thought of in terms of glory lost and glory regained. On our definition, for example, hiddenness and disclosure involve considerably less than this. In particular, on our definition it is not necessary that the evils of the world be removed in order for God to be disclosed. Therefore, if the notion of a presumptuous response to Divine disclosure is, for Pascal, bound up with the classical picture of the Fall, as I have indicated it might be, this can only lessen the force of any responses to the argument of this book that are based upon it.

It seems, however, that on Pascal's view, there is *other* inductive evidence as well, namely, the arrogance of philosophers who take themselves to have found *proofs* of God's existence. And so the Pascalian might argue in response as follows: "The notion of proving God's existence seems perfectly compatible with living in a world filled with evil and suffering. Therefore Pascal's notion of a presumptuous response is capable of being *detached* from the notion of a restored pre-Fall glory. Even if we reject the notion of a Fall, and think of hiddenness and disclosure in terms not connected with it, the problem of presumption remains."

But even if we ignore the fact that to disclose himself (in the relevant sense) God need only provide evidence sufficient for belief, and set aside the possibility that he could provide *nontheoretical* evidence, we must say that this claim is only weakly supported by the consideration it cites. As Penelhum writes, referring to the corrupt motives Pascal ascribes to philosophers, "one must surely say that sometimes the attempt to prove the existence of God has not been undertaken from such motives as these. When Pascal thinks about dogmatic philosophers and their attempts at proof, he thinks too readily of Descartes."[18] If now we *recall* the fact that God need only provide evidence sufficient for belief, and *reintroduce* the possibility of nontheoretical evidence—if, for example, we think in terms of experiential evidence of the sort described in Chapter 2—then the support provided for the Pascalian's claim by the arrogance of philosophers becomes negligible.

Four points may be noted here. First, the notion of proof carries

18. Penelhum, *God and Skepticism*, p. 95.

with it an air of finality, whereas that of evidence sufficient for belief does not (evidence of the latter sort may fall well short of proof). Those who construct a proof therefore always have more reason to boast than those who find themselves with evidence sufficient for belief, and hence are more likely to become arrogant. Second, religious experiences of the sort in question, unlike theoretical proofs, are commonly viewed as coming from "outside"; the subject of a theistic religious experience does not perceive herself to be in *control* of her situation. Hence experiential evidence would be less likely to inspire a sense of *achievement* in the one to whom it was made available. Since the sense of significant achievement and control is often involved in arrogance, this suggests that recipients of experiential evidence would not be as likely as others to respond arrogantly (especially if those *near* the experients were clearly *also* receiving experiential evidence). Third, religious experience has its own distinctive psychological effects, and arrogance is not very naturally construed as one of them. Feelings of gratitude, joy, reassurance, astonishment, guilt, or dismay seem more likely. This third point is of course closely related to the second in that the feelings mentioned are ones we would naturally associate with a *communication* from a higher, moral source, whereas arrogance is more likely where there is no sense that one is the recipient of such a communication. Finally, and most important, part of what God might communicate to us through religious experience is *the very message of wretchedness and corruption* that Pascal suggests a Divine disclosure would inhibit. Religious experiences, it can be argued, are not all likely to provoke an arrogant response, inasmuch as they would awaken in us a sense of our wretchedness and corruption (a state *incompatible* with arrogance). This fourth point is made all the more interesting by the fact that Pascal, writing his *Pensées*, seems at times to have recognized it:

> The God of the Christians is a God of love and consolation: he is a God who fills the soul and heart of those whom he possesses: he is a God who makes them inwardly aware of their wretchedness and his infinite mercy: who unites himself with them in the depths of their soul: who fills it with humility, joy, confidence and love: who makes them incapable of having any other end but him. [Fragment 449, p. 169]

The Christians' God is a God who makes the soul aware that he is its sole good: that in him alone can it find peace; that only in loving him can it find joy; and who at the same time fills it with loathing for the obstacles which hold it back and prevent it from loving God with all its might. Self-love and concupiscence, which hold it back, are intolerable. This God makes the soul aware of this underlying self-love which is destroying it and which he alone can cure. [Fragment 460, p. 178]

What should we make of this? Why did Pascal not see these claims as providing a counterexample to the Presumption Argument? Why were they not seen as suggesting an *alternative* to theoretical proof (and, for that matter, to the restoration of primeval glory) and, hence, as rendering otiose the appeal to philosophical arrogance? Whatever the reason may actually have been, it seems clear that if religious experience can have the effects Pascal describes, it could, if given, *rule out* a presumptuous response; and, therefore, that God's disclosure (in the relevant sense) need not at all provoke such a response. That it can have these effects is strongly suggested not only by Pascal's own reports but also by the testimony of *many* believers to experiences apparently of God which brought home to them their corruption—experiences which were unexpected and unsought, but which changed the direction of their life and (on their interpretation) led to a deep and fulfilling relationship with God. The critic of Pascal therefore has strong inductive evidence of his own, evidence which seems to render irrelevant the evidence adduced by the Pascalian in support of his claim and, indeed, to positively establish the contrary claim.

I would suggest, therefore, that in focusing on the effects of proofs on philosophers, Pascal has failed to take into account other possible sources of evidence, in particular, the evidence of religious experience, which, so far from provoking an arrogant response, seems likely to produce its opposite. We could also vary the emphasis and say that he is wrong to focus on the effects of any evidence whatever on *philosophers*. If God were going to make evidence sufficient for belief generally available, he would not likely provide evidence of the sort that (sometimes) makes philosophers arrogant, namely, theoretical proofs, but rather evidence assimilable by anyone, no matter how sophisticated or lacking in sophistication. If religious experience fits this description, as it seems to do, and if God could through religious experience make us aware of our wretchedness and move us in the direction of humility, then, again, the Pascalian solution seems to lack plausibility.[19]

How might the Pascalian respond to these claims? Could he argue that even religious experience would, at least in *some* cases, provoke a presumptuous response if given too early, and that it must therefore (in these cases at least) be postponed until individuals have come a long way on their own? Can he say that even when the evidence is experiential, the threat of presumption is such that God must be patient, waiting until evidence will be religiously efficacious?

When I think about these possible rejoinders, my first inclination is to reiterate points already made and to suggest that evidence could *always* be provided in such a way as to avoid a presumptuous response. Surely an experience apparently of God—a loving, holy God—would not inspire such a response in anyone. But let us suppose for the sake of argument that the Pascalian's claim is plausible. Does it follow that the extended Presumption Argument provides the required rebuttal? As it seem to me, it does not. For we may still reject a claim which must be plausible if it is to succeed as such, a claim which I have hitherto assumed to be correct, namely, that a loving God would indeed withdraw to the extent in question if this were necessary to prevent a presumptuous response. Even if we accept the former claim, we may show the unacceptability of the Pascalian explanation as a rebuttal by providing reasons for rejecting the *latter*; and this I propose to do.

But first we must be clear about what it is we are rejecting. If it could be shown that, given evidence sufficient for belief, at least some human beings would be *forced* to respond presumptuously, with no hope of ever being able to do otherwise (unless God again became hidden), then I would agree that a loving God, wishing to establish a proper relationship with human beings, would remain

19. Pascal himself offers support for the antecedent of this claim: "Do not be astonished to see simple people believing without argument. God makes them love him and hate themselves. He inclines their hearts to believe" (*Pensées*, fragment 380, p. 138).

withdrawn. But I hope it will be obvious that this is not the case.[20] Given all the considerations I have adduced, it seems unreasonable to suppose that in the circumstances in question, anyone would ever have more than an inclination to respond arrogantly or presumptuously—an inclination, moreover, capable of being overridden. In other words, while some might be tempted to respond inappropriately, everyone would be free not to. The most, therefore, that a defender of Pascal could ever plausibly claim is that, given good evidence, some might be *inclined* to respond presumptuously, and it is the claim that God would remain withdrawn to prevent humans from yielding to such an inclination that I reject.

My reasons for rejecting this claim are drawn from the discussion in Chapter 5. There I assumed, with Swinburne, that a loving God would wish to give us a choice with respect to our own destiny, and that to do this, he must, inter alia, give us a range of natural inclinations to act badly which it is up to us to yield to or to suppress. He must leave us morally free. Now if God remained withdrawn in the face of a possible presumptuous response to theistic evidence, he would in effect be preventing us from choosing how to handle the gift of Divine disclosure; he would be rendering us *morally unfree* in this respect. And in preventing us from choosing how to respond to Divine disclosure, he would be removing the possibility of an explicit choice with respect to our relationship with himself—a choice which many theologians have considered to be essential to a choice of destiny.

Perhaps it will be replied to this that there are *other* possible choices one might make with respect to a relationship with God— a choice to *seek* God, for example—and that it is not at all a bad thing for God to be patient and to allow us to mature before permitting choices as significant as the one in question. But for this to be plausible, the danger of a presumptuous response—and what is more, a response with *continuing* relationship-inhibiting effects— must be quite great indeed, and we have already noted the defects of this view. Given the nature of human beings and the revelatory

---

20. Strangely, in order to suppose that it *is* the case, one must accept a claim about human beings that is directly opposed to the claim advanced by Hick and Swinburne (see Chapter 5): one must claim that humans would, in circumstances of the sort in question, be morally unfree in respect of certain *bad* actions.

options open to God, even in those few cases where a presumptuous response might seem possible (cases of nonbelief that might turn into presumptuous belief if evidence were given), the choices of the individuals in question could not be viewed as more likely to be relationship-inhibiting than relationship-building, and so I suggest that a God who values both our friendship and our freedom would not withdraw in order to prevent them from being made. (If he withdrew, although a presumptuous response would be prevented, friendship would be rendered impossible and freedom would be diminished, and so it seems clear that he would produce neither an outweighing nor an offsetting good by doing so.) To withdraw under such circumstances would betray not so much patience as an un-Godly wariness and mistrust.[21]

My assessment of Pascal's contribution to our discussion is therefore a negative one. When we consider that only evidence sufficient for belief is required, that this could be provided without removing the evil of the world, through religious experience, that religious experience could communicate to us our corruption and need for humility, and finally, that the danger of human presumption, even were it to exist, would only provide opportunity for a significant exercise of moral freedom—when we consider all these things, I say, our judgment must be that the Pascalian solution does not succeed.[22]

Arguments Possibly or Actually Attributable to Kierkegaard

In the case of Kierkegaard, even more than in the case of Pascal, a certain tentativeness in interpretation is required. Although here there is no shortage of completed works, there is a shortage of

21. Interestingly, if some human beings might respond presumptuously to good evidence of God's existence, and if so doing (or not so doing) would constitute an important exercise of moral freedom, we are provided with an additional reply to the arguments of Hick and Swinburne. These writers hold that good evidence would *remove* moral freedom. Here, however, we have an exercise of moral freedom that *requires* for its existence that the evidence be good.

22. This conclusion is further supported by the discussion in the penultimate section of Chapter 7, where I argue that there is room for a sort of Divine withdrawal *within the context* of a Divine-human relationship.

works in which the author's ideas are clearly stated. This is because
Kierkegaard preferred an *indirect* style. He wrote under pseudo-
nyms and filled his books with parable, metaphor, irony, humor,
and poetry, hoping that by forcing his readers to toil for results, he
would cause them to become *subjectively involved* with the matters
discussed. Such involvement, he held, was necessary for the apprehension of ethical and religious truths.[23]

I have more than one reason for noting here these features of
Kierkegaard's writing style. For Kierkegaard's most general intentions as a writer seem also to have been intentions he ascribed to
God, by reference to which he thought the hiddenness of God
could be explained. His (apparent) view was that God communi-
cates with *us* indirectly in order to stimulate the proper sort of
subjective involvement in our existence as human beings, and in
order to prevent situations and states incompatible with such involvement. I will take it as my task to clarify and develop this view
and the reasons for Divine hiddenness it suggests, and to assess the
force of these reasons against the argument of Part 1.[24]

23. For a discussion of Kierkegaard and indirect communication, see Louis P.
Pojman, *The Logic of Subjectivity* (University, Ala.: University of Alabama Press,
1984), pp. 148–154.

24. It should be noted that another, apparently conflicting, view on Divine hiddenness is also suggested by Kierkegaard, namely, that each of us *knows* there is a
God and that if God seems hidden, this is because we have stifled or suppressed
such knowledge: "There [has] never been an atheist, even though there certainly
have been many who have been unwilling to let what they know (that the god
exists) get control of their minds" (*Philosophical Fragments*, Howard V. Hong and
Edna H. Hong, eds. and trans. [Princeton: Princeton University Press, 1985], "Se-
lected Entries from Kierkegaard's Journals and Papers," pp. 191–192). On this
view, acceptance of God's existence must be understood in terms of knowledge,
not of faith. As Kierkegaard writes, "I do not believe [i.e., have faith] that God
exists . . . , but know it; whereas I believe that God has existed" (ibid., p. 222).
But this distinction is not upheld in other of his writings, where, as we will see,
God's existence is said to be objectively uncertain and hence, like the paradox of
the Incarnation, a suitable object for faith; and the reasons for Divine hiddenness he
offers elsewhere emphasize not sin, but a Divine withdrawal which causes difficulties even for those who are *not* "unwilling" to become aware of God. Clearly
there is a problem of interpretation here. I will not, however, attempt to solve it,
but will assume for the sake of argument that Kierkegaard did not espouse a Calvinist position on this matter (if he did, he is adequately answered by considerations adduced in Chapter 3), and develop the other reasons for Divine hiddenness
suggested by his writings.

As suggested in the preceding paragraph, the basic structure of
the explanation I am (tentatively) attributing to Kierkegaard
closely resembles the basic structure of Pascal's account. Like Pascal, Kierkegaard seems to have assigned to the hiddenness of God
both a positive and a negative function: Divine hiddenness, on his
view, both intensifies subjectivity and prevents certain situations
and states that would inhibit it.

In a moment I will be adding detail to this basic structure, but
before I do so, it will be useful to reflect for a moment on how
"hiddenness" and "subjectivity" are to be understood in this context. As I indicated earlier, the latter term, as used by Kierkegaard,
implies, minimally, *involvement* in one's existence. But how can
this involvement be further characterized? An attempt at exhaus-
tive characterization is of course out of the question, but perhaps
the following points, drawn from Kierkegaard's *Concluding Unscientific Postscript*, will help make this notion a little clearer.[25]

The subjective individual, as portrayed in the *Postscript*, focuses
his interests on some idea and, through his own decisions, brings
his life into conformity with it. As Louis Pojman explains, "the
important thing in [Kierkegaardian] subjectivity is *appropriation*,
the resolution and integration of an idea in one's life."[26] The objective individual, by contrast, pursues learned *inquiries* into ideas, to
see, for example, whether they are really instantiated. But as he
does so, Kierkegaard writes, the "infinite, personal, passionate interest of the subject . . . vanishes more and more, because the
decision is postponed, and postponed as following directly upon
the results of the learned inquiry" (p. 28). "All decisiveness, all
essential decisiveness, is rooted in subjectivity. A contemplative
spirit, and this is what the objective subject is, feels nowhere any
infinite need of a decision, and sees no decision anywhere. This is
the *falsum* that is inherent in all objectivity" (p. 33). Subjectivity,
unlike objectivity, involves an "internal decision in which an individual puts an end to the mere possibility and identifies himself
with the content of his thought in order to exist in it" (p. 302).

25. Søren Kierkegaard, *Concluding Unscientific Postscript*, David F. Swenson and
Walter Lowrie, trans. (Princeton: Princeton University Press, 1941). Further references to this work, in both text and notes, will be made parenthetically.
26. Pojman, *Logic of Subjectivity*, p. 66.

The decisions made by the subjective individual involve *risk* and *cost*; the ideal is that of persistent exertion and striving (p. 110). This costly exertion and striving in the face of great risk Kierkegaard calls "passion" (p. 381).[27] In passion the individual takes control of his life; so far from letting his thought and action be determined from without, he is *self*-determined and *self*-directed. Instead of drifting along, responding automatically to inclinations, he "transforms his entire existence in relation [to his idea], and this transformation is a process of dying away from the immediate" (p. 432).

The highest passion of all, according to Kierkegaard, is the passion of *faith* (p. 118). Here we have the greatest risk, the absolute venture. The one who has faith stakes his whole life on an objective uncertainty (indeed, in the case of the idea of the Incarnation, on an *absurdity*). Faith's venture is to believe against all odds that there is a God and that, although eternal, he has entered time in the Incarnation. Since these are the most difficult of ideas to appropriate, they require the highest degree of decisiveness. As Kierkegaard puts it: "Christianity . . . requires that the individual risk his thought, venturing to believe against the understanding . . . this is the absolute venture and the absolute risk" (p. 384). "The absurd [must] stand out in all its clarity—in order that the individual may believe if he wills it; I merely say that it must be strenuous in the highest degree so to believe" (p. 190). "There can be no stronger expression for inwardness than . . . when . . . facing the tremendous risk of the objective insecurity, the individual believes" (p. 188).

Although it is easy to miss this point, it seems that for Kierkegaard, subjectivity has (what we may call) a definite direction. The individual who exercises it will realize her *potential for the infinite*, that is, her potential for a relationship with God. God is the infinite Subject, and so it is only to be expected that those who come to know him will do so by transcending the finite in subjectivity. This occurs in the moment of highest passion—when one believes

27. For a good discussion of this notion, see Robert M. Adams, "Kierkegaard's Arguments against Objective Reasoning in Religion," in Steven M. Cahn and David Shatz, eds., *Contemporary Philosophy of Religion* (New York: Oxford University Press, 1982), pp. 221–227.

in God against all reason. In that moment one is closest to God: "It is only momentarily that the particular individual is able to realize existentially a unity of the infinite and the finite which transcends existence. This unity is realized in the moment of passion" (p. 176). "God is a subject, and therefore exists only for subjectivity in inwardness" (p. 178). The subjective individual, to realize her potential, must believe "against the understanding," and feel "the peril of lying upon the deep, the seventy thousand fathoms, *in order there to find God*" (p. 208, my emphasis).

Kierkegaard's notion of subjectivity is notoriously difficult, and this account of it is doubtless incomplete in some respects. But it conveys, I think, some of his most important emphases and will suffice for our purposes. What now of the notion of God's "hiddenness"? How is *it* understood?

Kierkegaard himself hardly ever uses the term, but it is clear that what it is commonly taken to mean is expressed by him in other ways. He speaks in the *Postscript* of the "objective uncertainty" of God's existence (by which he means, at the very least, the *improbability* of God's existence) and of God's "elusiveness" (pp. 218–219). As the term "elusive" suggests, Kierkegaard apparently holds that many of the epistemic difficulties we may face vis-à-vis God's existence are a result of God's intentional withdrawal. It is suggested that God *could* (in some sense) reveal himself more clearly but chooses not to.[28] Since it is not just human blindness but God's intentional withdrawal that lies behind Divine hiddenness, the anxiety and uncertainty humans may feel with respect to God's existence are not (at least not in the first instance) necessarily signs of culpability.[29] And so we may say that Kierkegaard's understanding

28. This view is suggested most clearly in the famous parable of the king and the humble maiden. In his application of this parable to theology, Kierkegaard writes of God's dilemma: "Who grasps the contradiction of this sorrow: not to disclose itself is the death of love; to disclose itself is the death of the beloved. . . . How grievous it is to have to deny the learner that to which he aspires with his whole soul and to have to deny it precisely because he is the beloved" (*Fragments*, p. 30). Here again we encounter the "patient God."

29. I say "at least not in the first instance" because Kierkegaard suggests that a failure to develop subjectively, and so a failure to *come* to believe that there is a God, may be culpable (see *Postscript*, pp. 363, 379).

of Divine hiddenness entails our own, that is, entails that God has permitted the occurrence of reasonable nonbelief.[30]

Keeping these comments about "subjectivity" and "hiddenness" in mind, we may now return to the sketch of Kierkegaard's explanation given earlier and begin to fill in some of the detail. It was suggested that he assigns to Divine hiddenness both a positive and a negative function. I will begin with the former.

An argument for the view that divine hiddenness fulfills a positive function is implicit in the following passage from the *Postscript*:

> *An objective uncertainty held fast in an appropriation-process of the most passionate inwardness is the truth,* the highest truth attainable for an *existing* individual. . . . The truth is precisely the venture which chooses an objective uncertainty with the passion of the infinite. I contemplate the order of nature in the hope of finding God, and I see omnipotence and wisdom; but I also see much else that disturbs my mind and excites anxiety. The sum of all this is an objective uncertainty. But it is for this very reason that the inwardness becomes as intense as it is, for it embraces this objective uncertainty with the entire passion of the infinite. . . .
>
> But the above definition of truth is an equivalent expression for faith. Without risk there is no faith. Faith is precisely the contradiction between the infinite passion of the individual's inwardness and the objective uncertainty. If I am capable of grasping God objectively, I do not believe, but precisely because I cannot do this I must believe. [P. 182][31]

30. Of course, Kierkegaard would not say, as I would, that it follows that evidence sufficient for belief has not been provided, for this statement, as I have defined it, presupposes that belief is involuntary, and Kierkegaard denies that this is so.

31. Alastair Hannay has some helpful comments on this passage which relate also to our emphasis: "Faith is being certain *in spite of* the objective uncertainty. . . . In describing faith as the 'contradiction' . . . between the 'infinite passion of inwardness' and the 'objective uncertainty,' Kierkegaard is referring to the conflict between the subjective, or personal, certainty one seeks, and has found, on the one hand, and the objective uncertainty, on the other, which has made the finding of the former depend on a strenuous personal choice. The passion of inwardness is the active passion of someone who has decided upon a risky course of action and knows that the determination with which he pursues it would give way to despair were he to fall back on the impersonal authority of reason. The objective uncer-

It is clear from this passage that on Kierkegaard's view, the objective uncertainty of God's existence is necessary for intense inwardness in relation to the idea of God's existence and hence for faith. But the claim that God's existence is objectively uncertain entails the claim that God is hidden. Therefore, Kierkegaard can conclude, God's hiddenness is necessary for faith and accordingly fulfills a positive function in relation to it.

This argument is a Kierkegaardian version of Pascal's ill-fated Stimulus Argument. But we can see (without committing ourselves to its success) that it is a much stronger argument, in the sense that it can claim more. Given his understanding of faith, Kierkegaard can claim that faith, unlike an awareness of wretchedness, *logically* requires Divine hiddenness: if we accept his concept of faith *at all*, we ipso facto accept the necessity of Divine hiddenness for its instantiation. (If Pascal could have claimed this much, no doubt his argument would not have fared so badly.)

I move now to Kierkegaard's apparent claim that Divine hiddenness has an important negative function—that it prevents certain situations and states that would *inhibit* subjectivity. This claim is more complex than the former claim and will take a little longer to develop. My procedure will be as follows. I will first let Kierkegaard speak for himself by quoting at some length from the *Postscript*. Then I will present what I take to be the important points (implicit and explicit) in a somewhat more systematic fashion, concluding with a brief comparison of Kierkegaard's thoughts on this subject in the *Postscript* with those expressed in the *Fragments*.

> Precisely because he himself is constantly in process of becoming inwardly . . . , the religious individual can never use direct communication, the movement in him being the precise opposite of that presupposed in direct communication. Direct communication presupposes certainty; but certainty is impossible for anyone in process of becoming, and the semblance of certainty constitutes for such an individual a deception. [P. 68, n.]

---

tainty is neither replaced nor obscured by the subjective certainty, rather it is a *necessary condition* of the latter" (*Kierkegaard* [London: Routledge and Kegan Paul, 1982], p. 127, my emphasis).

No anonymous author can more cunningly conceal himself . . . than God. He is in the creation, and present everywhere in it, but directly he is not there; and only when the individual turns to his inner self . . . does he have his attention aroused, and is enabled to see God.

Nature is, indeed, the work of God, but only the handiwork is directly present, not God. Is not this to behave, in His relation to the individual, like an elusive author who nowhere sets down his result in large type, or gives it to the reader beforehand in a preface? And why is God elusive? Precisely because He is the truth, and by being elusive desires to keep men from error. . . .

If God were to reveal himself in human form and grant a direct relationship, by giving Himself, for example, the figure of a man six yards tall, then [we] would doubtless have [our] attention aroused. But the spiritual relationship to God in truth, when God refuses to deceive, requires precisely that there be nothing remarkable about the figure. . . . When God has nothing obviously remarkable about him, [we are] perhaps deceived by not having [our] attention aroused. But this is not God's fault, and the actuality of such a deception is at the same time the constant possibility of the truth. But if God has anything obviously remarkable about him, he deceives men because they have their attention called to what is untrue, and this direction of attention is at the same time the impossibility of the truth. [Pp. 218–220]

The argument suggested by these passages is the following: "If strong objective evidence of God's existence were made generally available, we would be *deceived* in two related ways.[32] First, we would be deceived into thinking that we had a proper understanding of religious truth—that the answers were clear, and striving unnecessary. Second, we would be deceived into thinking that God could be fully understood in terms of objective categories, and that an external, prudential response to God was sufficient to establish a proper relationship with him. The results of such deception would be disastrous for beings disposed (as we are) to avoid the strenuosity of subjectivity.[33] For we would become *complacent*,

32. Kierkegaard means "deceived *by God*": God, fully aware of our disposition to avoid subjective strain, would, in providing objective evidence, be *knowingly* causing the formation of false beliefs.

33. Kierkegaard writes, "In general it is quite inconceivable how ingenious and inventive human beings can be in evading an ultimate decision" (*Postscript*, p. 379).

thinking that we had arrived when really there was still a lot to be done, failing to recognize that the religious life, rightly pursued, is subjectively demanding, and hence failing to pursue it rightly. Our knowledge of God would be *superficial*, since the most that can be known of God objectively is still radically incomplete: God is Spirit and can only really be known through the activation of our own spirit in inwardness. Our relationship with God would be *shallow*, not deep, personal, and strenuous as befits a relationship with the infinite Subject. We would remain happily within our finite parameters, relating to God transactionally, not inwardly, and hence not really relating to him at all."[34] It is only a short step from this argument (the Deception Argument, as I will call it) to the claim that if God is hidden, the deception in question and its subjectivity-inhibiting corollaries will be prevented. Therefore, Kierkegaard can claim that the hiddenness of God fulfills an important negative function in relation to the life of faith.

It may be useful to note, before concluding this part of the discussion, that the main emphasis of the Deception Argument seems also to be traceable in the *Philosophical Fragments*.[35] In chapter 2 of that work, Kierkegaard presents his famous parable of the king and the humble maiden. The main point of this parable is often taken to be that God must come among us incognito if our *freedom* is to be preserved.[36] Kierkegaard, in other words, is often viewed as a precursor of Hick. But while I do not wish to deny that such an emphasis may be found in the *Fragments*, it is important to note that it is not the only emphasis. In particular, the claim that, were God to be openly revealed, we would be *deceived* and consequently fail to reach a proper *understanding* of God, is also to be found:

> The learner is in untruth . . . and yet he is the object of the god's love . . . the god wants to be his teacher, and the god's concern is to bring about equality. If this cannot be brought about, the love be-

34. On relating to God transactionally, see ibid., pp. 378–379.
35. This finding, of course, is to be expected if my interpretation of Kierkegaard so far has been on the right track (for the *Postscript* is a "postscript" to the *Fragments*). If a similar emphasis can be found in the *Fragments*, this provides confirmation for my interpretation here.
36. See, for example, Penelhum, *God and Skepticism*, p. 79.

comes unhappy and the instruction meaningless, for they are unable to understand each other. . . .

The poet's task is to find a solution, a point of unity where there is in truth love's understanding . . . for this is the unfathomable love that is not satisfied with what the object of love might foolishly consider himself blissfully happy to have. [Pp. 28–29]

What wonderful self-denial to ask in concern, even though the learner is the lowliest of all persons: Do you really love me? For he himself knows where the danger threatens, and yet he knows that for him any easier way would be a deception, even though the learner would not understand it.

For love, any other revelation would be deception, because either it would first have had to accomplish a change in the learner . . . and conceal from him that this was needed, or in superficiality it would have had to remain ignorant that the whole understanding between them was a delusion. . . . For the god's love, any other revelation would be a deception—if I pleaded with him to change his resolution, to manifest himself in some other way . . . then he would look at me and say: Man, what have you to do with me. . . . Or, if he just once stretched out his hand to bid it happen . . . I would then very likely see him weep also for me and hear him say: To think that you could become so unfaithful to me and grieve love in this way; so you love only the omnipotent one who performs miracles, not him who humbled himself in equality with you. . . .

The situation of understanding—how terrifying, for it is indeed less terrifying to fall upon one's face while the mountains tremble at the god's voice than to sit with him as his equal, and yet the god's concern is precisely to sit this way. [Pp. 33–35]

It is natural to interpret these passages as suggesting that, were God to be clearly revealed, we would be caused to acquire false beliefs about him—beliefs which made the inward awareness of God all the more difficult to realize; and that God, in view of this, remains patiently withdrawn so that a *proper* relationship and a *proper* understanding in inwardness may be achieved.

In bringing this expositon of Kierkegaard to a close, we may note that his arguments do indeed provide possible rebuttals for the prima facie case we are considering, for each suggests that God has reason *not* to put his existence beyond reasonable nonbelief for all human beings at all times. Whether they provide at least one *actual* rebuttal as well is the question to which I now turn.

A Critique of Kierkegaard's Arguments

The Kierkegaardian Stimulus Argument, stated informally in the last section, can be stated more formally as follows:

(1) Intense inwardness in relation to the idea of God is essential to faith.

(2) Such inwardness requires that one choose to believe that there is a God in the face of objective uncertainty (improbability).

(3) One can only choose to believe that there is a God in the face of objective uncertainty if God is hidden.

(4) Divine hiddenness is necessary for intense inwardness in relation to the idea of God. (From (2) and (3))

(5) Divine hiddenness is necessary for faith. (From (1) and (4))

This argument turns into a possible rebuttal of the argument from the reasonableness of nonbelief if we add the assumption that faith (in Kierkegaard's sense) is plausibly viewed as an outweighing good or is clearly an offsetting good (in the senses of Chapter 4). For then we may plausibly draw the further conclusion that God has reason to hide himself. But as it seems to me, the argument ultimately fares no better than its Pascalian counterpart. For it is not at all clear that faith in Kierkegaard's sense *is* a good of the sort required. It is, for example, hard to see why such an *intense* form of inwardness should be idealized. Indeed, it would seem that a properly balanced view of the religious life requires that intensity of the sort valued by Kierkegaard *not* be idealized. Such intensity seems too narrow, excluding as it does many other good things in life which a loving God might wish us to experience and enjoy. As Robert Adams puts it:

> Certainly much religious thought and feeling places a very high value on sacrifice and on passionate intensity. But the doctrine that

it is desirable to increase without limit, or to the highest possible degree (if there is one) the cost and risk of a religious life is less plausible (to say the least) than the view that *some* degree of cost and risk may add to the value of a religious life. The former doctrine would set the religious interest at enmity with all other interests, or at least with the best of them. . . . In a tolerable religious ethics some way must be found to conceive of the religious interest as inclusive rather than exclusive of the best of other interests—including, I think, the interest in having *well-grounded beliefs*. [My emphasis][37]

Kierkegaard seems to have an "all-or-nothing" view—either we focus entirely on risk and sacrifice, striving subjectively with an infinite passion and, as part of this, deciding to believe religious propositions against all reason, or else we live a life that is religiously worthless. But surely this view is mistaken. A life of gradual development and transformation, involving risks and sacrifices but other goods as well, including the good of evidence for one's beliefs, seems to more nearly conform to the Christian ideal. But if so, then intense inwardness in relation to the idea of God is not essential to faith (i.e., the first premise of Kierkegaard's argument is false) and, consequently, Kierkegaard's argument does not succeed.

It seems that the only way Kierkegaard can escape this objection is if he can show that *all* subjective endeavor would be ruled out by God's self-disclosure. If no subjective advance of any kind would be possible given strong evidence of God's existence, then the more moderate view I have advocated (which presupposes that *some* subjectivity is *compatible* with well-grounded belief in God's existence) would not represent a genuine alternative. But this is to say that his argument is, at best, dependent on the Deception Argument, yet to be considered. We will discuss this argument in due course, but before doing so we must consider one other objection to the Kierkegaardian Stimulus Argument—the most serious objection, in my opinion.

Kierkegaard's understanding of faith seems clearly to presuppose that belief is voluntary: we are told that to have intense inward-

---

37. Adams, "Kierkegaard's Arguments against Reasoning," p. 227.

ness, we must choose to believe propositions viewed as improbable. But this presupposition is not one we are in a position to accept. For as I argued in the Introduction, there is very good reason indeed to suppose that belief is (logically) involuntary. But if so, Kierkegaard's argument must be rejected as containing an incoherence: it makes no sense to suppose that what he recommends can be done, or that God would wish it to be done.

The most that Kierkegaard can affirm, in light of this objection, is a *revised* understanding of intense inwardness, according to which we may choose to *accept* the claim that there is a God in the face of objective uncertainty, that is, act *as if* it were true. Acceptance in this sense does not entail belief and is indeed possible. But such a modification would not significantly improve the quality of Kierkegaard's argument. It is true that acceptance of God's existence in the face of objective uncertainty requires that God be hidden, but now we must ask why God would consider a state of affairs in which such acceptance was possible to have a value as great as the value of a situation in which *belief* was possible. As I argued in Chapter 1, belief is a *logical precondition* for certain theological benefits and certain valuable religious states commonly associated with faith. (Kierkegaard seems to agree, for he places great emphasis on the notion of subjective conviction.) Hence, other things being equal, we must suppose that the faith God would value entails belief.

Because of these considerations, I would suggest that the revised understanding of intense inwardness is little better than the unrevised. Indeed, it seems that the modified version of Kierkegaard's argument is also ultimately dependent for its success (in this context) on the Deception Argument. For only if the provision of evidence sufficient for belief would greatly inhibit progress toward a deep and personal relationship with God could acting-as-if be seen as an attractive alternative. It is therefore to the Deception Argument that we must direct our attention. For the purposes of discussion, let us state it a little more formally:

(6) If strong, objective evidence of God's existence were made available to them, human beings would form (false)

beliefs entailing that subjectivity is of no great importance.

(7) Human beings are disposed to avoid the strenuosity of
subjectivity.

(8) Individuals who are disposed to avoid the strenuosity of
subjectivity and who believe that subjectivity is of no
great importance will not become subjective.

(9) Therefore, if strong, objective evidence of God's existence were made available to them, human beings would
not become subjective.

I will assume here that God would indeed wish to facilitate the
exercise of subjectivity, even, if necessary, at the cost of permitting
reasonable nonbelief, meaning by this that some degree of risk and
sacrifice and commitment to the pursuit of genuinely religious
goals (including the goal of a relationship with God) are essential to
the most valuable kind of religious life. (I do *not* mean that God
would wish us to attempt to believe at will what we take to be
improbable propositions; we have already seen that the notion of
such "believing" is incoherent.) I will also assume that premises (7)
and (8) of the Deception Argument, as stated above, are true, for
their claims seem clearly correct. This leaves premise (6). What can
be said about it?

I would suggest that, whereas premise (6) must for our purposes
be taken as referring to evidence sufficient for belief, it is only
plausible when given the stronger interpretation that Kierkegaard
himself seems inclined to give it. If we think in terms of theoretical
proofs and striking displays of Divine power, as he seems to do,
we can begin to see how someone could come to assert it. For if
we were allowed access to such phenomena, we might indeed tend
to form false beliefs of the sort Kierkegaard mentions. If we wit-
nessed an exhibition of Divine power, perhaps we would feel that
there was nothing left for us to do, that all that was required of us
was to stand back and watch *God* work, applauding at appropriate
moments, like observers at some celestial fireworks display. Perhaps if we were granted access to a successful theoretical proof, we
would be drawn away from the inner life and into a maze of arguments, thinking that this was the Divinely appointed way of ac-

166]   The Force of the Argument

quiring further knowledge of God. In these ways our attention
might indeed be called to what is "untrue." But it cries out for
demonstration that these are the *only* ways evidence sufficient for
belief could be provided. In particular, we must once again stress
that *religious experience* could provide the necessary evidence, and
that, so far from leading to the formation of beliefs entailing that
subjectivity is of no importance, such experience could *inspire* subjectivity. The Kierkegaardian claims that evidence sufficient for belief would hinder us from turning to our inner self, but if God
could *meet us there* in a way that motivated us to respond to him in
love and trust but also provided evidence sufficient for belief, then
it seems that his claim must be rejected.

Therefore, my response to the Deception Argument is as follows: Evidence sufficient for correct belief need not lead to the
acquisition of false beliefs about God and so God need not deceive
us in providing it. Such evidence could, indeed, produce *true* beliefs, beliefs entailing that subjectivity is of *great* importance, by
revealing God to us as personal, holy, and loving. Hence Divine
hiddenness is not necessary in order for humans to have the opportunity to become subjective. Anyone who remained complacent or
inappropriately objective upon experiencing Divine self-disclosure
would not be deceived by God but would be, at most, *self*-de-
ceived.

I suggested earlier in this section that well-grounded belief, if
compatible with subjectivity, is to be preferred to acting-as-if
which—although it makes possible a distinctive sort of inwardness—cannot rival the value made possible by belief. In other
words, God might choose not to facilitate well-grounded belief if
this entailed a loss of subjectivity, but if it did not, he would
greatly prefer it.

We are now in a position to claim that well-grounded belief is
not incompatible with subjectivity and, therefore, to draw the relevant conclusion. But no doubt those who favor Kierkegaard's arguments will wish to argue that although there is an inwardness of
belief, the inwardness of uncertainty is much deeper and more pro-
found—that it is only if I construe the two kinds of inwardness as
unequal in value that I get my conclusion, and that this is not the
case. In drawing the chapter to a close, I attempt to articulate this
complaint and give my final response.

Experiential evidence, the Kierkegaardian will say, is just like any other evidence in that it would, if given, diminish the value of the religious life by vastly reducing the cost and risk entailed by it. It is only when one seeks for God without any assurance that he is there that one is truly in a position to *venture*, to risk all. If we were never required to seek, we would never be required to strive inwardly to achieve the knowledge of God; and surely it is a valuable thing for persons in process of becoming to strive in this way.

To this I respond by suggesting that if the God met in experience is the infinite Subject of Kierkegaard's writings, there will be no end to the process of "coming to know God" even for the one who has believed from the start. There will always be new facets of the Divine nature to discover and appreciate. No matter where one begins, therefore, a lifetime of striving is only a start upon the way. Thus, surely, there is no need for God to remain hidden so that we can strive to know him!

As for cost and risk, these also exist for the believer, although, again, in a different form. The one who believes that there is a God has open to her a lifetime of worship and costly service. If she fully commits herself, she as surely "exists in" the idea of God as the one who, yet uncertain, undertakes to act-as-if. And since she also has belief, and so has access to the valuable states it *alone* facilitates, we must conclude that her state is, all things considered, much to be preferred to that of the one who is (only) in a position to act-as-if.

[7]

Investigation, Diversity, and Responsibility

In the foregoing, I have closely examined certain influential discussions of Divine hiddenness in an attempt to find a plausible response to the problem of reasonable nonbelief. But in each case my conclusion has been negative: the best-known attempts at an explanation of our situation in terms of the hiddenness of God fail to provide a rebuttal for the argument of Part 1. In this chapter I consider a motley set of less well-known arguments. Some of these, although clearly important in their own right, are related to arguments already discussed; others suggest entirely new lines of thought. Only the first—Joseph Butler's Probation Argument— exists in developed form. The others have not heretofore been developed by anyone and are at most hinted at in some passage or other. Nevertheless, my aim with respect to each argument is the same: to give to it a clear shape and assess its force.

Butler on Intellectual Probation

Joseph Butler devotes the better part of a chapter (part 2, chapter 6) of his greatest work, *The Analogy of Religion*,[1] to a problem in

---

1. The full title is *The Analogy of Religion, Natural and Revealed, to the Constitution and Course of Nature*. I have used the J. H. Bernard edition of Butler's works (*The Works of Bishop Butler*, 2 vols. [London: Macmillan, 1900]). Volume 2 con-

many ways similar to our own, the problem posed for Christians by the following skeptical claim: "If the evidence of revelation appears doubtful, this itself turns into a positive argument against it, because it cannot be supposed that, if it were true, it would be left to subsist upon doubtful evidence."[2] Now, as his formulation of this claim suggests, the problem to which Butler addresses himself and the problem of reasonable nonbelief do differ in at least one respect: the evidence Butler refers to as appearing "doubtful" (whose apparent doubtfulness he attempts to explain) is evidence adduced in support of Christian revelatory claims and not the evidence of theism (with which we have been concerned).[3] Hence to see what force Butler's arguments have in the context of our discussion, it will be necessary to adapt them for our purposes—to set on one side the question of doubtfulness attaching to revelatory claims, and focus instead on whether the explanations he offers succeed as explanations of apparent doubtfulness in *theistic* evidence. I will accordingly assume hereafter that the evidence to which Butler refers is evidence of this latter sort.[4]

A central claim of Butler's *Analogy* is that we are subjected to temptation in this life so that we may become fitted, through the development of good moral character, for the life to come. Ours is a "state of probation . . . intended for moral discipline and improvement." We have been placed in it so that we might "qualify ourselves, by the practice of virtue, for another state, . . . a future state of security and happiness."[5]

It will be noticed that this view in some ways parallels the claim of Swinburne, discussed in Chapter 5, with respect to the relation between temptation and a genuine choice of destiny. This may in-

---

tains the *Analogy*; and Butler's fifteenth *Rolls Sermon*, to which I will also refer, is to be found in volume 1. The numbers appearing in my references to the *Analogy* are for the part, the chapter, and the paragraph, respectively. In references to Sermon 15, only the paragraph number appears.

2. Butler, *Analogy*, 2, 6, 1.

3. The reason for this difference is that the evidence for God's existence did not appear doubtful to either Butler or his opponents, the deists.

4. I will, however, return to the distinction between evidence for theism and evidence for Christian revelatory claims at a later stage of the discussion. As we will see, it is a distinction that the critic of (the adapted) Butler can exploit.

5. Butler, *Analogy*, 1, 5, 1.

cline us to ask whether the two views of Divine hiddenness also
have something in common. Is it Butler's opinion that we would
not be subject to temptation and, thus, not in a state of probation if
our epistemic situation were improved? Some passages suggest
that this is so. For example, in the fifteenth of Butler's *Rolls Ser-
mons*, "Upon the Ignorance of Man," we read the following:

> Now if the greatest pleasures and pains of the present life may be
> overcome and suspended, as they manifestly may, by hope and fear,
> and other passions and affections; then the evidence of religion, and
> the sense of the consequences of virtue and vice, might have been
> such, as entirely in all cases to prevail over . . . afflictions, diffi-
> culties and temptation; prevail over them so, as to render them ab-
> solutely none at all. But the very notion . . . of a state of discipline
> and improvement, necessarily excludes such sensible evidence and
> conviction of religion, and of the consequences of virtue and vice.[6]

To this version of the Probation Argument, it seems to me, the
responses to Swinburne urged in Chapter 5 apply equally well, and
so I will consider it no further. But there is a second version of the
argument in Butler's writings, which makes an independent claim,
and to which he gives much more attention. In Sermon 15, its
point is made briefly:

> Religion consists in submission and resignation to the divine will.
> Our condition in this world is a school of exercise for this temper:
> and our ignorance, the shallowness of our reason, the temptations,
> difficulties, afflictions, which we are exposed to, all equally contrib-
> ute to make it so. . . . Therefore difficulties in speculation as much
> come into the notion of the state of discipline, as difficulties in prac-
> tice: and so the same reason or account is to be given of both.[7]

In the *Analogy*, it is made at greater length:

> The evidence of religion not appearing obvious, may constitute one
> particular part of some men's trial in the religious sense; as it gives
> scope for a virtuous exercise, or vicious neglect of their understand-

6. Butler, Sermon 15, 9.
7. Ibid.

ing, in examining or not examining into that evidence. There seems no possible reason to be given, why we may not be in a state of moral probation, with regard to the exercise of our understanding upon the subject of religion, as we are with regard to our behaviour in common affairs. The former is as much a thing within our power and choice as the latter. . . . Thus, that religion is not intuitively true, but a matter of deduction and inference; that a conviction of its truth is not forced upon everyone; this as much constitutes religious probation, as much affords sphere, scope, opportunity for right and wrong behaviour, as anything whatever does.[8]

Temptations render our state a more improving state of discipline, than it would be otherwise: as they give occasion for a more attentive exercise of the virtuous principle, which confirms and strengthens it, more than easier or less attentive exercise of it could. Now speculative difficulties are, in this respect, of the very same nature with these external temptations. For the evidence of religion not appearing obvious is to some persons a temptation to reject it, without any consideration at all; and therefore requires such an alternative exercise of the virtuous principle, seriously to consider that evidence, as there would be no occasion for, but for such temptation. And the supposed doubtfulness of its evidence, after it has been in some sort considered, affords opportunity to an unfair mind of explaining away, and deceitfully hiding from itself, that evidence which it might see. . . . [Such temptation], as it calls forth some virtuous efforts, additional to what would otherwise have been wanting, cannot but be an additional discipline and improvement of virtue.[9]

The claim of the second version of the Probation Argument, as indicated by these passages, concerns not moral temptation and moral probation simpliciter, but *one particular sort* of moral temptation and *one particular sort* of moral probation. These we may, following Penelhum, call intellectual temptation and intellectual probation. If God's existence were made more obvious, (the adapted) Butler argues, the choices with respect to theistic evidence of (in Penelhum's words) "frivolous inattention, easy rejection and heedless negativity" and, on the good side, "serious scrutiny, lengthy

8. Butler, *Analogy*, 2, 6, 8.
9. Ibid., 2, 6, 12.

reflection and wrestling with unwanted doubts" would not be open to us.[10] But, it is implied, it is a good thing that humans are subject to these additional choices and temptations, since they provide further opportunity for the development of moral character. Therefore (the conclusion follows), God cannot be expected to make his existence any more obvious than it is.[11]

Butler might seem to be on firmer ground here than with the first argument. For does not intellectual probation, as here defined, *by its very nature require* that God's existence be less than obvious? How could we be in doubt about something that has been made clear to us? Hence it might seem that even if moral probation of other sorts is compatible with a clear indication of God's existence, *intellectual* probation is not, and thus that even if Swinburne's argument and the first version of the Probation Argument do not succeed, *this* argument may.[12]

10. Terence Penelhum, *Butler* (London: Routledge and Kegan Paul, 1985), pp. 195, 196. Penelhum is one of very few recent writers who give attention to Butler's philosophy of religion, and I have been greatly helped by his careful study.

11. Whether Butler considered this argument to be an *extension* of the other or a *narrower version* of it depends on whether or not, in the final analysis, he endorsed the latter. The first passage from Sermon 15 quoted above suggests that he did. But it is important to note that the *Analogy*, which treats these matters at much greater length, seems to favor a contrary view. There it is clearly implied that "real immoral depravity and dissoluteness" is perfectly compatible with a "distinct conviction" of the truth of religion (*Analogy*, 2, 6, 8), and from this it follows that clear evidence would *not* necessarily remove moral temptation. For this reason, it seems to me preferable to suppose that Butler viewed the second Probation Argument as a narrower, more acceptable, version of the first.

12. Swinburne appears at times to recognize the possibility of extending his "choice of destiny" argument to choices with respect to investigation of theistic evidence (see, e.g., *Faith and Reason* [Oxford: Clarendon Press, 1981], p. 86). He also suggests the possibility of construing as valuable the *cooperative* investigation of theistic evidence (*The Existence of God* [Oxford: Clarendon Press, 1979], pp. 188–189). The arguments I deploy against Butler can, however, be applied to these arguments with little adaptation. One possible response to the latter argument is suggested by Swinburne himself when he notes that "men seem only to be beginning to take the opportunities which exist for co-operation for long-term practical ends" (ibid., p. 189). There would appear to be endless opportunities for human cooperation on important matters even if the question of God's existence does not need to be cooperatively investigated, and so—especially given that doing so would preclude, in many cases, the great good of personal relationship with God in this life—it seems unlikely that God would withdraw his presence on this account.

I will have occasion to question this distinction later in the chapter, but for now let us suppose that apparent doubtfulness in theistic evidence is necessary for intellectual probation and see how Butler's argument fares, given this assumption. It seems to me that even if we accept (as I am prepared to do) that a loving God might well subject human beings to a period of moral probation, we need not accept the further claim that such a God would impose *intellectual* probation. If we assume, as we must, given the arguments in Chapter 5, that a wide range of temptations to do bad actions would remain even for individuals provided with evidence sufficient for belief (and thus that the provision of such evidence is compatible with moral probation), and if we recognize, as we should, given the arguments of Chapter 1, that apparent doubtfulness in theistic evidence must (by virtue of its inhibition of belief) remove, for as long as it persists, the possibility of an explicit personal relationship with God, and all that entails, we should regard as at any rate initially suspicious the claim that God would wish to add to the aforementioned temptations the intellectual temptations attendant upon apparently doubtful evidence. Because of its negative effects and apparent superfluity, intellectual probation surely requires more in the way of support than Butler's claim—namely, that the temptations attendant upon it give further occasion for "discipline and improvement of virtue"—seems capable of providing. Given this justification alone, intellectual probation seems clearly the lesser of the two goods and so cannot provide the basis for a rebuttal of the sort we require.

In light of these points, it seems that if his claims are to go through, Butler must show that we have *special* reasons for supposing that God would wish to impose on at any rate some individuals a period of intellectual probation, reasons additional to the reasons we have just by virtue of the fact that such probation is a form of moral probation and so provides further occasion for "improvement of virtue." And toward the end of his discussion, Butler does indeed seem to suggest such reasons:

[There does not] appear any absurdity in supposing, that the speculative difficulties, in which the evidence of religion is involved, may make even the principal part of some persons' trial. For as the

chief temptations of the generality of the world are the ordinary
motives to injustice or unrestrained pleasure; or to live in the neglect
of religion from the frame of mind, which renders many persons
without feeling as to anything distant, or which is not the object of
their senses: so there are other persons without this shallowness of
temper, persons of a deeper sense as to what is invisible and future;
who not only see, but have a general practical feeling, that what is
to come will be present, and that things are not less real for their not
being objects of sense; and who, from their natural constitution of
body and of temper, and from their external condition, may have
small temptations to behave ill, small difficulty in behaving well, in
the common course of life. Now when these latter persons have a
distinct full conviction of the truth of religion, without any possible
doubts or difficulties, the practice of it is to them unavoidable, unless they will do constant violence to their own minds; and religion
is scarce any more a discipline to them, than it is to creatures in a
state of perfection. Yet these persons may possibly stand in need of
moral discipline and exercise in a higher degree, than they would
have by such an easy practice of religion. Or it may be requisite, for
reasons unknown to us, that they should give some further manifestation what is their moral character, to the creation of God, than
such a practice of it would be. Thus . . . what constitutes . . . the
probation . . . of some persons may be the difficulties in which the
evidence of religion is involved; and their principal and distinguished trial may be, how they will behave under and with respect
to these difficulties.[13]

The argument here is that for *some* people, intellectual probation
is not, as we have assumed, just an added form of probation but
the *only* form; without it, they would not be subjected to serious
temptation at all. These are people of an intellectual bent who are
not troubled by the "ordinary" motives to injustice, unrestricted
pleasure, and the neglect of religion in favor of immediate (sensual)

13. Butler, *Analogy*, 2, 6, 13. It is interesting to note that this passage also suggests a reason for denying the (apparent) claim of Sermon 15 (viz., that a much
improved epistemic situation would rule out moral temptation and probation).
Butler suggests that many people, if provided with a proof of the truth of religion,
would still neglect it "from that frame of mind which renders many persons without feeling as to anything distant, or which is not the object of their senses." This
is essentially the same point I made toward the end of Chapter 5, namely, that it is
often quite difficult to give up short-term pleasure for the sake of long-term goals.

fulfillment, people who would not have any difficulty with the practice of religion should a demonstration of its truth become known to them. Therefore, if they also require a period of moral probation (and Butler assumes they do), such individuals should not be provided with a demonstration of religion, but should be required to face the temptations attendant upon *difficulties* in the evidence.[14] In this way they too may be disciplined and provided with an opportunity for the improvement of virtue.

What should we say in response to this argument? Does it make plausible the view that a loving God would require at any rate some individuals to investigate the question of his existence before arriving at evidence sufficient for belief? As it seems to me, it does not, for the following reasons.

First, individuals of the sort Butler describes must be exceedingly few in number, if they exist at all. No doubt there are persons of an intellectual bent who have a "deeper sense as to what is invisible or future" and who recognize that things are "not less real for their not being objects of sense." But how many are also free from the temptations to which objects of sense give rise? Suppose, however, that there exist individuals who combine these qualities. Now we must ask why Butler considers them to be in need of discipline and improvement of virtue. If their virtue is apparent, why should they be subjected to additional tests? Surely God would only sacrifice personal relationships for the sake of intellectual probation, even for a short while, if there were individuals who stood in *need* of it. Let us, however, also grant that the individuals in question are in need of discipline. The question that then arises is how intellectual probation could ever provide it if *other*

14. Note that Butler's point here is not just a narrower version of Swinburne's prudential claim, that is, his point is not that this particular class of individuals should not be provided with strong evidence because of their special sensitivity to its prudential implications. His point is rather that clear evidence should not be provided because the individuals in question stand in need of intellectual probation, and this (logically) necessitates *difficulties* in the evidence. According to Butler, these individuals would find religious practice easy in the circumstances described, not for any reason directly associated with the availability of a demonstration of religion, but because of their general rationality and freedom from sensual desire. They are inclined to do what is right even if it goes *against* short-term interests and so, seeing religious practice to be morally right, would not be tempted to do anything else.

forms of moral probation do not. Butler attempts to move us on to intellectual probation by demonstrating that these individuals are not subject to other temptations, but it is unclear how apparent doubtfulness in the evidence could tempt anyone to be frivolous or dismissive or to avoid serious scrutiny who was not in the "common course of life" inclined to reject long-term goals in favor of short-term pleasures or to give up in the face of difficulty. Those for whom intellectual temptations can arise must, it seems, be individuals who would be tempted in other contexts of life as well. Butler seems therefore to be faced with a dilemma: either the individuals in question cannot be subjected to temptation at all, finding *no* "difficulties," intellectual or other, to be a source of temptation, *or* they can be subjected not only to intellectual but also to other forms of probation. Whichever alternative is chosen, the special importance of intellectual probation falls away. Let us now go one step farther, however, and suppose that even this point can be answered, and that (despite what has been said) intellectual probation *is* a genuine possibility for the persons in question. It seems to me, finally, that Butler is wrong in thinking that the extraordinary individuals he describes could be put to the test in no *other* way, and thus that intellectual probation is in the end unnecessary even for them. In particular, it seems he underestimates the difficulties likely to be encountered by those who give themselves wholeheartedly to the life of faith. One who was undeterred by the "ordinary" temptation to neglect religion would surely, upon being apprised of its truth, seek to follow closely in the footsteps of its most exemplary practitioners, who continually perform supererogatory actions and sometimes give up life itself for the sake of others; and such a form of life could not be "easy" for *anyone*.

It seems, therefore, that Butler's argument does not go through. Given that intellectual probation would have side effects such as a loving God would seek, other things being equal, to avoid, and given that its possible good effects would be superfluous (i.e., given that other forms of probation, suitable for everyone, abound), God would surely not view its existence as having a value as great as the value of a strong epistemic situation in relation to theism, and so would not impose it on anyone.[15]

15. Perhaps it will be claimed that even if the *instrumental* value of intellectual probation is not comparatively very great, the choices it makes possible have great

There is another route to this conclusion, which, before moving on, I would like briefly to indicate. We have so far assumed that apparent doubtfulness in theistic evidence is necessary for intellectual probation—that, unlike moral probation of other sorts, intellectual probation is not compatible with a clear indication of God's existence. But this assumption may be challenged, and in two ways. The first retains the connection between intellectual probation and theistic evidence, and suggests that temptations with respect to this evidence would persist *even if* it supported a theistic conclusion. The second proposes a broadening of the notion of intellectual probation to allow for temptation arising with respect to evidence adduced in support of *other* important religious propositions.

Beginning with the first of these, we may note that its central claim is one we have already encountered several times in Part 2. This is Penelhum's point, that self-deception is possible even when good evidence for theism presents itself and that temptations to self-deception may therefore arise not only when the evidence is obscure but also when it is clear. In Penelhum's book on Butler, the point is made in the following ways:

> If we do have the freedom to respond or not to respond to the signs of God, this freedom exists if the signs are clear, as well as if they are not. It is very well known (and Butler, who says such wise things about self-deceit, certainly knows it) that people can ignore obvious facts, can fail to attend to what stares them in the face, and can invent, or eagerly grasp on to, difficulties that would not impress them at all if they were not biased against learning unwelcome truths. The very facts about us that make intellectual probation a

---

intrinsic value. There is value in free choices to pursue the good quite apart from the value of the improved character to which such choices may lead. But to this we must reply that the intrinsic value of such additional free choices surely does not exceed the intrinsic value of personal relationship with God. And *since*, as we have seen, God would value such relationship not *only* for the good—instrumental *or* noninstrumental—it would produce in the life of the believer, but also for its own sake, we must conclude that, all things considered, intellectual probation would not be viewed by God as facilitating a good as great as the good that would (apparently) need to be sacrificed in order to make it possible.

real possibility show that it could exist quite well, in all the forms Butler suggests for it, if the signs of God's presence were clear.[16]

> It is just mistaken to suppose that there are no moral tests involved in acknowledging a fact which we know for certain, as opposed to one which we judge to be merely probable. If the acknowledgement is a painful one, showing our failures and defects to the world, there are no limits to the ingenuity with which we will persuade ourselves that we do not know it after all, or will distract ourselves from paying attention to it.[17]

It seems, therefore, that even if God's existence were made more obvious—if, say, evidence sufficient for belief were made available—many of the choices with respect to theistic evidence listed earlier, namely, frivolous inattention, easy rejection, heedless negativity, serious scrutiny, lengthy reflection, and wrestling with doubt, would remain open to us. Theistic evidence would *continue* to be a source of intellectual temptation, and thus intellectual probation would still be possible: the bad choices mentioned would remain tempting for many and the good choices difficult.

Penelhum's argument succeeds, I think, in showing that many individuals would find theistic evidence to be a source of moral temptation even if its verdict were much clearer than it is. But what of those extraordinary individuals, described by Butler, who would happily begin the practice of religion if convinced of its truth? Surely they would be immune to the temptations outlined by Penelhum. Surely they would require evidence that could be *reasonably* doubted. Now it seems to me that the criticisms already given of Butler's claims with respect to these individuals suffice to show that, were they to exist, they would not require intellectual probation at all. But suppose that these objections can be answered. We may yet deploy the second criticism, mentioned above, of the view that doubtfulness in theistic evidence is necessary for intellectual probation. Returning to the distinction between the evidence of theism and the evidence of revelation, we can argue that apparent doubtfulness in theistic evidence is not required for intellectual probation because the evidence of *revelation*

16. Penelhum, *Butler*, p. 195.
17. Ibid., p. 197.

may appear doubtful, and hence may—if the notion of intellectual probation is suitably broadened—provide the basis for a fully satisfactory form of intellectual probation. There is no reason to suppose that if the question of God's existence has been settled, all related questions—such as whether God has in some way revealed himself and his purposes for humankind more fully—must also be settled: good evidence for God's existence may coexist with a *paucity* of evidence for revelatory claims.[18] But if the evidence relevant to such claims (e.g., the claim that God is revealed in Christ) may remain open to reasonable doubt, then even if the evidence for God's *existence* no longer is, we may still be put in a state of intellectual probation with respect to the truth of religion.[19] Therefore, even if there are individuals who require a stronger form of intellectual probation, this does not at all imply the need for apparent doubtfulness in theistic evidence.

Now perhaps one objection to this argument will be that if the individuals in question were provided with good evidence for God's existence, their motivation to pursue questions about a Divine revelation would be much greater—they would wish to know God's will in order to be in a position to conform their lives to it—and so the tests represented by such questions would be much less severe than I have suggested. But in claiming that these individuals *would* be tempted were the doubtful evidence *evidence concerning God's existence* and that they require such doubtfulness for probational purposes, the critic has in effect already conceded that they would not automatically do what they saw reason to do. (They would see that serious investigation of theistic evidence was called for but be tempted not to pursue it.) And so he cannot claim here that finding good reason to investigate the evidence of *revelation*, the individuals in question would have no desire to do otherwise. Since the only more general justification for this claim would seem

18. Some may wonder whether we are not committed by the terms of the argument developed in Part 1 to the claim that any evidence of revelation would also be clear. They are referred to the end of Chapter 1, where a response to this sort of objection is provided.

19. I assume that the evidence of revelation *may* remain open to reasonable doubt. If, as I have argued, God's *existence* may be reasonably doubted, this would seem to be true a fortiori with respect to more specific claims about God's action in the world.

to require the acceptance of arguments discussed in Chapter 5, which I have rejected, I suggest that it is an unsuccessful claim.[20]

In consequence of the arguments just given, we are, it seems, in a position to conclude once more that given its negative implications and the superfluity of its good effects, a loving God would not impose intellectual probation vis-à-vis theistic evidence on anyone.[21] Indeed, now we may claim that various forms of probation including intellectual probation would be *preserved* even if God's existence were beyond reasonable nonbelief. Butler's arguments therefore do not provide the rebuttal we require.[22]

20. In defense of this assessment, we may also call as witness the (unadapted) Butler, for he and his opponents *presupposed* the existence of God, and yet the difficulties in which the evidence of revelation is involved concerned them—in particular, were taken by Butler as providing intellectual probation. The fact that God's existence was already (in his opinion) well-evidenced did not in his view in any way lessen the value of the intellectual probation provided by doubtfulness in the evidence of *revelation*.

21. It may be claimed that questions about God's existence—about whether there is a religious reality *at all*—are far deeper and more serious than questions that presuppose the truth of the theistic claim, and so ones God would wish to be among those we are given the opportunity of investigating. For this reason, it may be said, it is a mistake to put both forms of investigation into the same category, as I have done. Investigation of God's existence would be viewed by God as the more valuable of the two. But I suggest it is not at all obvious that the investigations into religious matters we would be in a position to pursue were we in possession of strong evidence for God's existence and (perhaps) growing in relationship with God would be any less interesting, deep, serious, and so on, than the investigation of questions concerning God's existence. If we suppose there to be a God who is infinitely rich and inconceivably great, we may surmise that there is no limit to the number of interesting and fruitful religious investigations it is possible to pursue even after having satisfied ourselves that there is a God, and so that there is no way to legitimately judge, from our perspective, that one such investigation is significantly "deeper," more "serious," and so on, than another. Even if there *is* such a difference, however, I would claim that investigation of revelatory claims provides a *reasonable substitute* for theistic investigation, and that since the former investigation is compatible with theistic belief and the goods for which it is necessary, whereas the latter is not, we must view a loving God as preferring it, all things considered.

22. For an argument similar to Butler's, which defends an understanding of religious doubt as *trial*, see J. R. Lucas, "Doubt: A Sermon," in *Freedom and Grace* (London: SPCK, 1976), pp. 120–122. But Lucas also suggests an answer to this argument, construed as an argument against the prima facie case I have developed, namely, that the doubt in question may occur and have the desired effects *within the context* of a relationship with God, and so need not occur prior to its development. I look more closely at suggestions of this sort in the penultimate section of this chapter.

The Diversity Argument

I turn now to a very different response to our problem, which we may call the Diversity Argument.[23] It can be formulated as follows:

(1) Religious diversity is at least as great a good as the good God would sacrifice by allowing reasonable nonbelief to occur.

(2) Diversity in religion would be vastly reduced if our epistemic situation in relation to theism were a strong one.

(3) Therefore, it is plausible to suppose that God would not allow such a situation to obtain.

The term "religious diversity" which appears in this argument admits of at least two interpretations. It can be seen as referring to the actual concrete religious traditions (Judaism, Christianity, Islam, Buddhism, Hinduism, and so on) or to the free expression of religious imagination, creativity, and devotion, which (in their better moments) these traditions represent. We have, that is, the following alternative constructions of (1) and (2):

(1′) The existence of Judaism, Christianity, Islam, Buddhism, Hinduism, and other actual religious traditions is at least as great a good as the good God would sacrifice by allowing reasonable nonbelief to occur.

(2′) The map of the actually existing religious traditions would be greatly changed if our epistemic situation in relation to theism were a strong one.

(1″) The free expression of religious imagination, creativity, and devotion is at least as great a good as the good God would sacrifice by allowing reasonable nonbelief to occur.

(2″) The expression of creative religiousness would be greatly inhibited if our epistemic situation in relation to theism were a strong one.

We may begin by assessing the force of the second set of premises. As it seems to me, the most vulnerable member of this set is

23. I am grateful to Robert Adams for pointing out to me the possibility of such a response. The formulation of it that appears here is, however, my own.

(2″).[24] It is clear that religious diversity in its sense is exemplified at a (perhaps infinite) number of possible worlds. In particular, it is clearly exemplified at those possible worlds in which the epistemic situation of humans in relation to theism is a strong one. But if so, then (2″) is false, and this version of the Diversity Argument is unsuccessful.

Let us consider how this response can be developed. The claim to which it is opposed can be expressed as follows: "If a strong epistemic situation in relation to theism were to obtain, human religiousness would be reduced to a narrow and stifling uniformity." Unless some such claim can be shown to be true or plausibly viewed as true, we have no reason to be deterred by (2″). But it seems to me that all such claims are false. We may note, first of all, that what is likely to follow from God presenting himself to the experience of all individuals capable of recognizing him in the manner described in Chapter 2 is not a uniform pattern of religiousness, but rather patterns of religious life that are (at one level at least) *compatible*, united under a common acceptance of God as personal and loving. Even this may be saying too much. For if humans would remain free to reject God, as I have argued they would, there would presumably remain the possibility of religious beliefs and practices *in*compatible *at all levels* with traditions built up on the experience of God, resulting directly or indirectly from the rejection of that experience by some individual(s) at some point in time. Suppose, however, that the "compatibility" claim *is* one to which the critic of the Diversity Argument is committed. (2″) is still false; for compatibility of the sort in question does not rule out diversity. Even within a *particular* tradition such as Christianity, where the various denominations are united not only under a common acceptance of God as personal and loving, but also under a common acceptance of Jesus of Nazareth as in some sense revelatory of God, there is room for diversity—for the expression of creative religiousness. To take but the most obvious example: even though all denominations make some connection between "Jesus" and "God," the connection is not by any means the same in all

24. I will assume here that (1″) is true. Religious diversity in its sense can be viewed as *intrinsically* valuable or as having value for the sort of reason discussed in Chapter 5.

cases. Indeed, disputes rage. This suggests that, were a strong epistemic situation in relation to theism to obtain, religious diversity (in the sense in question) would not at all be ruled out. Quite the contrary. If the object of the experiences in question were indeed the inexhaustibly rich source of existence, we would expect traditions that arose on the basis of such experiences to (potentially) reflect this richness.[25] While a certain direction might be given to religious creativity, creativity could hardly be restricted in any important sense. (And if such direction would not prevent diversity, its presence should be seen as an *advantage* of the situation in question, rendering it preferable, all things considered, to the actual situation; for creative *chaos* is surely not the religious ideal.) When all of this is taken into account, it seems clear that where "religious diversity" is understood as in (1″) and (2″), the Diversity Argument fails.

Can a more favorable judgment be rendered if the premises of the Diversity Argument are (1′) and (2′) instead of (1″) and (2″)? It seems to me that the answer must again be a negative one. Here the problem is not the second premise but the first. It is not the second because it is likely that any world in which a strong epistemic situation in relation to theism obtained would be one in which the map of the religious traditions was different. If God had always followed a policy of presenting himself to the experience of individuals capable of recognizing him, then (it is likely) various traditions now existing would not have arisen and/or various traditions *not* now existing *would* have arisen (and/or various traditions now existing would have existed in different form). Such an important input into the religious life of humankind would surely have had some effect.

Let us assume on the basis of this consideration that (2′) is true. What is to prevent us from accepting (1′) as well and declaring the argument sound? In response to this it can be argued, first of all, that (1′) would appear to derive any plausibility it has from (1″). If the actual religious traditions have value, it is because they in some way instantiate the free expression of religious imagination, cre-

---

25. In line with this point, we should recall what was mentioned in Chapter 2, that in the situation in question there would be nothing preventing individuals from having experiences apparently of God of other sorts.

ativity, and so forth. But then, given that there are various possible traditions that might have existed instead and that might also have instantiated religious creativity, including religious traditions compatible with a strong epistemic situation in relation to theism, and given the extra value we must associate with traditions of the latter sort, we must surely conclude that the existence of the actual religious traditions is *not* as great a good as the good their existence precludes, and so that (1′) is false.

Perhaps it will be replied that Judaism, Christianity, and other religious traditions are valuable not just in the sense of the preceding paragraph but also in an *instrumental* sense, constituting (to appropriate a Christian term) important "means of grace" for their adherents. But surely we must answer, again, that many other possible traditions, had they existed instead, would have performed the same function. In particular, if God exists and all experiences of grace are ultimately traceable to his benevolence, then, as I have argued, possible situations in which the religious life of humankind and explicit belief in God's existence are more closely linked than in ours must be ones in which the grace of God is more readily appropriated. For these reasons and the reasons given above, I conclude that (1′), which implies that God might wish the religious life of humankind to be just as it is, is false. The argument from (1′) and (2′) is therefore no more successful than the argument from (1″) and (2″), and so the Diversity Argument fails.

Reasonable Nonbelief and Actual Existents

An argument in some ways related to the second version of the Diversity Argument but sufficiently independent to warrant separate treatment can be derived from Robert Adams's essay "Existence, Self-Interest, and the Problem of Evil."[26] In this essay, Adams argues, following Leibniz, that we owe our existence to past evils:

> I could not have existed without past evils that have profoundly affected the course of human history, and especially the "combina-

26. Robert Adams, "Existence, Self-Interest, and the Problem of Evil," chap. 5 in *The Virtue of Faith* (New York: Oxford University Press, 1987).

tions of . . . people and marriages." . . . A multiplicity of interacting chances, including evils great and small, affect which people mate, which gametes find each other, and which children come into being. The farther back we go in history, the larger the proportion of evils to which we owe our being; for the causal nexus relevant to our individual genesis widens as we go back in time. We almost certainly would never have existed had there not been just about the same evils as actually occurred in a large part of human history.[27]

Adams claims that it follows from this that "God has not wronged *us* in causing or permitting those evils, if he is going to see to it that we will have lives that are worth living on the whole. What right could I have against satisfying the necessary conditions of my coming to be, and how could I be injured by satisfying them, if my life will be worth living?"[28] On Adams's view, this argument makes a significant contribution to theodicy, for if all those who claim they have been wronged by God in fact owe their *existence* to the evils God has allowed (and live a reasonably good life), the possibility of justified complaint would seem largely ruled out.

Critics of the case developed in Part 1 who are impressed by this argument will wish to argue by analogy as follows: "If it were not for the fact that God has *not* always followed a policy of presenting himself to the experience of all human beings capable of recognizing him, we—that is, the actually existing human beings, including those constructing and evaluating this argument—would very likely not have come into existence. The absence of such an important input into the life of humankind, though it may seem regrettable, has in fact affected 'the course of human history' (including especially the religious life of humankind) and (consequently) the 'combinations of . . . people and marriages'; and we would almost certainly not have existed had things been otherwise." Since we are referring here to an alleged evil of omission rather than an evil of commission, this point is perhaps more naturally put the other way around: "Had God always *followed* the policy in question, we would likely not have come into existence. For such an important input would have affected the 'combinations of . . . people and

27. Ibid., p. 66.
28. Ibid., p. 67.

marriages,' resulting in the existence of human beings other than ourselves." Either way, the conclusion which may seem to follow is that since the evil of which we complain is in fact a necessary condition of our existence, God cannot be said to have wronged us in preventing a strong epistemic situation in relation to theism from obtaining.

I find this argument unsatisfactory for more than one reason. I have argued (in Chapter 1) that what a perfectly loving God would do cannot in all cases be determined by considering what are his obligations. Thus, even if nothing which it would be wrong of God to allow happens to me, difficulties may remain. But let us set these on one side. It seems to me that the argument is in much deeper trouble than this. As we have seen, Adams states that the problem of evil must be understood in terms of God having (allegedly) *wronged* us. This suggests that the alternative which the one who argues from evil has in mind is a situation in which she (or some other individual) is *not wronged*. On this view, the arguer is claiming, in effect: "If God existed, I would exist and suffer no evil of this kind." But this claim entails that a situation in which God exists and does no wrong is one in which *the existence of the complaining individual* is preserved. It is for this reason that Adams's argument seems so effective. For if, as he claims, these evils must exist if the arguer is to exist, then the arguer is not in a position to claim that God would bring about a situation in which she exists and suffers no evil. The situation she is saying God might be expected to bring about is in fact impossible.

Adams's (apparent) view of the position of one who argues from evil is mistaken, however. It is mistaken, first of all, in supposing the following claim to be coherent: "God exists and has wronged me."[29] If, as Adams assumes, God is essentially perfectly good and so cannot wrong anyone, this claim is in fact *in*coherent. Furthermore, why would anyone seeking to argue from evil to the nonexistence of God make *this* claim? It is, after all, a claim entailing that God exists. Perhaps Adams would reply that what he assumes to be coherent and attributes to his arguer is not this, but rather

29. Adams suggests his acceptance of the coherence of this claim by arguing against it at length.

something like: "An evil has befallen me which it would be wrong of God to allow." But if this is the arguer's claim, it does not entail that a situation in which God exists and does no wrong is one in which the arguer's existence is preserved. On this interpretation of her claim, the arguer may, indeed, allow that if there were a God, other human beings would exist *instead* of her.

My point here can perhaps be made clearer if we bring to bear the distinction between de re and de dicto readings of propositions. Consider the following proposition:

> (4) If there were a God, all human beings would live a life unblemished by evil *e*.

Adams's arguer appears to accept a de re reading of this proposition, expressible as follows:

> (5) If there were a God, all human beings (that is, all of the human beings who *actually exist*) would live a life unblemished by *e*.

I have suggested, however, that the arguer from evil need not claim this much. What she may accept instead is the following de dicto reading of the proposition in question:

> (6) If there were a God, all human beings (that is, all existing human beings, *whoever* they might be) would live a life unblemished by *e*.

If (5) is true, then, if God exists, I exist. But the same need not be said about (6), and so (6) is not subject to Adams's criticism. Having noted this, we can now consider:

> (7) Josie Bloggs (a human being who actually exists) lives a life blemished by *e*.

This proposition brings us back once more within the ambit of the de re. But it is important to note that while it clearly follows from (7) and (5) that there is no God, the same conclusion follows from (7) and *(6)*. That is, *actual* suffering can count against the existence of a perfectly good God even if in a world created by such a God, the sufferer would not have existed. Josie Bloggs, as suggested above, need not exist for God to exist, and so she need not be among the human beings mentioned by (6) who would come into existence and live a life unblemished by *e* if there were a God. But if Josie Bloggs *does* exist, it follows from (6) that unless she lives a life unblemished by *e*, God does not exist. To put it another way: if (6) is true, God does not coexist with human beings who live lives blemished by *e*, and so if Josie Bloggs's life is blemished by *e*, God does not coexist with Josie Bloggs. We can therefore recommend to the arguer that she choose a proposition like (6) to express her claim; she clearly is not limited to propositions like (5).

The application of this reasoning to the problem of inculpable nonbelief should be apparent. The one who argues from the reasonableness of nonbelief claims that

> (8) If there were a God, the epistemic situation of human beings in relation to theism would be a strong one.

He means by this, not the de re proposition,

> (9) If there were a God, the epistemic situation in relation to theism of *actually* existing human beings would be a strong one,

but rather the de dicto proposition,

> (10) If there were a God, the epistemic situation in relation to theism of existing human beings, *whoever* they might be, would be a strong one.

This, however, does not prevent him from adducing as a further premise the de re proposition,

> (11) The epistemic situation in relation to theism of the human beings who actually exist is not a strong one,

and deriving

> (12) God does not exist.

For although the human beings who actually exist need *not* exist for God to exist, and so need not be among the human beings mentioned by (10) who would come into being and benefit from a strong epistemic situation if there were a God, if they *do* exist, it follows from (10) that unless their epistemic situation is a strong one, God does not exist. As (10) states, God and human beings in a weak epistemic situation do not coexist, and so if actual human beings exist in such a situation, God and *actual human beings* do not coexist.

If this is correct, the Adams-type objection can be easily circumvented. For then anyone can consistently claim both that the situation of reasonable nonbelief in which she finds herself poses a problem of evil, and that, had things been otherwise, she would not have existed.

Perhaps it will be replied to my argument that I have missed the point of the Adams article. Adams's point, it may be said, is that if we consider our existence to be on the whole a good thing, the fact that conditions *necessary* for our existence have been satisfied must also be viewed by us as a good thing, even if the satisfying of those conditions can be seen by us to have involved the occurrence of what is in itself evil. But to this it seems right to respond by saying that the existence of individuals who would have come into being had these evils not occurred and the necessary conditions of our existence not been satisfied might *also* have been a great good. Indeed, where the evil in question is the existence of reasonable nonbelief, the well-being achievable by them would have been much greater than the well-being that actually existing individuals are in a position to achieve. Would not God then have preferred their existence to ours?

But a response to Adams need not rest on this point alone. (If it did, it might be weakened by his claim that "God could be perfectly good and . . . cause or permit *evils* that are necessary for good ends that he loves, even if those goods are not the best states of affairs obtainable by him."[30]) We can point out, in addition, the value God (if he exists) places on personal relationship *for its own sake*. Adams speaks of the creatures God creates as creatures he *loves*, but as the discussion in Part 1 indicates, if God loves, then the creatures he creates will (for reasons of well-being *and* the intrinsic value of personal relationship) exist in the presence of evidence sufficient for belief, other things being equal. And as an attempt to fill out this ceteris paribus clause, Adams's argument seems inadequate. It provides a good to compete with the good of personal relationship with God only if our existence would have some special value that the existence of individuals in a better position, epistemically, to relate personally to God would not have. But it seems that this condition is not satisfied: there seems no reason for God, in advance of our existing, to decide in favor of *us* and attempt to steer things our way.[31] Indeed, Adams himself veers from his chosen course at the last moment. After having suggested that God might well have wished to bring *us* into being, and so permitted the evils in question, he writes: "I am suggesting, in effect, that the existence of *creatures such as we are*, with the characteristic, subtle, and sometimes bittersweet values and beauties of human life, may also be a good of the relevant sort that is loved by God" (my emphasis).[32] But if in the end Adams wishes to say only "creatures such as we are," as apparently he does, and as it seems he *ought* to do, then his whole argument collapses. For no reasons have been given or could be provided for supposing that exactly those evils that have occurred are necessary for the existence of creatures such as we are; only for supposing they are necessary for *our* existence. And if creatures other than ourselves but such as we are could be as valuable as ourselves—as surely we must admit— then given all the points made above, we must conclude that there is here no rebuttal for the argument of Part 1.

---

30. Adams, *Virtue of Faith*, p. 72.

31. Indeed, the view suggested here seems slightly absurd. While it is one thing to speak of the various evils with which history is littered as necessary conditions of our existence, it is another altogether to claim that God has allowed these evils with a view to bringing us—the humans beings who actually exist—into being.

32. Adams, *Virtue of Faith*, p. 72.

The Responsibility Argument

An explanation of reasonable nonbelief in terms of the value of human responsibility has not been explicitly developed by anyone. But the possibility of such an explanation is suggested by certain passages in the literature and so must be considered. Swinburne, for example, writes that "a God has reasons for creating a world in which humanly free agents have deep responsibility for each other—provided by the opportunity to harm each other in various ways, e.g. by curtailing each other's knowledge, freedom and power, and the opportunity to benefit each other in converse ways."[33] Swinburne gives special emphasis to the view that it is good that humans have the power not just to benefit but also to harm:

> A world in which agents can benefit each other but not do each other harm is one where they have only very limited responsibility for each other. . . . [If] I cannot harm you, you will be moderately all right whatever I do. Your well-being will not then depend greatly on me. God has reason for going beyond that. A God who gave agents only such limited responsibility for their fellows would not have given much.[34]

Taking these points into account, the critic may once again proceed by analogy and suggest that there may well be opportunities to harm or benefit which require for their existence that some individuals for some period of time be (or possibly come to be) in a state of reasonable nonbelief.[35] We must now look at how such a suggestion could be filled out.

(i) The most obvious development of this suggestion would in-

---

33. Swinburne, *Existence of God*, pp. 190–191.

34. Ibid., p. 189. There is an obvious connection between Swinburne's points about responsibility and his "choice of destiny" arguments: emphasized here are deep and significant *choices* affecting other human beings. In more recent writing Swinburne more explicitly connects the two discussions, referring to the value of a "free and responsible choice of destiny." See his "Knowledge from Experience, and the Problem of Evil," in William J. Abraham and Steven W. Holtzer, eds., *The Rationality of Religious Belief* (Oxford: Clarendon Press, 1987), p. 154.

35. The nature of the alternative state of affairs suggested here will be clarified when we come to the second form of the Responsibility Argument.

volve the claim that it is a good thing that some individuals be in a
state of reasonable nonbelief so that others, more favored in this
respect, are given the opportunity to benefit or harm them by providing them with evidence sufficient for belief, or else failing to do
so. In providing some human beings with this opportunity, God
gives to them a deep responsibility for the well-being of their fel-
lows. He gives to them the power to assist them toward a personal
relationship with God, and all that entails, or to leave them in ignorance of God's existence; and it is a good thing that such responsibility be given.

But this explanation has an air of unreality about it. For it to
succeed, the opportunity in question must be one that some human
beings in our world in fact have, and if they are to have it, they
must be possessed of evidence that *clearly* supports God's existence
and that honest inquirers will *see* to support God's existence.[36] But
this does not seem to be the case. The evidence that various individuals have claimed to provide support for God's existence is often evidence that inculpable nonbelievers who fail to believe even
after long investigation and soul-searching have considered. Thus,
even if there is a God, the evidence of those who believe in him is
not clearly such as to render plausible the view that they have the
responsibility in question.

Despite this problem, let us suppose that there exists the possibility of responsibility of a sort. Perhaps some inculpable nonbelievers would have evidence sufficient for belief if they heard
what believers could tell them, even if others would not. The question we must then face is whether it is plausible to suppose that a
loving God would consider the value of the responsibility given to
convinced theists by the presence of inculpable nonbelief to be
great enough to allow it to occur.

One point which suggests itself is that since our world is one in
which human beings clearly already *have* great responsibility for
each other's well-being, and since giving this spiritual form of re-

36. For surely, if God deprives *A* of evidence so that *B* can have the opportunity
of benefiting or harming *A* by bringing evidence to him or failing to do so, it is to
be expected that the evidence *B* is actually in a position to give *A* will be strong;
otherwise there is no sense in the supposition that *B* is in a position to *benefit* or
harm A.

sponsibility to some would prevent others from gaining access to God, a loving God might be expected to refrain from giving this additional responsibility. The claims of Swinburne and others about the value of responsibility are large claims even when (as is usually the case) claims about the value of spiritual responsibility are not seen as entailed by them. Because this is so, and because of the value that would go unrealized if God gave to some this further responsibility, special reasons for supposing God to value it seem clearly required.

We can go farther as well. For, having noted the many forms of deep responsibility we have independently of the responsibility in question, it may seem to us that a loving God would not wish to withdraw his presence to facilitate additional responsibilities, but would in fact wish to do the opposite: because the responsibilities we have are so great, God, like a good parent, would wish to make it possible for us to draw on the resources of a personal relationship with him, in order to better enable us to *fulfill* our responsibilities.

To these arguments it may be replied that according to the explanation in question, the human beings to whom this extra responsibility is given are ones who *have* become to some extent aware of God's presence and who therefore *are* in a position to relate personally to God and to draw on the resources provided by such relationship: those who are asked to share their evidence of God's presence with others must, logically, first have it themselves. But it is hard to see how this point mitigates the difficulties faced by the proponent of the Responsibility Argument. Let us look once more at the responses outlined above. I have suggested (in the second response) that a personal relationship with God would help us *successfully manage* our responsibilities. I have not suggested that it would make things *easy*; unless the arguments of Chapter 5 can be successfully refuted, such a suggestion cannot be upheld. Thus, even the individuals who according to the Responsibility Argument *are* given access to God cannot be viewed as finding life unchallenging; far from it. And of course, either way, those who inculpably fail to believe and so do *not* have such access must be viewed as lacking an important resource. We can therefore argue as follows. Since, even in the absence of the extra responsibility suggested as appropriate for them by the Responsibility Argument, very considerable responsibility-related challenges would remain for humans given access to God, and since, were this responsibility given to them, others would be prevented from experiencing such relationship and would suffer the lack of an important resource for the fulfilling of *their* responsibilities, a loving God would *not* consider the value of the responsibility given to convinced theists by the presence of inculpable nonbelief to be great enough to warrant allowing it to occur.

Other points can be adduced in support of this conclusion. First of all, as was suggested in the discussion of Butler, even if all human beings were to arrive at belief in a loving God, their understanding of God and of his relation to the world would remain imperfect, and so some of what they had yet to learn might well be specially revealed by God. If God were to reveal himself further in this way, then even if he wished to give to some human beings additional spiritual responsibilities, he would not need to deprive anyone of evidence for belief in his existence but could instead leave it up to certain individuals historically and geographically well-placed (and evidentially well-fortified!) whether the *special revelation* became generally known or not.[37]

It seems to me that there are reasons for supposing that, given a choice, a loving God would in fact *prefer* to tie the spiritual responsibilities of human beings to the dissemination of a special revelation. For one thing, as I noted in Chapter 2, perhaps the most religiously efficacious way of coming to believe in the existence of a loving God is through one's own experience; and so if there is a God, we have some reason to suppose that he would provide human beings with experiential evidence of his existence. Of course, once the experiential foundation, so to speak, was laid, a variety of ways of growing in spiritual understanding, of building on that foundation, might be appropriate and religiously efficacious, including ways associated with the communications of *other* human

37. And given that God's existence was well-evidenced, no one would be in a position to claim that God should, for reasons of personal relationship, have made this special information available to everyone. For as I have argued, personal relationship with God is to be *developmentally* understood, and belief in God's existence is sufficient to enter upon such relationship.

beings in contact with God. To put this point another way: there is some reason to suppose that a loving God would wish to provide evidence for belief in his existence directly, not through some human intermediary; for otherwise the acceptance of evidence would perhaps not be as likely to evoke a personal response, and further information about God, however provided, would not be as readily assimilated and spiritually appropriated. A second reason to suppose that God would prefer to tie the spiritual responsibilities of human beings to the dissemination of a special revelation is that it is possible (some would say likely) that many human beings would *fail* in their spiritual responsibilities, or that the fulfillment of these responsibilities would be long delayed. Taking this into account, a loving God would surely wish those for whom others had been made spiritually responsible to be provided with *some* basis for communion with himself in the interim—a more general knowledge of God's existence and loving nature which would allow them to experience at any rate some of the benefits associated with a personal relationship with God.

Much of what I have said about general and special revelation and human responsibility for dissemination of the latter matches traditional Christian thinking about God's self-revelation and the nature of the missionary task. It will be noted, however, that on the traditional view, the all-important message of God's love and forgiveness is not a part of the general revelation but is intimately connected to the story of Christ. And so it may seem that my distinction between the two notions is incorrectly drawn. Indeed, it may seem that since the evidence for God's existence I have been mentioning is evidence for the existence of a perfectly *loving* God, there is really no distinction left at all: what I am asking for *includes* the special revelation of Christianity (or at least its major theme), and so there is no "further revelation" for me to appeal to as an alternative source of spiritual responsibility.

To this I would reply by saying that I have been describing what seems to be the policy a perfectly loving God would pursue, and if this conflicts with traditional Christian thinking, so be it: traditional Christian thinking on these matters may be internally inconsistent. The message of a God of love Christians have (in the actual world) tried to convey has sometimes not taken root in the experience of those to whom it was delivered because other concepts had taken root instead. If there *were* a loving God, things would, it seems, be otherwise; then, surely, this message would *precede* the missionaries. Does this mean that there would be nothing left for missionaries to convey? Would there then be no filling out of the general revelation to which various individuals could contribute? It seems not. In such a situation we might still, for example, be able to speak of the responsibility of some to bring to others the news of one who wonderfully *exemplified* the agapeistic character of God, who provided the basis for a community of love in the body of his teachings. And even leaving aside the traditional Christian connection between a fuller knowledge of God and the person of Christ, we could speak of the responsibility of those who had experienced God's presence and grown in interpersonal relationship and in relationship with God to seek to enter into dialogue with members of other communities and share their experiences and the fruits of their spiritual labors. In this way *all* human beings could (potentially) have spiritual responsibilities. We could go farther still and suggest that if, as has been argued, some humans might very well reject the evidence for God's existence with which they were provided, inculpable nonbelief need not exist in order for humans to have "missionary" responsibilities. If belief could be rejected, there would be opportunity for others who did not reject it to admonish, exhort, awaken, or else fail to do so. There would be nonbelief for believers to address, even if not *inculpable* nonbelief.

Given these points, we may add to the previous argument (which is, I think, sufficient in itself to defeat this form of the Responsibility Argument) the claim that various forms of spiritual responsibility would in fact be *facilitated* by a strong epistemic situation in relation to theism. Not only do humans have many forms of deep responsibility. If God were self-disclosed, certain others would be added to the list. There is therefore no reason to suppose that a loving God would for reasons of human *responsibility* deprive anyone of awareness of his presence. The value he would realize in so doing would be far less great than the value he would give up.

(ii) A second version of the Responsibility Argument can also be developed. It claims that humans have been given responsibility for the spiritual well-being of *future generations*, and that some or all present-day cases of inculpable nonbelief are due to past abuses of this responsibility. Bad human choices over time—in particular, the choices of humans to rebel against God and to reject the good evidence given them by God—have gradually reduced the level of religious awareness, resulting ultimately in a secular society in which exist human beings who have never seen any need to attend to the possibility of a religious dimension, beings who find the idea of God alien, foreign, even ridiculous and so (in many cases at least) inculpably fail to believe that there is a God. In theological terms, this is the view that some of those who fail through no fault of their own to believe in God are nonetheless inhibited by sin in the (indirect) sense that they have inherited (biologically and/or culturally) and now express involuntarily dispositions and values inimical to belief.

In responding to this form of the argument, we may once again wish to point out the difficulties faced by the one defending the empirical claim on which it depends, namely (in this case), that at some time in the past, humans had in their possession good evidence of the sort in question. It is unclear how we are to be led to the conclusion that this claim is plausible. If it is plausible, it must be plausible to suppose that there was a time when inculpable nonbelief was impossible. But there seems no non-question-begging way to defend this view; that is, it seems that any such view depends on the prior assumption of (at least) the plausibility of supposing God to exist, an assumption the argument of this book (to which the Responsibility Argument is a response!) casts into question. For the empirical evidence seems to provide no reason to suppose that there have not always been individuals who have inculpably denied the existence of God or remained agnostic or unreflectively failed to believe, and so seems to provide no reason to suppose that evidence of the required sort has *ever* been generally available. Furthermore, in this case it will not suffice to say that at any rate *some* individuals at some time knew of considerations that, although not obviously good evidence, would have constituted evidence sufficient for belief for *someone or other* in a future generation. If the evidence human beings had in their possession was not such as *no one* could inculpably reject, there is the clear possibility of arguing that the present decline in belief is due

to the judgments *upon careful investigation* of certain individuals at
certain times that the evidence available to them was not support-
ive of belief. And from this it follows that it is clearly possible that
individuals *have* always passed on the considerations that seemed to
them good evidence, but that reasonable nonbelief arose *despite*
this, which is to say that humans never had the responsibility in
question, for it was not in their power to ensure that individuals in
the next generation would not reasonably fail to believe: despite
their best efforts, reasonable nonbelief might come to exist. I conclude, therefore, that there are serious difficulties in the way of
showing that the empirical claim in question is plausible. But if it is
not plausible, then the argument to which it belongs does not constitute a rebuttal.

We can argue not only that the claims of the second version of
the Responsibility Argument seem not to square with the facts, but
also that there is reason to suppose that the facts on which it depends would not be *permitted* to obtain by a loving God. Humans
already have deep responsibilities for the well-being of future generations and regularly abuse them.[38] If future generations exist, we
will have wronged them in many ways, for example, in our obses-
sive concern for material goods, leading to poor management of
the fragile environment in which they will live. Given the deep
responsibilities we already have and our propensity to abuse them,
a loving God, concerned to enter into personal relationship with
human beings of all generations, recognizing the difficulties humans of all generations must face, would, we might expect, not
give us the further responsibility in question. It is important to
note that nothing in this argument implies that the human beings
to whom God reveals himself *in each generation* should not be in a
position to reject God and a personal relationship with him *for
themselves*; by granting humans freedom, God makes it possible for

38. This fact is the one we must emphasize in response to those who would
claim that the opportunity to prevent others from coming to believe that there is a
God constitutes a much *deeper* and therefore much more valuable form of responsibility than those here mentioned. It *would* be a great responsibility. But the harm
that might well—and I should say, would *probably*—result, would be commen-
surately great, and so I suggest a perfectly loving God, concerned not only to give
human beings responsibility, but also to enter into personal relationship with
them, would rest content with giving other responsibilities.

them to reject him. But by the same token, it seems that a loving God would not give anyone the opportunity to put others in a position where neither explicit acceptance *nor* explicit rejection is possible. God, if he exists, is concerned to make it possible for each human being, at all times at which she or he exists and is capable, to be personally related to himself, and will, other things being equal, see to it that this is the case, unless *that individual* chooses otherwise. Given the deep responsibilities humans could have even given such a strong epistemic situation in relation to theism, the second version of the Responsibility Argument does not seem to me to be capable of adducing considerations strong enough to off-set this concern.

We may conclude this section with the following observation. There is a tendency among some writers to value the giving of freedom and responsibility almost limitlessly: their view seems to be that if having some of these commodities is a good thing, then more must always be better. But this is to forget that the context for all theistic talk about these matters must be the love of God, and that love not only grants freedom and responsibility, but desires personal relationship. A balanced view, it seems, must allow for the realization of the *relational* aspirations of love, *if* their realization is compatible (as I believe it clearly is) with the giving of much freedom and responsibility. Because of the nature of Divine love, we may expect to find ourselves with freedom and responsibility, but by the same token, not in unlimited measure.

The Cognitive Benefits of Doubt

Most of the counterarguments we have considered suggest that the cognitive deprivation represented by the reasonableness of non-belief is tolerated by God for the sake of some *noncognitive* good, such as moral freedom or deep responsibility.[39] The argument taken up in this section chooses a different tack. It focuses on the reasonableness of doubt, suggesting that the deprivation it represents facilitates certain *cognitive* benefits: inculpable doubt, although

39. I say "most" because Kierkegaard's Deception Argument, inasmuch as it suggests that reasonable nonbelief would ward off *false beliefs* about God, can be construed as referring to cognitive benefits.

it can be seen as depriving one of proper access to God, can also be seen as creative of a fuller, deeper, more perfect understanding of God and of God's relation to the world.

This argument can be filled out as follows: "Inculpable doubt involves a careful probing of issues surrounding the proposition(s) over which one is in doubt. In the case of theism, doubt—if inculpable—will result in a deeper understanding of the claim that there is a God, and of the nature and proper conduct of the religious life. The reasonable doubter, through long thinking combined with deep religious concern, will clarify to herself (and perhaps also to others) the meaning of such propositions as 'God is good,' 'God is loving,' and so forth, and as a result of her investigations, will grow to appreciate more fully the character and potential depth of the life of faith. There is consequently a sense in which, even in the midst of doubt, one may be coming to know God better. Though as doubters we may complain that our knowledge of God is restricted, were God to reveal himself to us, we would have to say that we knew him better than we otherwise could have; the personal relationship with God into which we would then enter would not have been *hindered* by our (previous) doubt but would be the fuller and the richer for it. We have reason, therefore, to suppose that God would wish inculpable doubt to obtain, and so have reason to suppose that if there is a God, a strong epistemic situation in relation to theism will *not* obtain."

This is an interesting argument. Unlike many of the others I have considered, it addresses directly the central difficulty represented by the reasonableness of nonbelief, namely, its relationship-inhibiting effects, and seeks to show that these can be *mitigated.* Although it cannot be argued that while in a state of doubt the doubter enters fully into personal relationship with God, the results of her sojourn in the wilderness can be seen as contributing directly to such a relationship by providing her with the deeper understanding of spiritual things required for its flourishing. She may arrive at a more adequate conception of the religious life *just because* she is barred from fully entering into it herself. It may seem, therefore, that we have here a good that God would wish to facilitate even at the cost of the goods for which belief is required. Indeed, it may seem that no real sacrifice would be incurred; for until a deeper grasp of spiritual things is acquired, there can be no significant progress in the Divine-human relationship and so no real movement toward the benefits of such relationship outlined in Chapter 1.

Must we say then that the argument from the cognitive benefits of doubt is successful? Does it provide a rebuttal for the argument of Part 1? It seems to me that despite what has been said, the answer must once again be a negative one; although of considerable interest, this argument ultimately fails.

Let me begin my defense of this claim by pointing out that in order for the argument to succeed, reasonable doubt must be plausibly viewed as not just sufficient, but *necessary*, for the benefits to which it refers. Even if God would value the deeper understanding in question, if it could be achieved in other ways, he would not (for reasons the reader should by now be able to supply) for its sake subject anyone to doubt. But this condition does not seem to be satisfied; reasonable doubt is apparently unnecessary for such a deeper understanding. Although it involves a careful probing of relevant issues, such investigation may also be the result of, for example, experiences apparently of God. Surely many of those who would experience God if our epistemic situation were in relevant respects improved would be motivated by their experience to seek to know God more fully and to explore the various possibilities of the religious life. They would begin in a relationship with God *and* grow in it. And so it seems that although there will be progress in relationship with God only if one is developing a deeper grasp of spiritual things, and although reasonable doubt may facilitate this, the further claim that *without* doubt the relationship must stagnate cannot be upheld. Many would be properly motivated by an experience of God, and so a sacrifice would indeed be incurred if belief were postponed.

But it is possible for the proponent of the argument under consideration to make his claim more clear and precise, and so (apparently) to avoid this difficulty. It is indeed "many," he may say, who would be prompted by their experience of God to embark upon a deeper quest, and not "all." There are also individuals who would take God and their experience of God largely or completely for granted and settle down into an undemanding and relatively shallow religious life; and it is only to such individuals that the argument from the cognitive benefits of doubt applies. In *their* case a period of investigation motivated by doubt is plausibly viewed as essential to the achievement of the benefits in question, and in *their* case no real sacrifice would be incurred if belief were to be postponed.

This qualified version of the argument faces a serious problem, however. For it would seem that the individuals in question, if likely to respond inappropriately—in particular, without religious zeal—to experiences apparently of God, could hardly be relied on to conscientiously investigate the question of God's existence in the *absence* of such experience. Inculpable doubt, which requires careful investigation, clearly implies just the sort of attentiveness and concern for the truth which the individuals in question are said to lack. And if it is replied that doubt about God, unlike experience *of* God, motivates to inquiry, we may point out that such doubt commonly already involves a measure of religious concern. If the individuals in question really would settle into spiritual indifference upon experiencing God, we would expect (in the absence of clear evidence for God's existence) to find them not among the doubters but in the company of unreflective nonbelievers, and so would not expect them to be reaping any cognitive benefits of the relevant sort at all. The proponent of the (clarified) argument therefore faces a dilemma from which his argument apparently cannot escape unscathed: either the individuals in question would not in fact benefit from the absence of clear evidence, because inclined to be apathetic and religiously unconcerned, or (if they *are* alert and concerned) they do not require an interval of doubt, because likely to be sufficiently motivated to inquiry by religious experience.

But perhaps the proponent of the (clarified) argument will reply by suggesting that it is *presumption* that is at issue—presumption of the sort likely sometimes to be inspired by religious experience, even in individuals who would otherwise (in particular, if in doubt) pursue careful investigation. But if this is the sort of reasoning on which the argument depends, we are back to considerations dealt with in Chapter 6. In effect, a version of Pascal's Presumption Argument is then being deployed to defend the view that doubt may be necessary in some cases: growth in spiritual understanding, it is suggested, is incompatible with the sort of presumptuousness sometimes exhibited by those who have been granted proximity to God. If, however, the Pascalian's moves fail in Chapter 6, they cannot be revived here. Humility is at least as likely to be the human response to religious experience as presumption, and religious humility is a close ally of investigative zeal. In any case, God would not seek to predict our likely response and prevent all situations in which inappropriate responses might occur, but would allow us an explicit choice with respect to relationship with himself and respect our decision, working within the parameters it established.

This response is greatly strengthened by a fourth, very powerful, consideration available to the critic of the argument from the cognitive benefits of doubt as clarified above. Suppose that what is in fact quite unlikely is shown to be plausible, namely, that individuals exist who would be properly motivated to religious inquiry in the absence of clear evidence, but who would settle into presumption if granted proximity to God. We may yet point out that there is a sort of Divine withdrawal that is compatible with a strong epistemic situation in relation to theism. What I have in mind here is analogous to a state often referred to as "the dark night of the soul"—a sense of God's absence which severely tests the believer's faith and, in particular, works against the sort of easy assurance and presumption in question.[40] God may for a time leave the believer in relative darkness, intending this to result in doubts, even if not in doubt, that is, intending the believer to be troubled by questions that shake her confidence and motivate her to examine more closely the content of her belief.[41] And surely such a pe-

40. Such an interruption in the experience of God's presence need not result in inculpable doubt because it is not necessary to lose evidence sufficient for belief in order to be so tested. Although it may seem that if the primary evidence of God's existence is experiential, I must always sense God's presence in order always to have evidence sufficient for belief, this is not the case. I may be forced to depend on *past* experience, to remain true to it; and this past experience, together with the past and present experience of others and nonexperiential evidence, may be perfectly sufficient for some degree of belief.

41. Now perhaps the believer *will* come to doubt, unreasonably. Does this mean that, contrary to the argument of Chapter 1, doubt is compatible with a personal relationship with God? I would say no, for the believer, since she has

riod of withdrawal would facilitate the same cognitive benefits as
are facilitated by doubt. Indeed, there is some reason to suppose
that God would *prefer* the former approach to the latter. The believer, having had experiences apparently of God, may have more
in the way of motivation because she senses a *loss*, and so may be
inspired to explore matters of faith even more deeply than the one
who is in doubt.[42]

We are therefore in a position to argue as follows: Given that, as
the previous argument shows, God would not second-guess human responses to evidence of his presence but leave humans free to
explore more deeply the nature of faith or to sink into spiritual
nonchalance, we must expect that God would not subject to doubt
those who antecedently seem likely to fall into the latter category.
But this does not mean that there is no way for God to prompt
those who in fact *do* respond inappropriately to a deeper inquiry:
something analogous to "the dark night of the soul" *after* belief
may readily substitute for doubt *prior* to belief, and may indeed
have a stronger effect. Since this is the case, there is no reason to
suppose that God would, for the sake of its cognitive benefits,
leave anyone in a state of inculpable doubt, and so the argument
from the cognitive benefits of doubt fails.

---

responded presumptuously to her belief, may not have been in a personal relationship with God in the first place. But even if she was, if she doubts unreasonably
and so fails to believe or to experience the benefits of belief, the individual has
withdrawn *herself* from the relationship. (I assume here for the sake of discussion
that God exists.) It may seem that we should say she is still in the relationship, but
this, I think, is because the individual, while in doubt, is likely to be influenced in
various ways by her prior belief. Her life is still strongly affected by her having
been personally related to God, and indeed, she may once again *become* personally
related to God. We need not say that she still *is* so related to account for this.

42. The view I have been defending is well expressed, from the perspective of
theological commitment, by John Macquarrie: "As happens also in some of our
deepest human relationships, the lover reveals himself enough to awaken the love
of the beloved, yet veils himself enough to draw the beloved into an even deeper
exploration of that love. In the love affair with God (if we may so speak) there is
an alternation of consolation and desolation and it is in this way that the finite
being is constantly drawn beyond self into the depths of the divine" (*In Search of
Deity* [London: SCM Press, 1984], p. 198).

A Cumulative Argument

We have seen that available counterarguments fail to show the plausibility of supposing that a perfectly loving God would allow the occurrence of reasonable nonbelief. There is still one last response we must consider—a *cumulative* argument that can only be clearly formulated now that the claims of each of the other arguments have been brought out into the open. It suggests that if we view the good to which the good of belief is opposed as the *conjunction* of the various states of affairs for which the occurrence of reasonable nonbelief is necessary, it will become quite obvious to us that we have a good greater than or equal to the good sacrificed by allowing reasonable nonbelief to occur, and (given that reasonable nonbelief *is* logically necessary for it) that the argument from the reasonableness of nonbelief can therefore be rebutted. Which are these states of affairs? Given the conclusions reached in the relevant chapters, they would seem to be the following: (i) the possibility (for many) of a Kierkegaardian subjectivity of uncertainty; of venturing, risking all, in the search for God; (ii) the possibility (in many cases) of choosing to investigate God's existence (or failing to do so) in the absence of any clear reason to believe that there is a religious reality at all; (iii) the existence of the actual religious traditions, that is, Hinduism, Buddhism, and so forth; (iv) the existence of those human beings who actually exist; and (v) the responsibility (for some) of transmitting evidence sufficient for belief to individuals who would otherwise lack it and so lack the benefits made possible thereby.[43] Is the conjunctive state of affairs represented by (i)–(v) plausibly viewed as having a value greater than (or alternately, does it have a value clearly equal to) the value that is sacrificed in allowing reasonable nonbelief to occur?

The correct answer to this question, it seems, is no. We may point out, first of all, what various arguments in Part 2 have already suggested, namely, that quite apart from facilitating personal relationship with himself, in providing evidence for all, God would ipso facto bring about the existence of various states of affairs that

---

43. As I suggested earlier in this chapter, it seems less than plausible to suppose that this state of affairs obtains, but for the sake of argument, I include it.

would otherwise not have obtained, many of which are *broadly of the same type* as those the objector is (correctly) claiming would have to be given up in order for such evidence to be provided. Let us briefly compare these states of affairs and the value they would bring into the world with those mentioned by the objector, remembering that the latter are *incompatible* with the former—that the former states of affairs and the value they represent are included in what is sacrificed in allowing reasonable nonbelief to occur. The alternative list looks like this: (vi) the possibility for all (and so also for those who would otherwise have been in a position to develop the subjectivity of uncertainty) of cultivating the inwardness of belief; of striving to know God more fully; (vii) the possibility for all who did not resist the evidence with which they were provided of pursuing questions concerning the nature and activity of a God already believed to exist; of pursuing (to the extent that circumstances and abilities allowed) the way of "faith seeking understanding"; (viii) the existence of religious traditions instantiating religious creativity, imagination, and the like, no doubt differing in many respects from those that actually exist, but perhaps in many cases more closely attuned to the truth; (ix) the existence of creatures other than ourselves but "such as we are"; and (x) the opportunity for those who would have failed to believe, had circumstances been otherwise, to grow in relationship with God, to share, or fail to share, the fruits of their spiritual labors with others, and to awaken, or fail to awaken, others to a realization of the importance of faith.

What can we say about the comparative values of the conjunctive states of affairs represented by (i)–(v) and (vi)–(x)? Obviously such judgments are difficult to make. But this, I would argue, is just the point we should emphasize: it seems that there is little to choose between the two alternatives; that their value is approximately equal.[44] And I would go on to point out that we have reached this conclusion *without* taking account of (xi) the possibility for all at all times of personal relationship with God and the great instrumental and noninstrumental value this represents—which

44. Further support for this conclusion is to be found in the detailed arguments of Chapter 6 and previous sections of Chapter 7.

surely tips the balance decisively in favor of the second list. That is, the conjunctive state of affairs represented by (vi)–(xi) (for the existence of which the absence of reasonable nonbelief is necessary) seems quite clearly the state of affairs we should (and a loving God *would*) prefer. A perfectly loving God would not be deterred by considerations of the sort the objector can marshal from bringing about, as he would naturally be inclined to do, the state of affairs represented by (xi), realizing that what would be sacrificed in so doing could in large part be made up in other ways.

So it seems that a cumulative argument must also fail. Indeed, in putting it forward, the objector helps bring the larger picture more sharply into focus, enabling us to see more clearly the force of the original claim.

Conclusion

Our investigations into the question of reasonable nonbelief have come to an end. As we have seen, in the case of each of the arguments discussed in the previous three chapters, it is possible to show that there is no logical connection of the required sort between the permission of reasonable nonbelief and the good offered for our consideration, and/or that the state of affairs said to be of great value does not in fact constitute an outweighing or offsetting good, and/or (in one or two cases) that the state of affairs is not plausibly viewed as obtaining. Since, as we saw in Chapter 4, all the conditions here mentioned (the actual existence of the state of affairs, the logical necessity of reasonable nonbelief for its existence, and its status as an outweighing or offsetting good) must be plausibly viewed as satisfied (and in the case of the existence of an offsetting good, *clearly* satisfied) if there is to be a rebuttal, we may conclude that there is no rebuttal among the available counterarguments. That is, premise (2) of the argument from the reasonableness of nonbelief, as stated in Chapter 4, can apparently withstand all available challenges, and so there seem to be good grounds for supposing it to be true, and hence for concluding that the argument is sound.

How ought believer and nonbeliever to regard this conclusion? The answer, it seems to me, is likely to be different for different cases, depending on the extent to which the various claims I have made are accepted and on whether the fifth assumption of the Introduction, namely, that the relevant evidence (exclusive of evidence adduced in this book) does not clearly favor either theism or atheism, is accepted or denied. Let us suppose, however, that my claims are fully accepted by some individual S. What should be the effect of this on the belief of S concerning God's existence? Consider first the situation in which S takes the relevant (independent) evidence to strongly *favor* the claim that there is a God (perhaps she has had powerful religious experiences or considers herself to be in possession of a simple deductive proof of God's existence). Must S, to be rational, deny or come to doubt the existence of God because of the undefeated argument from the reasonableness of nonbelief? It may seem not. For S's situation would appear to be analogous to that of Jim, who believes that he has just been running with an acquaintance Joe in the city park and then is told by very reliable witnesses that Joe died in a plane crash the previous day. Surely the testimony must be denied in this case. Jim, it seems, must believe that the apparently reliable witnesses are in fact deceitful or deceived. And something similar, it may seem, must be said about S. S must believe that there are countervailing considerations even though she can find none, because of the force of her other evidence for God's existence (i.e., for the denial of the conclusion of the argument from the reasonableness of nonbelief).

But consider the following expansion of this analogy. Suppose that Jim, out of curiosity, travels to the site of the plane crash, reads the local newspapers, which mention Joe's name in connection with the crash, talks to more witnesses, including members of Joe's family, who tell him Joe has indeed died, and finally goes to the funeral chapel and sees what is to all appearances the body of Joe. At some point the conflicting considerations must put him (at least!) in a state of doubt as to whether it was really Joe he was with in the park, and we would surely be inclined to say that any other response to the evidence would be unreasonable. What does this suggest concerning the rationality of S continuing to believe that there is a God? It seems to me to suggest that if S's other evidence remains the same, only up to a certain point will it be reasonable for S to say, because of the force of her other evidence, that there must be a theologically acceptable explanation of the occurrence of reasonable nonbelief even though she can find none. Here too there may come a time when it suddenly becomes clear that the evidence provided by the occurrence of reasonable nonbelief is at least as weighty as contrary evidence. This would be the case, for example, if S came to believe very strongly that if there *were* a good served by reasonable nonbelief, this information would be available to her. Such a belief might result from additional evidence suggesting that any good served by reasonable nonbelief would be logically possible to know; that God, if he exists, would reveal to earnest inquirers any good served by reasonable nonbelief; that the relevant moral facts were known to S, and so forth. Beliefs of this sort, if formed by S, might very well cause her to view her other evidence with some suspicion, or simply lead to perplexity about which evidence was weightier. Either way, just as in the case of Jim and Joe, doubt could at some stage be the reasonable result. Now of course, both in the case of S and in the case of Jim and Joe, the contrary evidence may *not* remain constant. Jim may, a few days after the crash, bump into a living, breathing Joe while running in the park, and come (reasonably) to believe it was all a hoax, and S may happen on yet another apparent proof of God's existence! The point remains, however, that even for one who considers herself to be in possession of extremely good contrary evidence, the argument from the reasonableness of nonbelief, if undefeated, must continue to exert a certain evidential pressure and cannot be ignored.

This conclusion holds a fortiori for anyone who is *less* strongly convinced on independent grounds that there is a God. In particular, the many who believe that the relevant (independent) evidence does *not* clearly favor either theism or its denial must, if my argument seems to them to be undefeated by available counterarguments, come to believe that there is no God. In their case, there is little for the new evidence for atheism to overcome. The situation of an individual S who is a member of *this* group is comparable to that of Kim, who catches a glimpse of a person in the corner of the park who appears to be Flo, but might very well not be, and then is told by reliable witnesses that Flo died in a plane crash the previous day.[1] Kim, if reasonable, will surely judge on the basis of her total evidence that it was probably not Flo whom she saw. In this case, there is no significant presumption for the new evidence to defeat. And if Kim goes to the park again the next day and has the same experience—that is, again has a fleeting glimpse of an individual resembling Flo—she, unlike Jim, who *bumps into* Joe and sees him face to face, will judge, if reasonable (and if no other evidence has come to light), that the individual she briefly sees is *probably not* Flo. Although here too there are possible alternative explanations of the witnesses' testimony, given that her evidence for believing that it was Flo she saw *is not strong in the first place*, Kim has no reason to appeal to such possibilities. So too in the case of S, if she finds herself without other reasons that clearly suggest the existence of God. Without strong independent evidence for the denial of my argument's conclusion, S has no reason to appeal to the possibility of an explanation unknown to her, perhaps beyond her grasp. Without the indirect support for an appeal to the possibility of unknown explanations afforded by strong independent evidence of God's existence, S must, if she agrees with this argument, come to believe that there is no God.

My conclusion has important implications for a number of positions and arguments in contemporary philosophy of religion. I will mention two here—the positions of agnosticism and nonevidentialism.[2] Nonevidentialism was originally and most famously endorsed by Pascal.[3] On this view, one is pragmatically (as opposed

---

1. The analogy might be a closer one if we said that Kim is informed that had it been Flo, she would have caught more than just a glimpse—that Flo likes to walk out in the open where everyone can see her! But it is the point about independent evidence I am emphasizing here, and for that, the present analogy will suffice.

2. The second of these positions, albeit familiar, does not seem to go by any one name. I call it "nonevidentialism" to contrast it with a view popularly known as "evidentialism"—the view that belief is rational only if based on adequate evidence.

3. I am of course referring to Pascal's famous "wager" argument. See his *Pensées*, A. J. Krailsheimer, trans. (Harmondsworth: Penguin, 1966), fragment 418. William James, while disagreeing with Pascal on specifics, reaches a similar conclusion. See William James, *The Will to Believe and Other Essays in Popular Philosophy* (New York: Dover Publications, 1956). For more recent restatements of this view, see Stephen T. Davis, *Faith, Skepticism, and Evidence* (Cranbury, N.J.: Associated University Presses, 1978); Robert M. Adams, "Moral Arguments for Theistic Be-

to evidentially) justified in believing that there is a God if one has legitimate ends the pursuit of which is facilitated by such belief, and if the question of God's existence cannot be settled on evidential grounds. Now it will be apparent that if the argument we have considered succeeds, nonevidentialism is, if not false, irrelevant. For if that argument is correct, "the question of God's existence cannot be settled on evidential grounds" represents an impossible state of affairs, and so what is according to nonevidentialism a necessary condition of justifiably believing in God on pragmatic grounds can never be realized. Any apparent inconclusiveness in the evidence must, if that argument succeeds, *itself* be taken as a consideration (evidentially) justifying the conclusion that God does not exist.

Agnosticism would seem to be in the same boat. The agnostic says that when the evidence appears inconclusive, one must suspend judgment—that in such circumstances, neither theism nor atheism is a rational belief. But again, if the argument we have considered succeeds, this position must be rejected as, at best, irrelevant. For if that argument is correct, individuals who find the evidence inconclusive (and hold the argument to *be* correct) must ipso facto become atheists: the weakness of theistic evidence—a fact they will take to be confirmed in their own experience—must in their case be viewed as *itself* a consideration that tips the balance in favor of atheism. Hence neither the pragmatic leap nor the agnostic slump is justified for anyone who accepts the argument from the reasonableness of nonbelief as sound.

Of the various points that strengthen the argument of this book, one stands out, and it may be useful, in drawing the volume to a close, to bring it more clearly into focus. This point is the following: the reasons for Divine self-disclosure suggested by reflection on the nature of love are not reasons for God to provide us with some incontrovertible proof or overwhelm us with a display of Divine glory. Rather, what a loving God has reason to do is pro-

lief," in C. F. Delaney, ed., *Rationality and Religious Belief* (Notre Dame: University of Notre Dame Press, 1979); and Nicholas Rescher, *Pascal's Wager* (Notre Dame: University of Notre Dame Press, 1985).

vide us with evidence sufficient for belief. One of the consequences of this is that moral freedom, perhaps the most important good we have discussed, need not be infringed in order for God to be disclosed in the relevant sense. If this were not so, we could add to the list of goods for which the occurrence of reasonable nonbelief is necessary, "the possibility of morally free choice," and in that case, the argument from the reasonableness of nonbelief would be defeated: if God's hiddenness were required for the preservation of moral freedom, we might indeed expect a hidden God. But as it is, the kind of revelation that would remove moral freedom need not at all be associated with an argument of the sort presented here. That various writers have been little exercised by the relative weakness of theistic evidence is, it seems to me, largely due to a failure to recognize this point. To put it another way: the relevant (epistemic) alternatives to our actual situation have not been properly delineated. By specifying, as I have, what we might expect our epistemic situation to be like if a loving God exists, I hope to have set up a standard by which various attempts to solve the problem of weak theistic evidence can be evaluated. Many such attempts seem only to show that some overwhelming manifestation is not to be expected, and so provide no reason at all to suppose that God should not be self-disclosed when the latter concept is more carefully and adequately defined.

I stated in the Introduction that it was my aim in this book to show the importance of the argument from the reasonableness of nonbelief for the philosophy of religion. This, I think, I may fairly claim to have done. As we have seen, it is an implication of our discussion that individuals who doubt or weakly believe must, if they accept this argument, come to believe that there is no God, and that even those who consider themselves to be in possession of strong independent grounds for belief in the existence of God ought to take it seriously, and seek to answer it or to acquire additional grounds for belief. I myself have been unable to find reason to suppose that it is so much as plausible that a perfectly loving God would be hidden, and so the prospects for a future counter-argument that would remove this threat to theism and revive the possibility of belief must appear dim (however much one may feel that the existence of such an argument, given the profundity of the notion of Divine love, would be an immensely good thing). But it may be that new evidence will turn up. Perhaps stronger counter-arguments can be devised. I hope that because of my efforts, others will be inspired to show that this is indeed the case.

Index

CPSIA information can be obtained at www.ICGtesting.com
Printed in the USA
BVOW07s0723190115

383629BV00001B/3/P